Lesbian Origins

Lesbian Origins

Susan Cavin

ism
∞
press

San Francisco

Library of Congress Cataloging-in-Publication Data

Cavin, Susan, 1948-
   Lesbian origins.

   Originally presented as the author's thesis
(Ph. D. — Rutgers University) under the title: An
hystorical and cross-cultural analysis of sex ratios,
female sexuality, and homo-sexual segregation versus
hetero-sexual integration patterns in relation to the
liberation of women.
   Bibliography: p.
   Includes indexes.
      1. Lesbians — Cross-cultural studies.   2. Sex ratio —
Cross-cultural studies.   3. Matriarchy.   I. Title.
   HQ75.5.C38   1985   306.7'663   85-18158
   ISBN 0-910383-16-2
   ISBN 0-910383-15-4 (pbk.)

Ism Press, Inc.
P.O. Box 12447
San Francisco, CA 94112

Editor: Daniel Fogel

Portions of this book have previously appeared in
Sinister Wisdom, Big Apple Dyke News, and *Lesbian Ethics.*

Manufactured in the United States of North America

Acknowledgments

I wish to thank Maricla Moyano and Mary Risk Cavin for their financial and emotional encouragement of this book — as well as my dissertation committee, Adrienne Rich, Rhoda Blumberg Goldstein, Mary Hartman, and Martin Oppenheimer, for their constant criticisms and engagement in this thesis, which greatly improved it.

Further, I am indebted to the New York Public Library, 42nd Street branch, for desk space in the typing room during 1977-78; to Pamela Wright, curator of the *Human Relations Area Files (HRAF)* at City University in New York (CUNY), and to CUNY reference librarians Carol Fitzgerald and Kay Finney, for their consideration and expertise in facilitating my use of the *HRAF*.

I am also grateful to Maricla Moyano and Marsha Segerberg for discussing the thesis with me for several years. I must finally thank the international lesbian feminist movement for providing the inspiration for my research.

Most importantly, I thank Laura Zeidenstein, my lover, for all the tangible and intangible help she gave me, for the final push to transform the dissertation into book form by encouraging me to do it and loving me through it, for giving me hope and making me happy. Without Laura, I don't think I could have finished.

●

Thanks to Hayden Herrera, author of *Frida: A Biography of Frida Kahlo* (New York: Harper & Row, 1982), for providing photographic reproductions of the five Frida Kahlo paintings included in this book. Among these, "Roots" is reproduced courtesy of a private collection, Houston, Texas, and "Self-Portrait with Cropped Hair" is reproduced courtesy of the Museum of Modern Art, New York City (gift of Edgar Kaufmann, Jr.).

Pathfinder Press, 410 West Street, New York, NY 10014:

WOMAN'S EVOLUTION, by Evelyn Reed
Copyright © 1975 by Pathfinder Press, Inc.

Prentice-Hall, Inc., Englewood Cliffs, NJ 07632:

HOMOSEXUAL BEHAVIOR AMONG MALES: A CROSS-
CULTURAL AND CROSS-SPECIES INVESTIGATION,
by Wainwright Churchill
Copyright © 1967 by Wainwright Churchill

CULTURAL ANTHROPOLOGY, 3rd Ed., by Carol R.
Ember and Melvin Ember
Copyright © 1981

Princeton University Press, 41 William Street, Princeton, NJ
08540:

Myth, Religion, and Mother Right, by J.J. Bachofen
Translated by Ralph Manheim. Bollingen Series 84.
Copyright © 1967 by Princeton University Press

Schocken Books Inc., 200 Madison Avenue, New York, NY
10016:

GODDESSES, WHORES, WIVES AND SLAVES,
by Sarah Pomeroy
Copyright © 1975

WOMEN UNDER SOCIALISM, by August Bebel
Copyright © 1971

Viking Penguin, Inc., 40 West 23rd St., New York, NY 10010:

WOMAN'S BODY, WOMAN'S RIGHT: A SOCIAL HISTORY
OF BIRTH CONTROL IN AMERICA, by Linda Gordon
Copyright © 1976 by Linda Gordon

Table of Contents

Heterosexism (1) — Lesbianism (2) — Lesbian Feminism (3)
Female Society: Gynosociety (4) — Prehistoric Mysteries: The
Origin Debates (6) — Terminology (7) — Sex Ratios (7) — Female
Sexuality (8) — Straight (10) — Gynosociety (10) — Homosex
Segregation (10) — Heterosex Integration (11) — Chapter
Summaries (12) — Part I: Sex Theory (12) — Part II: Cross-
Cultural Sex Data (13) — Part III: Lesbian Feminist Praxis (13)

Demystifying Sexual Ideology (17) — Hystory versus History (19)
Patriscience is Heterosexist (21) — Link Between the Origin of
Society, Origin of Women's Oppressions, and Theory of
Liberation (22) — The Matriarchal School (25) — Bachofen's
Evolutionary Sequences (25) — Engels' Evolutionary
Sequences (26) —19th Century 'Predetermined Evolution' (27)
20th Century Matriarchists (27) — The Patriarchal School (28)
The Ideology of Patriarchy is: Patriarchy is Progress (30) Who's
Who in Evolution (31) — Feminist Analyses of Male Supremacy
and Women's Oppression (33) — Lesbian Feminist Criticism of
Hetero-Feminists (34) — Lesbian Feminist Theory of Women's
Oppressions (35)

List of Illustrations

About the Artists
of *Lesbian Origins*

JEAN LOIS GREGGS, of Black/American Indian heritage, was born in Monroe, Louisiana and graduated from Grambling University with a degree in fine arts. She later received her M.S.W. from Adelphi University, New York. Ms. Greggs is a full-time gestalt psychotherapist in private practice in New York City and in Teaneck, New Jersey.

In her art work, Ms. Greggs often addresses the nature of spiritual journeys and personal evolvement. She works in wood, copper, oil, watercolor and magic marker, usually working simultaneously in two or three media. Ms. Greggs' oil painting, "The White Light" (43" x 60"), appears on the front cover.

JANET YACHT, born in Brooklyn in 1938, has been painting since 1969. She has lived in Greenwich Village for the last 20 years. Prior to that, Yacht lived in England, Santa Fe, and Wisconsin.

One of her favorite pastimes is to take long, stoned walks through Chinatown, the Wall Street area and the old Lower East Side. She derives indirect inspiration for paintings from these walks. She loves the narrow streets, and the strange ugly architecture provides some inspiration for her feeling for the surreal. Being an agoraphobic, she turns things that scare her into positive material for her paintings.

Yacht is a representational/surrealist painter who likes to make the extraordinary out of the ordinary. She loves the potential for horror at every corner. Her favorite painters are: Georgia O'Keefe, DeChirico, Hopper, Delveaux, Magritte, Van Gogh, and Ernst.

LAURA ZEIDENSTEIN is a lesbian feminist of Russian and Romanian Jewish heritage. She has lived in Nepal, Bangladesh, and Mexico, and has travelled widely. She is a martial artist with a black belt in Goju-ryu karate, and presently teaches self-defense to women. L.Z. is currently studying to become a nurse/midwife.

Her artwork is often influenced by the movement of martial arts and the colors of people and places of the life around her. She tries to integrate the creative process of midwifery with her martial and fine arts. She currently resides in Brooklyn with her lover.

List of Tables

Preface

Lesbian Origins begins at the origin of human society, which is now largely a theoretical realm of science, and ends in the future of women's liberation, another theoretical sphere. This book begins and ends in sex theory, although the middle of the book summarizes known empirical sex data.

Part I, Sex Theory, contains new theory on the origin of society as well as the origin of women's oppression. Part II, Cross-Cultural Sex Data (as well as Appendices A and C), contains new data summaries of societal sex ratios, lesbianism, and sex separation. Part III, Lesbian Feminist Praxis, concludes the work with new theories of women's liberation routes out of patriarchy.

Theory plays a crucial role in science. The classic hypothesis test begins with a theory, tests it against the real world of existing data, then returns to theory in the end to see if the theory fits the data. Following the dialectic between theory and data is a major pursuit of science—although in post world war 2 North American sociology, the emphasis is rather more empirical. Today, grand theory is frowned upon in North American mainstream sociology, although original 19th century European sociology was largely grand theory. This book is a return to grand theory.

One principle of science is that, when puzzled by data or the lack of it, a return to the drawing board (theory) is advisable. The science of prehistory is handicapped by the fact that written history extends back only a few thousand years, compared to the great unknown X *million* years humans have lived on earth without written record. In the study of prehistoric society, so much more is unknown than known empirically. Until an empirical breakthrough into the depths of the prehistoric unknown occurs, new theory is needed to provoke new discoveries.

—Susan Cavin
Poultney, Vermont
18 March 1983

Glossary

asexual—1) referring to a person having no sex or no sexual inter-course; includes celibates, but is not limited to celibacy, which implies a vow to remain nonsexual with either sex; 2) produced without sexual action, as in asexual reproduction.

avunculocal—referring to a married couple living with the maternal uncle of the husband.

bilateral—referring to the transmission of property rights or descent through both the female and the male line, in a manner which is either equal or does not emphasize either line of descent.

bilocal—referring to a married couple living near or with either spouse's parents.

bride price—valuables given to the father or other relatives of the bride, by the groom or his representatives. These valuables usually serve to recompense the bride's family for the loss of the woman's services and confirm the status of the marriage in society. They also guarantee that the husband will take good care of the new wife—since, if she returns to her parents' home badly treated, the husband loses the amount paid for her.

bride service—winning a wife by working for the parents of the bride, usually before the marriage takes place. This service is often in place of paying a bride price.

butch/femme—1) gender and sex role play in lesbian and gay culture which generally satirizes heterosexual masculinity/femininity dichotomies. Either sex can play either role. 2) referring to a complex cultural system of cross-gender mannerisms which may be adopted by either sex in lesbian and gay life. 3) Joan Nestle, co-founder of the Lesbian Herstory Archives in New York City, describes the lesbian butch/femme relationship as "an erotic partnership, serving both as a conspicuous flag of rebellion and as an intimate exploration of women's sexuality." 4) The butch/femme gender system is a continuum of ideal types of stylized masculinity/femininity at both extremes, while people in the the exact center of the continuum would be androgynous (role-less or playing both roles).

closet, in the—1) hiding lesbian or gay identity from oneself and/or other people and/or non-gay institutions. 2) method of political oppression used by straight society to deny lesbians and gays human rights. Keeping homosexuals *in the closet* constitutes the central core of lesbian/gay oppression in straight society.

coming out of the closet—1) first lesbian or gay sexual experience. 2) a life-long process of acknowledgment of lesbian or gay identity to oneself and to others in the private spheres of family and friends as well as in the public sphere. 3) the most significant rite of passage from the straight world into the lesbian/gay world. Crossing over to the other side. 4) radical transformation of the spirit, a quantum leap of consciousness; consciousness raising for everyone in contact with someone who *comes out of the closet*. 5) strategic act of lesbian/gay liberation; considered the most powerful political act on both the individual and collective level of lesbian and gay movement. The strategy is: if everyone came out of the closet, lesbians and gays could not be oppressed by straight society's intimidation, insults, denial of lesbian/gay existence, or social stigma when discovered— because "we are everywhere."

devolution—1) reversing the evolution of the state or returning a society, subculture or region back to the socio-political organization that historically preceded the rise of the state. Devolution can occur peacefully, as in the case of "Scottish home rule," which devolves the United Kingdom by parliamentary procedure—or by popular election, e.g., French-speaking Quebecois separatists devolving Canada. Devolution can occur violently, as in the case of the Basque and Catalan separatists trying to devolve Spain. Lesbian separatists attempt to devolve patriarchy. 2) reversing or collapsing hierarchy by anarchism.

ec(cop)tation—economic cooptation: neutralizing the content of a political symbol by capitalist advertisers in order to mass-market a product for economic profit.

egonomics, male—economy of the male ego, which in this study is the economy of patriarchy.

extended family—a family consisting of a series of close relatives along either the male or female line, usually not along both. The extended family is the most commonly found type of family in primitive societies.

gay—referring to homosexual culture and homosexual people of either or both sexes—although many lesbians think that the term is generally used to connote male homosexual life more often than lesbian life.

group marriage—a group of females married to a group of males. Engels thought that group marriage was the first marriage form to emerge in society, but 20th century anthropologists have found no evidence to substantiate this theory.

gynocide—patriarchy's direct and indirect, systematic mass murder of women's bodies and minds. Gynocide includes: female infanticide, as well as the systematic use of amniocentesis to abort females because males are preferred; the systematic underfeeding of females relative to the overfeeding of males at any point in the age cycle; cultural misogynous practices that physically maim or cripple females (such as clitoridectomy and footbinding) or limit their locomotion (corsets, high heels, tight clothing); systematic, unhealthy overuse or underuse of the female body that limits the life chances of females relative to males; systematic rape, wife battering, incest, sexual molestation of the female body, and the mass psychological warfare techniques used by patriarchal media/states and individual sexual terrorists to frighten the entire female population into submission. Economic gynocide includes the feminization of poverty, forcing women to work for no wages (housework, childcare, malecare) or lower wages than men over a lifetime. When each individual oppression of women is combined to form the socio-economic complex whole of patriarchy, it can be seen that the entire system of patriarchy amounts to gynocide.

gyno-defense—physical and emotional defense of women and female society.

gynoscientists—scholar/activists of female society who fight patriarchal biases in male academic disciplines, and who also contribute to the development of feminist science.

gynosocial relations—relations between females.

gynosocial variables—female social variables such as matrilineage, matrilocality, mother-headed households, lesbianism, feminism, female homosocial relations both within and outside the family, fertility rates, female marriage resistance, feminine gender play, female labor sectors, high-female/low-male sex ratios, abortion, birth control, etc. These variables indicate whether women have power or lack power to control their own destinies; they also shape the nature of sexual society. These variables are latent measures of potential areas of woman-controlled activities, which may or may not be actualized by women's organization and/or consciousness.

gynosociety—1) society created by females. 2) female society. 3) communal society of self-governing females. 4) the basic structure of society itself, female social structure. Gynosociety is typically homosexually segregated.

herstory—the history of women, particularly the history of women as told by women—as in the Lesbian Herstory Archives in New York City.

hetaerism—referring to the promiscuity prevailing in gynosociety before the patriarchal overturn and the rise of the state. (term used by J.J. Bachofen in *Mutterrecht*).

heterocentric—1) the false, biased belief by heterosexuals that heterosexuality is superior to all other forms of sexuality. 2) heterosexist ethnocentrism.

heterofeminists—non-lesbian feminists; heterosexual feminists. (term coined by Adrienne Rich)

heterosex integration—There are two types of integration of the opposite sexes within society: physical proximity (horizontal integration), and socio-economic proximity (vertical integration). When not otherwise specified, I am only referring to the physical proximity of the opposite sexes in social space. However, this term is totally defined as a societally rigid practice and preference for *no* physical and/or social separation of the sexes by custom or law in: residential quarters which encompass sleeping, eating, and living arrangements; social, political, or religious functions, clubs, associations, or political affiliation; participation in sports or recreational activities; ritualistic ceremonies, initiation rites; and the sexual division of labor.

heterosexism—1) an ideology of patriarchy which economically sanctifies heterosexuality, especially procreative intercourse, as sacred and ordained by imaginary patriarchal gods, as the *only* normal purpose of sex—while at the same time criminalizing homosexuality as a perversion, a sickness, an abnormality, or as a crime. This ideology becomes dominant in extremely homophobic societies. 2) the basis of male supremacy, according to lesbian feminist theory. Heterosexism lies at the root of patriarchy, women's oppression, and lesbian oppression; it must be eliminated before the liberation of lesbians and all other women can occur. 3) Heterosexist attitudes include the assumption that lesbians do not really exist.

heterosexist supremacy—the political rule over society, all social and economic institutions by heterosexists, who also control the mass social production of ideas. Related to male supremacy historically and ideologically, with the result that heterosexual males control the means of production and the social relations of production.

heterosocial relations—male/female social relations. In the family, they include: wife/husband, mother/son, father/daughter, uncle/niece, aunt/nephew, grandmother/grandson, grandfather/granddaughter, male/female cousins; non-family heterosocial relations include male/female associations, friendships, and loverelationships.

high-female/low-male sex ratios—54% or more of the societal population is female, while 46% or less of the societal population is male. This applies to both the total population and the adult population of society.

high-male/low-female sex ratios—54% or more of the societal population is male, while 46% or less of the societal population is female. This applies to both the total population and the adult population of society.

homophobia—1) an irrational hatred of homosexuals, an excessively violent negative focus on homosexuality. 2) usually associated with latent homosexuals who cannot consciously accept being identified with homosexuals. 3) a psychological syndrome or reaction formation which compounds desire/fear/aggression toward homosexuals. 4) a misguided and paranoid assumption that all homosexuals want to sleep with heterosexuals and turn them into homosexuals. 5) e.g., homophobes are typically "turned on" to homosexuals in an insulting, lascivious way but, unable to admit their desire directly, they instead turn it around, projecting their confused sexual fantasies onto homosexuals—so that the homophobe can then act disgusted by all homosexuals who he imagines are always after him. (term coined by George Weinberg in his book, *Society and the Healthy Homosexual*)

homosex segregation—By this term, I mean same-sex segregation, not the practice of homosexuality. Homosex segregation is a societally rigid practice and preference for the physical (horizontal) and social (vertical) separation of the sexes by custom or law: in residential quarters which encompass sleeping, eating, and living arrangements; in social, political, or religious functions, clubs, associations, or political affiliation; in participation in sports and recreational activities; in ritualistic ceremonies, initiation rites; and the sexual division of labor. The sexual division of labor is, by definition, the classic form of homosex segregation.

homosocial relations, female—social ties between females; female/-female social relations. In the family, they include: mother/daughter, aunt/niece, sisters, female cousins, grandmother/granddaughter. Non-family female homosocial relations include: female/female associations, friendships, and loverelationships.

homosocial relations, male—social ties between males; male/male social relations. In the family, they include: father/son, uncle/-nephew, brothers, male cousins, grandfather/grandson. Non-family male homosocial relations include: male/male associations, friendships, and loverelationships.

horizontal homosex segregation—spatial or physical separation of the sexes into same-sex groupings.

horizontal heterosex integration—spatial or physical intermixing of the opposite sexes within a given territorial space.

horticulture—hand tillage of the soil, using such implements as the hoe, which can be operated by human power. Women engage in a large part of horticulture. Shallow cultivation is generally the rule.

hysteconomy—1) female forms of economy, ranging from women-controlled businesses to entire sectors of an economy controlled by women, to the entire economy of a society dominated by women. 2) illegal-market female economies not recorded in capitalist patriarchal economic indexes. 3) the complex whole of women's work, both productive and reproductive, both wage and wageless, which is the basis of all economies, even patriarchal ones—although women's communities are disorganized and not in control of women's labor products in patriarchy. Hysteconomy lies at the root of all economies, whether they be hunting and gathering, horticultural, agricultural, industrial, post-industrial, capitalist, socialist, or non-aligned.

hystory — 1) the story of women as told by women-identified-women — as distinct from history, the story of men as told by male-identified-men. This means that objectively neutral history does not exist; rather, the recording or retelling of past events is ideologically dependent upon the sex, race, class, age, sexual preference, religion, politics, and other relevant sociological identifications of the author. Thus far, it is ideologically impossible to remove the observer from the observation. 2) the time of prehistory, pre-patriarchy, pre-recorded history—while history denotes the time of patriarchy. Some lesbian feminists prefer to use the term, *herstory*; but throughout this work, I will employ the term, *hystory*.

incest — sexual and/or emotional relations between kin so closely related that they are forbidden by law or custom to marry. I delineate between two major forms of incest, homosex and heterosex incest. Homosex incest describes the emotional and/or sexual relations between same-sex kin: mother/daughter, sisters, aunt/niece, female cousins, grandmother/granddaughter, father/son, brothers, uncle/nephew, male cousins, grandfather/grandson. Heterosex incest describes the emotional and/or sexual relations between opposite sex kin: mother/son, sister/brother, male/female cousins, grandmother/grandson, uncle/niece, father/daughter, aunt/nephew, grandfather/granddaughter.

lesbian feminism — a critical analysis of patriarchy and male supremacy, created by political lesbians in 1970 combining radical feminist ideology with "Radicalesbianism." It is a political analysis of the power of female sexuality, which contends that "women-identified-women," when organized at the grassroots level, have the power to create female societies free of hierarchical sex, race, class, age, and hetero-sexist oppressions. Also, it is a consciousness that originally derives from the historical intersection of two separate political movements: the women's liberation movement and the gay liberation movement. It is through the existence of feminist lesbians that these two movements have crossed each other's historical paths.

lesbian separatism — a vanguard ideology, strategy for lesbian liberation, as well as a way of life, a subculture for *avant garde*, radical lesbian feminists. The ideology was first publicly articulated in 1971 in the U.S., but is now international. The strategy for liberation articulated by lesbian separatists involves: 1) female non-cooperation with the patriarchal system and patriarchal men, ranging from a woman's choice not to be involved with men socially, emotionally, sexually, politically or economically, to physical separation from the institutions and jurisdiction of patriarchy. 2) recognition of the power of women to say "no" to men; the power of women to choose to

Lesbian Origins

control their own destinies outside the compulsory servicing of men required by patriarchy. 3) realization that lesbians and all other women who choose to rebel can collapse patriarchy by collectively withdrawing female labor, service, energy and emotional support from patriarchal institutions and men. This theory/strategy is based on the assumption that lesbians and all other women, like all oppressed groups, have been brainwashed (chiefly through internalized misogyny and internalized homophobia) to collaborate and cooperate with the oppressor in their own oppression. Lesbian separatism attempts to reverse this process by teaching the power of female sexuality and female separation outside of male control. (see Note #9 from the Introduction, pages 229-30, for more information on lesbian separatism).

lineal—referring to consanguine relatives (a blood related social group) connected by a line of descent. Two such relatives are never from the same generation.

loverelationships—social relations between lovers.

matriarchal school—group of 19th and 20th century scholars who subscribe to the matriarchal theory of human social origin, first formulated by J.J. Bachofen in 1861 (*Das Mutterrecht*), and who have made an intellectual contribution in this area of research. Several prominent members of this school are: Lewis Henry Morgan, Frederick Engels, Karl Marx, August Bebel, Robert Briffault, Mathias and Matilde Vaertung, Helen Diner, Elizabeth Gould Davis, and Merlin Stone. All of these scholars vary in their conceptions of matriarchal development, but all agree that historically, matriarchy precedes the development of patriarchy, mother-right precedes father-right, and patriarchy is a rather late historical development.

matriarchy—1) an early society, suggested by some writers, in which women constituted the major authority. 2) a socio-economic system ruled by women. 3) The following characteristics would imply that a society has a prehistory or hystory of matriarchy: extremely high-female/low-male sex ratios, matrilineage, matrilocality, female control of the means of production, sororal polygyny, mother-headed households and families. 4) Iroquois society is considered by the majority of anthropologists to be the "golden matriarchy."

matri-heterosex incest—sexual and/or emotional relations between male and female kin closely related in matrilineal and/or matrilocal societies—or in mother-headed households found in patriarchal societies. These relationships include: mother/son, sister/brother, maternal uncle/niece, grandmother/grandson, maternal cousins of opposite sexes.

matrilineal—referring to the transmission of authority, inheritance or descent primarily through females.

matrilocal—referring to a married couple's residing with the wife's family or kin group.

modal—referring to the statistical mode, the most frequent value in a frequency distribution.

nuclear family—referring to a married couple with their children.

patriarchal school—group of 19th and 20th century scholars who subscribe to the patriarchal theory of human social origin first formulated by Henry Maine in 1861. Prominent members of this school include: Edward Westermarck, Talcott Parsons, and Lionel Tiger. Patriarchal scholars in this tradition agree that matriarchy as a world historic stage never existed, and that matriarchy did not precede patriarchy. This school generally attributes women's oppression to female biology. Throughout this book, I refer to members of the patriarchal school as *patriscientists.*

patriarchy—1) a socio-economic system ruled by men. 2) a society where men are economically, politically and socially segregated *up* while women are segregated *down* as a caste generally, although some exceptions occur; a society largely characterized by vertical sexual segregation. Early patriarchal societies tended more toward horizontal (spatial and physical) segregation of the sexes, while late patriarchies such as U.S. and other industrialized societies in the late 20th century tend toward horizontal integration of the sexes. But all patriarchies, early or late, depend upon vertical sexual segregation. 3) a society which domesticates women and children along with animals—regarding all three as the property of men. 4) a society which oppresses women, particularly stigmatizing all nonheterosexual and/or nonmonogamous heterosexual women—because father-right, the father family and paternity itself, which are the bases of patriarchal society, depend upon the mass production of heterosexual, monogamous women for the mass reproduction of fathers and sons. 5) a society with either high-male/low-female sex ratios (typical of early patriarchy), or a society with near equal sex ratios (typical of late patriarchy).

patri-heterosex incest—sexual and/or emotional relations between male and female kin closely related in patrilineal, patrilocal, or patriarchal societies. These relationships include: father/daughter, brother/sister, paternal aunt/nephew, grandfather/granddaughter, paternal cousins of opposite sexes.

patrilineal—referring to transmission of name, property, or authority through males.

patrilinearity—referring to linear, unidirectional thinking, which is dominant in capitalist patriscience.

patrilocal—referring to the practice of a married couple's living in the husband's community or of a wife's settling in the home of her husband.

patriscience—1) father science; male science. 2) the predominantly white male scientific establishment in patriarchal societies where the apparatus for the social production of ideas is generally controlled by sexist, racist, classist, heterosexist, and ageist males who claim to be "objectively neutral," but are in fact ideologically biased—as is their research.

patriscientists—1) scholars in the patriarchal school. 2) scientists who are apologists for patriarchy. 3) may be male or female scientists who have been trained in the patriarchal tradition to believe that they are "objectively neutral," when in fact they are ideologically biased; their research generally justifies racism, sexism, classism, heterosexism and ageism.

patrisocial—referring to: 1) father relations, male-controlled social relations, based on the *paterfamilias* model in varying degrees. 2) the social relations of patriarchy. 3) types of social relations ideologically favored by, and most frequently found in patriarchal societies—e.g., heterosexual and male homosocial relations, father-controlled family forms.

poli-sex—1) political sex. 2) sexual politics based on the feminist line that "the personal is political" and the lesbian feminist line that "you are who you sleep with." 3) the intricate intertwinings between what is political and what is sexual.

political lesbian—a woman who adopts the politics of lesbian feminism and/or lesbian separatism without necessarily being a sexual lesbian, i.e., practicing sex with other women. (term coined by Ti Grace Atkinson)

polyandry—a marriage in which a woman has more than one husband at the same time.

polyandry, fraternal—a marriage of several brothers to one woman.

polygyny—a marriage in which a man has more than one wife at the same time.

polygyny, limited—referring to a society where a man may have more than one wife at the same time; however, due to financial reasons, less than 20% of the societal population practices polygyny.

polygyny, sororal—1) a marriage of several sisters to one man. 2) a man's marriage to his wife's younger sister.

prehistory—earth time prior to the development of writing—thought to include the longest period of human social development on earth, which is largely unknown. In this book, I use the term to mean pre-patriarchy as well.

sex ratios—1) the number of females relative to males in the population of a society. 2) *Total population sex ratios* refer to the number of females relative to males in the total population of a society. 3) *Adult sex ratios* refer to the number of adult females relative to adult males in the population of a society. In this study, I broadly define *adult* as anyone 15 years or older. (see also *high-female/low-male sex ratios* and *high-male/low-female sex ratios*).

sex variables — 1) elements or dimensions of sex that vary. 2) all socio-logical variables that are derived from biological sex, the variation/-differentiation of the human race into two sexes, male and female. Examples: sexual selection, sexuality, sex ratios, sexual preference or orientation, marital status, sex segregation/integration, marriage forms, fertility rates, number of offspring, gender, sexual practices, sexual taboos, sexual dimorphism, incest, marital residence, inheritance and lineage, positions of sexual intercourse, etc.

sexism — 1) sexual discrimination against women. 2) an ideology of patriarchy which values men and devalues women simultaneously. Sexism holds that women exist for the pleasure and assistance of men only; that female identity derives only from relations with men (father, brother, husband); that women are and should be dependent upon men for everything; that marriage and the family, the private sphere, is the only proper domain of women; and that women are not the moral, spiritual, and intellectual equals of men. This attitude stigmatizes women who do not marry, or who do not devote their primary energies to the care of men and their children. Association with a man is the basic criterion for a women's participation, status, and acceptance in patriarchal society. Women who refuse association with men are considered a threat to society. 3) Economic vertical segregation of women down the wage hierarchy, while segregating men up. 4) Political vertical segregation of women down the power hierarchy, while segregating men up.

sexolution — 1) sexual revolution, evolution, and devolution. 2) the developmental movement of the sexes in relation to each other; socio-sexual change in societal direction. 3) transformation of society by mass sexual-social change. This may be slow and gradual as in sexual evolution, taking centuries and millenia — or may be sudden and cataclysmic as in sexual revolution, occurring within a decade.

sexploitation — sex exploitation: the exploitation of females by males for profit. The pornography and prostitution industries are sensational examples of sexploitation. However, wageless female labor (e.g., housework) and underpaid female labor (e.g., clerical and service sectors of the economy) are also sexploitation.

sororal polygyny — see *polygyny, sororal.*

stem family — a nuclear family plus one or more related individuals who do not comprise a second nuclear family.

Stonewall rebellion — In late June of 1969, at the Stonewall Inn on Christopher Street (just west of 7th Avenue, near Sheridan Square) in Greenwich Village, New York City, the drag queens ("Sylvia" and others), lesbians, and gay male patrons of the bar (Ed Murphy and others) resisted arrest by police raiding the bar, and fought back. Three days of lesbian and gay resistance in the streets of the Village followed the Stonewall resistance, which then resulted in the formation of the Gay Liberation Front, and later Lesbian Feminist Liberation in New York. The lesbian/gay liberation movement was reborn in New York City in 1969, and quickly became national and international. Since 1970, every year on a Sunday late in June, lesbians and gays all over the world march to commemorate the anniversary of Stonewall, the rebirth of the movement.

straight—1) heterosexuals. 2) squares, conventional people. 3) bores, not fun. 4) oppressive types. 5) the bourgeois establishment of society. 6) anti-gay and anti-lesbian culture. 7) mainstream society. 8) white, male supremacist society that oppresses lesbians, gays, women, prostitutes, the handicapped or physically challenged, the young, the old, the working class, the poor, the lumpenproletariat, Asian Americans, Blacks, Hispanics, and American Indians. Patriarchy is a straight society.

straight feminist—a heterosexual woman who believes in feminism. (see also *heterofeminists*)

tribadism—a form of lesbian lovemaking where two women rub their bodies together, particularly their genitals and breasts, to orgasmic conclusion. From the Greek verb, *tribein* (to rub). Females who practice tribadism are known as *tribades*, or *tribads*.

uterine society—female society.

uxoribilocal—In this form of marital residence, the couple initially lives with or near the wife's kinspeople, and then settles down in the vicinity of either the wife's or husband's kinspeople.

uxoripatrilocal—In this form of marital residence, the couple initially lives with or near the wife's kinspeople, but then settles down in the vicinity of the husband's kinspeople.

Dedicated to Maricla Moyano,
my lover of ten years,
from 1973 through 1983,
who taught me how
"Lesbians Ignite!"

●

In memory of Sadie,
my cat, who sat on
this book for years.
18 July 1970—18 July 1985.

Introduction

I am a lesbian feminist sociologist. This book was originally my dissertation in political sociology at Rutgers University, October 1978. It is one of the first lesbian feminist doctoral dissertations in the United States. The dissertation is titled: "An Hystorical and Cross-Cultural Analysis of Sex Ratios, Female Sexuality, and Homo-Sexual Segregation Versus Hetero-Sexual Integration Patterns in Relation to the Liberation of Women."[1]

HETEROSEXISM

Lesbian Origins challenges the heterosexism of the social sciences because heterosexism is the major basis of male supremacy. Heterosexism is an ideology of patriarchy[2] which economically sanctifies heterosexuality, especially procreative intercourse, as sacred and ordained by imaginary patriarchal gods, as the *only* normal purpose of sex; while at the same time criminalizing homosexuality as a perversion, a sickness, an abnormality, or as a crime. Heterosexism is still ideologically dominant in the North American social sciences, reflecting a society which is extremely homophobic.[3]

A heterosexist social system gives straight people privileges, social status, economic incentives, and rewards to be exclusively heterosexual by taking away the civil rights and social status of lesbians and gay men.

1

Heterosexist attitudes include the assumption that lesbians do not really exist, as if heterosexual women are the only women in the world. Heterosexism is also the world view which assumes that butch/femme role play is biologically determined; as if butch and femme are the only sex roles humans can play.

Heterosexism intersects the economy and ideology of male supremacy in such a way that heterosexism may be the basis of sexism.† According to lesbian feminism, heterosexism lies at the root of patriarchy, women's oppression, and lesbian oppression. Thus, heterosexism must be eradicated before the liberation of lesbians and all other women can be achieved.

LESBIANISM

Lesbianism is a phenomenon quite different from lesbian feminism, and the two should not be confused. Lesbianism is: a state of intense sexual and/or emotional attraction and/or love relationship between two or more females; a sexual "ignition," according to Maricla Moyano, the New York radical lesbian feminist who in 1972 coined the phrases that turned into political movement buttons, "Lesbians Ignite" and "Dykes Ignite." Emotional lesbianism includes intensive love-friendships between females of all ages. Lesbianism is also the adjective and formal name of the women of Lesbos. Lesbianism is also associated with tribadism, the touching friction of one clitoris to another clitoris.

Lesbian subculture involves women marginal to mainstream patriarchal societies by virtue of their sexual love for other women. Lesbianism can occur inside or outside of the family. Within the family it is possible to find sexual attraction between female relatives such as sisters, mothers and daughters, aunts and nieces, females cousins; or deeply emotional ties between female relatives—which may, but typically do not ever reach sexual expression.

Lesbianism has been documented in the earliest written records of Western society, e.g., Sappho on Lesbos (c. 600 B.C.)[4], lesbian prostitutes in Athens (450 B.C.)[5], and lesbian relations

---

†Heterosexism is deeply rooted in the judaeo-christian tradition. The old testament mandates the death penalty against male homosexuality, "bestiality," and sorcery, whether practiced by a man or woman (Leviticus, chapter 20). The christian apostle Paul denounced homosexuality, both female and male (Romans, 1.26- 27). —*Editor*

among Spartan women.[6] (see chapters 2 and 6 in the text). Although lesbianism has been recorded since prostitution was first recorded in western history, literature, and art, lesbian feminism appears to be a later and rarer occurrence.

LESBIAN FEMINISM

Lesbian feminism is at once an international political movement, a political ideology, a praxis (theory in action), and an international society for the liberation of lesbians and all other women. One of the major principles of lesbian feminism teaches lesbians to "come out" of the closet as a necessary step toward individual and collective lesbian liberation. The straight closet is viewed as a source and method of lesbian oppression.

The lesbian feminist movement is composed of lesbians who generally are, or were, feminists at some stage of their political careers, who now work not only for the general liberation of women, but for the particular liberation of lesbians, celibate women, and spinsters as well. Lesbian feminists are regarded in movement circles as the vanguard of the women's revolution.

Lesbian feminism is a critical analysis of patriarchy and male supremacy created by political lesbians in 1970 by combining radical feminism with "Radicalesbianism."[7] It is a political analysis of the power of female sexuality, which contends that "women-identified-women," when organized at the grassroots level of society, have the power to create female societies free of hierarchical sex, race, class, and age oppressions.

Lesbian feminism is a consciousness that originally derives from the historical intersection of two separate political movements: the women's liberation movement and the gay liberation movement. It is through the lesbian feminist that these movements have crossed each other's hystorical paths.

In the 20th century, lesbian feminism has emerged twice as a political movement. 1) At the turn of the century, lesbian feminists—lesbians who worked in both the feminist and early homosexual rights movements (1864-1935)—appeared in Germany. Their political activity continued until the nazi regime carried out a mass arrest and deportation of homosexuals to the concentration camps, where they were forced to wear a pink triangle insignia. Over 200,000 gays perished in Hitler's camps.[8]

2) In 1969-70, lesbian feminism burst out again at the start of the gay liberation movement, after a few years of the second wave of feminism. The second wave of lesbian feminism in the 20th century has produced a much stronger and broader based international movement than the first.

The lesbian feminist movement was bound to happen, because neither the straight feminist nor gay male movements of the 19th and 20th centuries took adequate account of the lesbian, although lesbians have actively participated in both movements. Many feminist and gay male critiques of patriarchy neglect lesbian feminism and commonly omit lesbian society or the existence of all-female society from their social maps. Such is the hystorical and political predicament of the lesbian in straight society: recorded unreality or unrecorded reality. Because of this marginal position — first to straight society, then to the feminist movement and gay male movement—political lesbians learned that they had better speak for themselves or else they would not be spoken for!

In this process, a new political movement was built, which has been in existence from 1969 through the present, and is still growing at the time of this writing. Today, lesbian feminism is a world political movement of lesbians, which broadly encompasses all degrees of lesbian struggle for liberation from patriarchal oppression. The goals of this movement range from the moderate or liberal lesbian's efforts to obtain lesbian civil rights within current patriarchal structures, to the radical lesbian separatist[9] goal of overthrowing world patriarchy in order to liberate lesbians and all other women.

Perhaps the most hated concept in patriarchy is the concept of all-female societies; for example, actual lesbian society or hypothetical Amazon society. Why are lesbianism and Amazonism taboo subjects in the records of patriarchy (excepting early Greek patriarchy), never to be mentioned? This question will be analyzed in chapter 2, "Lesbian Origins," and chapter 3, "Amazon Origin Theories."

FEMALE SOCIETY: GYNOSOCIETY

A major preoccupation of this work is female society and its relation to society in general. I posit that female society is the constant base of all soceities, even patriarchies. In patriarchy, male society is always hierarchically superimposed on top of the

'Body—Mind—Spirit', by Jean Lois Greggs
(watercolor, 12" x 16")

productive and reproductive labor networks of female society. Quite simply, without female society, society does not exist at all. Due to both sexism and heterosexism, patriscientists[10] generally miss this point and falsely assume that society is sex neutral, when at base it is a female network.

Female homosocial relations are critical to the formation and maintenance of the family, community and society. By female homosocial relations, I mean social ties between females. These ties include the following familial relations: mother/daughter, aunt/niece, sisters, female cousins, grandmother/granddaughter. Outside the family, female homosocial relations take the form of female friendships and female loverelationships.

Heterosocial relations in the family include these relations: wife/husband, mother/son, father/daughter, uncle/niece, aunt/nephew, grandmother/grandson, grandfather/granddaughter. Outside the family, heterosocial relations comprise male/female friendships and male/female loverelationships.

In this work, I will contend that *female homosocial relations form the original base and constant cement of society.* Female/female relations hold society together. Original society is numerically high-female/low-male. These theories will be expanded in chapter 2, "Lesbian Origins."

PREHISTORIC MYSTERIES: THE ORIGIN DEBATES

The major purpose of this book is to search for the origin of society, the origin of lesbianism and all-female society, as well as the origin of women's oppressions. Aside from curiosity, the point of looking for these prehistoric mysteries is to find liberation routes out of patriarchy for lesbians and all other women.

The search for the origin of human society in the social sciences is analogous to the search for the origin of the universe in theoretical physics. Physical reconstruction of original events is all but impossible. To be sure, scientists are gravediggers, but when it comes to digging the original scene, no one knows exactly where to dig.

Faced with a monumental scarcity of original facts, there is a tendency among both physical and social scientists to fall back on their childhood cosmologies, or religious ideology regarding original society. Some speculate that the biblical book of Genesis is a true account of origin. This is not very original thinking.

Many social scientists insinuate that only heterosexuals are present at creation, without any evidence to back it up. To date, no scientist has the scoop on creation. Most of what is pontificated about social origin is still up for serious scientific debate. Still, the question of human origin is one of the most interesting mysteries to study in science.

The social science debates over human societal origin began in the 19th century and continue to rage unsolved in the 20th. The question of origin is especially current, due to the feminist renaissance in the arts and sciences in the 1970's and 1980's, which resulted from the poli-sex "ignition" of the women's liberation movement in the 1960's and 1970's.

The origin debates of the 19th and 20th centuries involve not only an academic search for the origin of the family, private property, stratification (class), and monogamous marriage, but for the very origin of social institutions themselves, such as language, community, the incest taboo, the sexual division of labor, and other societal bases.

The feminist and lesbian feminist interest in these origin debates is something else, however: to theoretically locate the origin of the oppression of women historically, in order to eliminate it in practice. These origin debates will be discussed in great detail in the first chapter.

In this book, I will offer new theories on the origin of society, as well as the origin of women's oppression, based on the study of three neglected sex variables: societal sex ratios, female sexuality, and sex segregation. Definitions of these variables and other important terminology will be helpful here.

TERMINOLOGY

Sex Ratios

The sex ratio of a society is the number of females relative to males in the population. The combined number of females added to the number of males equals the total population of society. It is my theoretical intuition that societal sex ratios are critical in determining the general condition of women in society. In other words, I theorize that the number of men relative to women in society effects both the oppression and liberation of women. No one has ever suggested this simple equation, and it has yet to be proven or disproven. Chapters 4 and 5 will make a theoretical and empirical case for this sex ratio theory.

There are several usages of the term, sex ratio, in the social sciences.[11] In census reports, the sex ratio of all age cohorts is a particular focus. In this book, the only age cohort I am interested in regarding sex ratios is the adult sex ratio of society. I use the term adult broadly here to mean anyone 15 years or older (see Appendix C for data on the adult sex ratio of society).

However, whenever I use the term *sex ratio* throughout most of this work, I refer to the *total* population sex ratio, unless otherwise specified. Now, aside from positing that societal sex ratios effect women's oppression and liberation, sex ratios also effect the types of social structure a society will have. Female sexuality is another critical social variable effecting the formation of society, women's oppression and liberation.

Female Sexuality

Whosoever controls female sexuality, in a real sense, controls the reproduction of society. The lesbian feminist position is that *no one* should control female sexuality, especially not men. Female sexuality should be free. However, if this lesbian feminist vision were reality, we would not be living in a patriarchy. At the "moment," and it has been a long "moment," patriarchy controls the female sexuality of its female population. Make no mistake about it, patriarchy must control female sexuality, or else patriarchy cannot exist.

Female sexuality lies at the basal structure of all societies. The only forms of female sexuality which involve males at all are: heterosex and bisex. Thus, males must control female heterosex and bisex if they are to control society at all.

The creation and maintenance of patriarchy or any other form of male-ruled society is based on the control of female sexuality. Female *a*sexuality (celibacy) and lesbianism function outside the control of patriarchy, because these sexualities do not involve men at all. Due to this fact, that by definition lesbianism and female celibacy omit male sexual participation/-control, these sexualities pose a threat to patriarchal control of female sexuality, and thus threaten patriarchal existence. Sexually, patriarchy depends upon the mass production and reproduction of straight women.

'Two Nudes in a Forest', by Frida Kahlo (1939)

Straight

In gay culture, straight refers to: 1) heterosexuals; 2) squares, conventional people; 3) bores, not fun; 4) oppressive types; 5) the bourgeois establishment of society; 6) anti-gay culture, mainstream society; 7) white, male supremacist society that oppresses lesbians, gay men, women, prostitutes, Blacks, Hispanics, American Indians, Asian Americans, the young, the aged, working-class people, the handicapped, the poor and lumpenproletariat. Female society, or gynosociety, is not so straight as patriarchy.

Gynosociety

By gynosociety, I mean: 1) society created by females; 2) female society; 3) communal society of self-governing females; 4) the basic structure of society itself; 5) female social structure. Female society, gynosociety, is almost by definition homosexually segregated.

Homosex Segregation

Sex segregation is one of the major sex variables of this study, along with sex ratios and female sexuality. I divide sex segregation into two ideal types: 1) homosex segregation, which is same-sex separation from co-ed society; and 2) heterosex integration, which is opposite sex interaction in society.

According to the principles of homosex segregation, the sexes are separated in society or from society in groups of the same sex — e.g., Boy Scouts, Girl Scouts, YMCA, YWCA. Separation of the sexes along homosex lines is experienced inside and outside society at all levels. Males and females can live separately inside the same society or they can live apart in two separate societies, one sex being the in-group, the other the out-group.

Homosex segregation is defined as a societally rigid practice and preference for the physical and/or social separation of the sexes into same sex groupings by custom or law: in residential quarters which encompass sleeping, eating, and living arrangements; in religious, social, recreational, and political organizations; in ritualistic ceremonies, initiation rites of passage; and in the sexual division of labor.

There are two types of homosex segregation: 1) horizontal; and 2) vertical. Horizontal homosex segregation refers to spatial or physical separation of the sexes into same sex groupings.

Vertical homosex segregation refers to social, economic, or political separation of the sexes in social stratification systems where one sex is segregated *up* to receive the lion's share of social status, rank, privilege, prestige, and income, while the other sex is segregated *down*.

Heterosex Integration

Heterosex integration is the physical or social integration of the opposite sexes within the same society. There are two types of heterosex integration: 1) horizontal; and 2) vertical. Horizontal heterosex integration refers to spatial or physical intermixing of the opposite sexes within a given territorial space. To a bourgeois feminist or academic, vertical heterosex integration refers to social, economic, or political equality of the opposite sexes in social stratification systems — where no one sex receives more social status, rank, privilege, prestige or income than the other. To a marxist, vertical heterosex integration refers to the revolutionary destruction of the existing social order and the elimination of social classes, breaking down the social division of labor between men and women in the process.

Heterosex integration is defined as a societally rigid practice and preference for no physical and/or social separation of the sexes by custom or law, in: residential quarters which encompass sleeping, eating, and living arrangements; social, political, recreational, or religious functions, clubs, associations, or organizations; ritualistic ceremonies, initiation rites of passage; and the sexual division of labor.

Rarely will any one society be *totally* heterosexually integrated or totally homosexually segregated. Most societies use a combination of integration/segregation forms for different purposes. For example, some societies use homosex horizontal segregation as a method of birth control, while other societies will simply delay the age of marriage to obtain the same result — e.g., Ireland, People's China. I am mainly interested in understanding which combination of heterosex integration and homosex segregation produces the most oppressive conditions — and which produces the most liberating conditions — for women in society.

It is my theoretical intuition that the ideal type of western patriarchy combines at its base vertical homosex segregation with horizontal heterosex integration: physically mixing men and women in *physical* space, but in *social* space segregating males *up* and females *down* the stratification system.

Now that I have defined the basic terms of this study, a brief summary of the chapters is useful before proceeding on to the text. Incidentally, any terms not defined in this introduction may be found in the glossary at the beginning of the book.

CHAPTER SUMMARIES

The major purposes of this book are: 1) to offer a new theory of sexual society; 2) to present a new sex theory on the origin of women's oppression; 3) to summarize the social scientific data which supports these theories; 4) to criticize the heterosexist biases of the social sciences; and 5) to present data and develop theory on women's liberation routes out of patriarchy. Briefly, the theoretical chapters of Part I, Sex Theory, contain the following information:

Part I: Sex Theory

Chapter 1, "Sex Devolution: Sexual Ideology on the Origin of Women's Oppression," represents a review of major 19th and 20th century literature on the subject. Various patriarchal, matriarchal, marxist, feminist and lesbian feminist theories of women's oppression are reviewed. I also examine the concept of evolution in relation to sexual ideology: Who's who in evolution? The ideology of patriarchy is: Patriarchy is progress. Is it really?

Chapter 2, "Lesbian Origins," presents my new theory on the origin of society, the origin of lesbian and women's oppression as well as new theory on incest. What roles do homosex incest and heterosex incest play in the development of the family? Why are there so many taboos surrounding original promiscuity and pre-state sex? Which came first: gay or straight sexuality? These questions emerge in the second chapter. Also, nonheterosexual origin myths, prehistoric lesbianism, and incest are discussed.

Chapter 3, "Amazon Origin Theories," includes a discussion of worldwide Amazon origin myths, Amazon sex ratios, and conflicting academic theories on Amazon phenomena. Both lesbians and Amazons are considered "mannish women" hated by patriarchy. Is there a relationship between the two hystorically?

Chapter 4, "Sex Ratio Theory," concludes the theoretical Part I of this book. Chaper 4 contains new theory regarding sex ratios and society. I also review relevant sex ratio literature and discuss the socio-numerical theories of Simmel, Engels, Bebel, Marvin Harris, Levi-Strauss, and others. Sex ratios and marriage forms are also discussed.

Part II: Cross-Cultural Sex Data

Chapter 5, "High Female Sex Ratios," summarizes sex ratio information on one hundred societies, a sample of world society, in the time period A.D. 1647 to 1971. I will discuss the sex ratios of extinction, i.e., when a people is dying out; and summarize the type of societies which have high-female/low-male sex ratios, as well as those which have near equal and high-male/low-female sex ratios. Some of this evidence supports my sex ratio theory of origin, although future research is needed.

Chapter 6, "Cross-Cultural Lesbianism," describes 30 societies where lesbianism has been recorded in the social scientific literature. These 30 societies cross over 2,000 years of recorded time, ranging from 450 B.C. to A.D. 1957.

Chapter 7, "Sex Separation," concludes the empirical Part II of this book. This chapter presents data on "female languages," the segregation of adolescent boys, post-partum sex taboos, and the sexual division of labor around the world.

Part III: Lesbian Feminist Praxis

Chapter 8, "Women's Liberations," ends the book. Chapter 8 contains 13 avenues toward women's liberation, a discussion of female power, and a lesbian feminist power scale. The conclusion is: Women's liberation cannot be achieved until female sexuality is set free at last.

Now consider *Lesbian Origins.**

—Susan Cavin

New York City

---

*Throughout my dissertation, I used the terms "matrilineality" and "patrilineality" and would still prefer to use my original terms throughout this book. However, the editor of this book has changed my original terms, "matrilineality" and "patrilineality" to his terms, matrilineage and patrilineage. —*Author*

Part I

Sex Theory

Chapter 1

Sex Devolution: Sexual Ideology on the Origin of Women's Oppressions

There is a logic to the ideology of sex. I use a critical method that is as simple as a coin toss to demystify sexual ideology. I divide society, history, sexuality or any other social phenomenon into two coins, a female and a male coin. Each coin has two sides, heads and tails. Heads is always the female version of the social phenomenon. Tails is always the male version of the same phenomenon. This is a lesbian feminist method!

DEMYSTIFYING SEXUAL IDEOLOGY

Using this approach, there are always at least four sides to every socio-sexual event to be discerned: 1) the female account of female events is ideally represented by lesbian feminists and lesbian separatists; 2) the female account of male events is ideally represented by straight or hetero-feminists[1]; 3) the male account of female events by classical male matriarchists and marxists; and 4) the male account of male events is ideally represented by capitalist patriarchists. This method may remind the reader of a Faulknerian story told from four perspectives, or the movie "Rashomon," which tells of a murder from several people's perspectives. On the next page is a coin toss paradigm of sexual ideology.

TABLE 1. Paradigm of Sexual Ideology as a Coin Toss		
COIN TOSS	**SEXUAL IDEOLOGY**	
Socio-Sexual Events: 2 Coins	Tails= Male Ideology	Heads= Female Ideology
Male Event= Male Coin (history)	1) capitalist patriarchists *(male version of history)*	2) hetero-feminists bourgeois feminists *(female version of male history)*
Female Event= Female Coin (hystory)	3) male matriarchists & marxists *(male version of hystory)*	4) lesbian feminists & lesbian separatists *(female version of hystory)*

Capitalist patriarchists, who dominate North American textbooks, sexually analyze society from the perspective of the male account of male events. This is a one-dimensional approach to a socio-sexual reality that has at least four dimensions. Patriarchists are playing with only one coin—moreover, only one side of one coin, male on male. Patriscientists do not acknowledge the existence of *hystory*—either *prehistorically*, or *running in simultaneous opposition to historical development.* In this sense, patriarchal ideology lives in what Sartre called "bad faith," or what Marx called false consciousness, so long as it denies the hystory of female existence (the female coin).

The straight feminist, or *heterofeminist* approach to society/-history is two-dimensional, already an improvement in consciousness of social reality. Heterofeminists tend to see *both* sides of the male coin: the male and female version of male events. The heterofeminist approach generally takes the form of: heads argue with tails, the prototypical battle of the sexes (e.g., de Beauvoir, Kathleen Gough, Juliet Mitchell, Susan Brownmiller). Now consider the female coin, hystory.

The classical historical materialists (Marx, Engels, Bebel, Morgan, Lenin, even Stalin) and the classical male matriarchists (Bachofen, Briffault) believe that matriarchy historically precedes patriarchy, while capitalist patriarchists (Parsons, Tiger, Aberle) deny matriarchal existence and hystory altogether. While arguing that matriarchy precedes patriarchy historically, male matriarchists and vulgar marxists view patriarchy as an evolutionary advance. They thus fall into the anthropological school of "predetermined evolution," which has been critically questioned by mainstream 20th century anthropologists and heterofeminists. Dialectical marxist materialists view the patriarchal transition as having a progressive and reactionary dynamic simultaneously.†

Lesbian feminism focuses on reconstructing the female version of female events. Lesbian feminism differs from the other three ideological positions in two basic ways: 1) It is a homosexual ideology, while the other three are all heterosexist ideologies. 2) It is a totally female ideology. Also, lesbian feminism takes account of the other three ideologies, in that it argues consciously against them—while capitalist patriarchists, male matriarchists, marxists, and heterofeminists generally fail to acknowledge the existence of lesbian feminist ideology at all.

The two male ideologies here are attached to land mass, geopolitical states. Both female ideologies are stateless, landless ideologies, purely consciousness. Thus far, feminism is just a state of mind.

HYSTORY VERSUS HISTORY

Hystory has several meanings. Hystory refers in one sense to the time of prehistory, pre-patriarchy, pre-recorded time; while history denotes the time of patriarchy and written records.

†Engels' dialectical conception, as developed in *The Origin of the Family, Private Property and the State*, was that the transition from matriarchy to patriarchy combined a progressive dynamic with a regressive dynamic: It involved an evolutionary advance in technology, leading to a dramatic increase in humanity's control over the forces of nature and to the development of the natural sciences—but at the expense and degradation of the vast majority of society (women and the laboring classes). In the last analysis, the transition to patriarchy can only be described as "progressive" to the extent that, by vastly increasing the social forces of production beyond the constrictive framework of the private property relations characterizing patriarchy, it leads to its own overthrow by the world proletariat it has created—opening the way for the liberation of women on the foundations of the most advanced technology inherited and developed from patriarchal capitalism ("negation of the negation"). This conception is distinct from the outlook of those "male matriarchists" who see matriarchy as "nice, but doomed and gone forever." Revolutionary marxists hold that the liberating features of ancient gynosociety will be *reasserted* in modern communism. (See Marx and Engels, *Selected Works*, New York: International Publishers, 1974, pp. 496-7, 503, 592-3). —*Editor*

'The Bathers', by Niger Medina (contemporary, Nicaraguan)

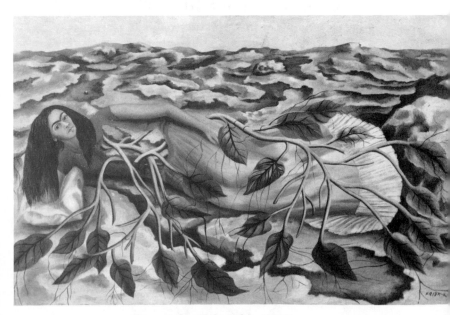

'Roots', by Frida Kahlo (1943)

Hystory is also the story of women as told by "women-identified-women" (herstory)[2], while history is the story of men as told by male-identified-males. History is distinctly male as hystory is distinctly female, ideologically.

According to these lesbian feminist usages, objectively neutral history does not exist. Instead, the recording or retelling of past events ideologically depends upon the sex, race, class, age, sexual preference, religion, politics and other relevant sociological identifications of the observer. Thus, it is ideologically impossible to remove the observer or his/her ideology from the observation.

Few sociologists or anthropologists trained in the patriscience tradition recognize female society or hystory, except in relation to the heterosexual institutions of marriage and the family. Nevertheless, *there is always hystory when there is human time, as there is always female society where there is human social space, regardless of patriscientific neglect to record female existence.*

PATRISCIENCE IS HETEROSEXIST

In the 1970's among the industrialized countries of the west, a feminist renaissance in both literature and science has risen to counteract the male supremacy over society and recorded history. To date, however, feminist critiques of patriscience and history have generally been written from a straight feminist perspective. A straight critique of straight society still makes the social universe seem straighter than it actually is.

A major problem with patriarchist, marxist, matriarchist and straight feminist approaches is that they all generally presume that all women are straight, thus omitting sexuality as a variable from their equations of women's oppression/liberation. In other words, they treat heterosexuality as a god-given constant that has no relation to women's oppression or liberation. This failure to realize the variation of sexuality leads straight scholars to ignore other crucial *sex variables*, i.e., dimensions of sex or elements of sex that vary.

The oppression of women is a *sexual oppression*, and cannot be fully understood or decoded without studying sex variables. Marxist theory generally focuses on economic variables (private property, inheritance, class society), while patriarchists generally focus on biological variables (differential sex organs, physical strength, and particularly the pregnancy factor) to explain women's oppression. Straight feminists are caught somewhere in the middle of marxist and patriscientific theories of women's oppression, without any comprehensive theory of their own.

Lesbian feminists focus on sexuality and offer sex theories to explain sexual oppression. In this book, I will offer new sex theories to explain women's oppressions, based on the study of three neglected sex variables in this debate: *sex ratios, female sexuality,* and *sex segregation.* First a discussion of the theoretical link between the origin of society, the origin of women's oppression, and the theory of women's liberation in sexual ideology is necessary here.

THE LINK BETWEEN THE ORIGIN OF SOCIETY, THE ORIGIN OF WOMEN'S OPPRESSION, AND THEORY OF LIBERATION

Any thorough analysis of the origin of women's oppressions implies at least some prior assumptions about social origin. For example, patriscientists think that no social form precedes patriarchy, which is the original form of society. They vigorously deny the possibility of a past age of women's liberation, and thus assume that women have always been oppressed since the origin of society.

Of course, this assumption has never been empirically proven; still it is dominant ideology in the North American social sciences. Following this patriarchal viewpoint, it appears that *no social change* can effect women's oppression because it is assumed to be a biological constant, rather than society's fault.

The patriarchal theory of social origin dooms women from the start, from the point of origin. Patriarchists blame women's oppression upon the victims, women—in particular, the female body. This is perhaps why patriarchists do not even bother to offer solutions to women's oppressions. What can they say? Cut out your ovaries or have a transsexual operation! The patriarchal, cavalier answer to women's oppression is: Become a man.

All anti-patriarchal theorists (marxist, feminist, lesbian feminist, matriarchist) agree that *women's oppression is not a biological constant, but rather a social variable*: Women's oppression varies according to social causes, and thus can be changed socially, economically, politically, ideologically, and historically.

There is considerable disagreement among these anti-patriarchists as to the exact form original society takes, but all agree that women were not systematically oppressed by men or the social structure in early prehistoric society. There is also a consensus among these anti-patriarchists or gyno-schools that women's oppression is the result of an historical event— namely, the rise of patriarchy—and clearly not the result of a doomed female biology.

Lesbian feminists think that the oppressed condition of women can be changed hystorically by the female development of alternative societies to patriarchy. This means that women's liberation can be achieved through hystorical revolution, or the evolution of new female societies, or perhaps the devolution of patriarchy back to prior female social forms, or a combination of these. The possibilities of freedom are infinite.

It has been reckoned by some feminist theorists that if women know how they originally became oppressed, then women will know how to undo that oppression. Other theorists in the movement do not think it matters whether women were ever liberated, free, or powerful in the prehistoric past. Their point is that liberations for women are the present necessities, and at the same time, female future visions. Since there is not only one oppression of women, neither is there only one liberation path for women. I refer to the plural oppressions of women, which demand plural liberations. Liberation is the topic of the last chapter of this book. Here, I must criticize the sexual ideology of the 19th and 20th centuries, the matriarchy/patriarchy debates, before proceeding to the development of feminist and lesbian feminist theory on the origin of women's oppressions.

The field of anthropology traces its own origin back to the 19th century debate over evolution of the patriarchal family. J. J. Bachofen (1861) first formulated the matriarchal theory of origin, and ironically "fathered" what later came to be known as the matriarchal school—the same year that Sir Henry Maine fathered the patriarchal theory of social origin through a study of Roman patriarchal law. I begin with the matriarchal school.[3]

Totonac goddess of subsistence and fertility: Veracruz, Mexico, A.D. 300-800.

MATRIARCHAL SCHOOL
Bachofen's Evolutionary Sequences

Using ancient myth as evidence, Bachofen posits that the patriarchal family evolved from: 1) an original pre-society state of promiscuity, *"Sumpfzeugung"* ("swamp procreation") or "hetaerism," whereby paternity is unknown, where lineage can only be traced through the mother—i.e., "mother right"; 2) The first human social order is created by Amazons through military defeat of "lustful males," and is based on the primacy of the mother, the feminine principle, reflected in mother goddess religions emphasizing fertility, culminating in the complete rule of women—gynaecocracy, the matriarchate. Amazonian matriarchy is original society; 3) conjugal matriarchy, the societal stage preceding the transition to patriarchy; 4) A stage of violent male revolt mythically linked to matricide and Amazon sex wars in defense of gynosociety characterize this patriarchal transition; and 5) The final establishment of patriarchy is built on the defeat of the Amazons.

Bachofen traces the origin of the patriarchal family back to the bloody transition from mother right to monogamy, where the woman belongs exclusively to one man. Monogamy invents paternity, "father right."

Bachofen has been criticized by 20th century patriscientists for lack of empirical data, and substitution of mythology for history. Engels (1884) criticized Bachofen's "mystic" lack of a material base for historical theory—although Engels certainly used portions of Bachofen's evolutionary schemes, incorporating them into his own theory of origin, minus the Amazons.

Both Bachofen and Engels have been criticized by 20th century patriscientists for their theoretical assumption of linear, universal evolutionary stages through which all human societies pass. Elizabeth Fee[4] (1974) and Adrienne Rich[5] (1976) criticize Bachofen from the feminist perspective that his theory of sexual and societal evolution is male supremacist, in that it places women and female society at the bottom of the evolutionary ladder while placing men and patriarchy at the top. Fee argues that Bachofen's evolutionary framework reflects the widespread Victorian effort to demonstrate that patriarchy is the "logical culmination of civilization," and that he used a prehistorical age of female power to support the patriarchal ideology of progress.

Lewis Henry Morgan[6] published "the first full field study of an American Indian tribe" in 1851, and became the "father of American anthropology."[7] Morgan's discovery of matrilineage (matrilineality) among the Iroquois, and his subsequent position in 1877 that matriarchy characterized the first line of descent in human social evolution, had an electric effect both on the early field of anthropology and on the writings of Marx and Engels. Engels combined the evolutionary approaches of Bachofen and Morgan in his 1884 *Origin of the Family, Private Property and the State.*[8]

Engels' Evolutionary Sequences

Engels accepted Bachofen's evolutionary theory that the matriarchal stage followed an original period of sexual promiscuity, where woman was the sole parent. Engels believed that the matriarchal stage was characterized by group marriage, mother right (matrilineage), matrilocal residence, and female supremacy in the household, which was the productive unit. Because women shared equally in social production, they were equal to men socially. Engels never states that women had political power as a group, however.

Morgan and Engels thought that the first stage of the family to develop out of the original promiscuity is the "consanguine family," which bans sexual relations between parents and children (here begins the incest taboo)—but allows indiscriminate mating among brothers, sisters and cousins.[9] Gradually, the "consanguine family"[10] is replaced by the "punaluan family," which excludes sex between maternal brothers and sisters.

The "punaluan family" was a group of sisters or close kinswomen from one tribe jointly married to a group of brothers or close kinsmen from another. It prescribed that women could only mate with men who were not their brothers, and men with women who were not their sisters. Engels thought that the increasing scope of the incest taboo eventually made group marriage impossible, and led to the rise of the pairing family. With the pairing family, the abduction and purchase of women begins.

The material basis for the oppression of women begins with the development of valuable productive resources, initially domestication of animals, then cultivated land.[11] Engels reckoned that animals, the earliest private property, must have been owned by men. Men acquired wealth in the form of herds, and wanted to pass this wealth on to their own children. This is the reason Engels offers for the male overthrow of mother right in favor of patrilineal inheritance. To think that the mass of women's oppression is based on the simple desire of the good shepherd to pass his old goat onto his sons!

Women's position in society declines as private property becomes the organizing principle of society. The change in property relations from communal to private, with inheritance traced through the male line, the institution of monogamous marriage and the beginning of class society led to what Engels termed the "world historic defeat of the female sex."

Engels is widely recognized as the most significant of the male theorists on women's oppression and liberation.[12] In the last chapter, I will criticize his theory of women's liberation.

19th Century 'Predetermined Evolution'

Morgan, Bachofen, Marx, Engels and Bebel all believed that patriarchal society evolved out of matriarchy, original society. Morgan's work, as well as Edward Burnet Tylor's[13] *Primitive Culture* (1872), express the first major concepts of the theory of "predetermined evolution" in cultural anthropology.

Following Franz Boas' 1896 publication of "The Limitation of the Comparative Method in Anthropology," patri-anthropologists shelved the evolutionist approach in favor of several subsequent schools of thought: from Boas' "historical particularism,"[14] to "diffusionism,"[15] "functionalism,"[16] "structural functionalism,"[17] "ethnoscience,"[18] and "cultural ecology."[19]

However, in the 1930's, Leslie A. White,[20] V. F. Calverton[21] and the "neo-evolutionists"[22] attacked Boas and argued that Morgan's and Tylor's evolutionary approach was correct from the start. Today, patri-anthropologists generally consider evolutionist theory[23] outdated and lacking empirical data to support its grand theory.

20th Century Matriarchists

Some of the major 20th century proponents of the matriarchal school are: Briffault (1927), Mathias and Matilde Vaertung (1923), Diner (1929), Gould Davis (1971), and Stone (1976).[24] These matriarchal researchers have presented an abundance of mother goddess archaeological evidence to support their contention that goddess worship is the most ancient of all religions.[25]

Patri-critics of the matriarchal school argue that even the existence of goddesses, no matter how well documented in the archaeological record, does not prove the existence of an entire social organization based on women's fertility—because it is problematic to argue directly from religion to social organization.

Yet feminist anthropologists, Rohrlich-Leavitt, Sykes, and Weatherford, contravene this critique of the matriarchal school on the grounds that it is "androcentric" and contradictory, as they write:

> ...Although it is generally accepted that religious practices reflect the secular life, when the archaeological record reveals the prevalence of goddesses, the corresponding secular dominance of women is denied despite the acceptance of a masculine secular supremacy when male gods are found to predominate.[26]

The 1978 "Ice Age Art Exhibition" at the Museum of Natural History in New York City, which is considered the oldest art in the world to date, contains a number of pregnant goddess figurines, which again supports the matriarchal school's contention of the prior age of goddess worship relative to god worship.

Speaking of male gods, it is time to move on to the patriarchal school of thought, which is based on the myths of male gods and other male superiority complexes.

THE PATRIARCHAL SCHOOL

Henry Maine (1861) and Edward Westermarck (1891) are the major 19th century proponents of the patriarchal theory of social origin. Both works are based on the premise that the patriarchal, heterosexual monogamian family is the primeval human institution, preceded by no other.

The 20th century proponents of the patriarchal school are numerous, and include most mainstream social scientists. Talcott Parsons' indirect biological assignment of "instrumental" (male) and "expressive" (female) roles in the family, is a major assumption of the social science patriarchal school. Lionel Tiger's direct genetic justification of male dominance hierarchies as part of the "male bonding" instinct also figures prominently in the patriarchal school.

Twentieth century anthropological data does not support the contentions of marxists, evolutionists, "neo-evolutionists," and matriarchists that matrilineage represents a universal historical stage in human society which precedes patrilineage.[27]

David F. Aberle (1962), a prominent patriarchist, studied the 84 matrilineal cases which comprise 15% of George Peter Murdock's 1957 "World Ethnographic Sample," and concluded that matrilineage is associated with horticulture, tends to disappear with plow cultivation, and vanishes with industrialization. Aberle thinks that matrilineage is a feature of perhaps "specific evolution," but not of general evolution.[28] Aberle found that matrilineal societies "are conspicuously underrepresented in the major areas of plow cultivation (Circum-Mediterranean and East Eurasia)" and most common in the Insular Pacific and North America. Matrilineal societies are also concentrated in Africa and South America. Aberle writes:

> Furthermore, among the matrilineal systems of the world, less than 50% are matrilocal or predominantly matrilocal. There is considerable variation among major areas. Matrilocality is common in North and South America, and avunculocality in Africa. The Insular Pacific is diversified, with matrilocal trends the modal type but making up less than 50% of the total... Although argument does not permit me to infer that matrilocal areas preserve matrilineal systems unchanged since their beginning, I am forced to consider that Africa in particular and the Insular Pacific to a considerable degree are areas where we are examining the conditions under which matriliny can survive rather than the conditions where it develops. Of Murdock's 60 minor areas, only 33 have one or more matrilineal systems. 37 of the total of 84 matrilineal cases are found in 5 of the 60 areas: Central Bantu, 7; Micronesia, 7; Western Melanesia, 8; Eastern Woodlands, of North America, 8; and southwestern United States, 7. These five areas are all horticultural.[29]

Incidentally, there is no clear anthropological evidence to support the patriarchal school's implicit contention that patrilineage precedes matrilineage. Kathleen Gough challenges the patriscientific assumption that hunters and gatherers were always patrilocal and patrilineal. She thinks there is some possibility that the earliest hunters and gatherers had matrilocal rather than patrilocal families.[30]

In *Sexual Politics*, Kate Millett summarizes the major themes of the patriarchal school in this way:

> Generally, the effect of this argument is to see in patriarchy the primeval, original, hence the 'natural' form of society, biologically based in the physical strength of the male, and the 'debilitating' effects of pregnancy in the female, working in conjunction with the environmental needs of a hunting culture to explain the subordination of women as the reasonable, even the necessary outcome of circumstances.[31]

Here it is important to debunk the ideology of the patriarchal school. One fatal flaw of patriarchal theories of male dominance based on the "debilitating" effects of female pregnancy is this: The presumptions that all women are both heterosexual and continuously pregnant, are erroneous.

These patriarchal theories carefully neglect the existence of the population of nonpregnant women, whether they are heterosexual, celibate, or lesbian. Not all women are geographically immobile, as patriarchal literature implies, due to pregnancy or child care. If the male-dominance/female-pregnancy theory can account for the oppression of pregnant women, it does not explain why nonpregnant women are also oppressed.

The Ideology of Patriarchy is: Patriarchy is Progress

The size of the male ego is a subject too large to discuss here. However, this much can be said: Patriarchal men cling desperately to the male supremacist myth that they are superior to women, nature, and animals. Patriarchal notions of progress are based more on male narcissism than on material reality.

Man is naturally, materially, biologically, socially, and historically dependent upon woman. But in patriarchy, the relations between the sexes are inverted artificially through the institutionalization of male dominance hierarchies on top of female society, and through the male ownership of female reproductivity and productivity. Female productivity controlled by patriarchy corresponds to all forms of female energy, service, and labor—whether it be wage or wageless—that is harnessed into a patriarchal economic force. The oppressed condition of women in patriarchal society will always correspond directly with that patriarchy's sexploitation, female "energy capture," and manipulation of female reproductivity and productivity. There is nothing mystical about it.

Patriarchists, male matriarchists, and vulgar marxists are all addicted to the male idea that whatever mass patriarchal events occur historically are progressive, destined, and could have happened in no other way. This is a self-serving male philosophy of history. The collective female imagination is full of *other* ways life might have been or could be.

Patriarchal oppression of women is neither progressive, nor necessary for women. Yet all male ideologies seek to justify patriarchy as a necessary evolutionary climb onward and upward.

Who's Who in Evolution

One problem with evolutionary theory is that is is sex relative. While men feel like they are going up from origin, women feel as if they are going backward. The evolution of patriarchy is based on the *devolution* of gynosociety. I reject the 19th century notion that evolution always moves forward in a linear progression, or that it is predetermined. Evolution may move in any direction. Perception of evolutionary direction is always relative to the sexual and political values of the observer.

Devolution is as likely to occur as evolution, and these two processes can occur simultaneously. Perhaps sexolution would be a better term to use here, since evolution is a value laden term connoting progress. By sexolution, I mean both sexual evolution and sexual devolution processes, the developmental movement of the sexes in relation to each other; or socio-sexual change in societal direction. When the sexes make a mass quantum leap to break through old, oppressive relationship patterns, sexolution becomes sexual revolution and transforms society. That is, in certain historical epochs sexolution leads to cataclysmic sexual revolution and sexual change; but usually sexolution moves as slowly over centuries as do the earth's plates.

The term evolution has become convoluted by the superimposition of male dominance hierarchies onto biological and sociological processes. The oppressors at the top of the male dominance hierarchies usually tend to see themselves as highly evolved, and view the oppressed as "unfit," unevolved. The oppressed at the lower levels of the hierarchies do not usually get the chance to define their oppressors in textbooks on evolution. Who's who in evolution is really more of an ideological matter than a biological one.

Sexual evolution in patriarchy seems more like a series of male-manic/female-depressive episodes than a steady progressive climb for both sexes. While men are going historically up, women are going down. High male status in patriarchy is obviously based on low female status. Patriarchy is the ultimate female down.

"In New York City on 21 October 1933, at 6 o'clock in the morning, Mrs. Dorothy Hale committed suicide, hurling herself from a very high window of the Hampshire House building. In her memory, this painting has been done by FRIDA KAHLO."

FEMINIST ANALYSIS OF MALE SUPREMACY AND WOMEN'S OPPRESSION

Feminists have widely criticized male writers in all academic disciplines, especially the social sciences, for submerging women under the listing: marriage and the family.[33] This is sexist in that it falsely assumes that all women are only wives and mothers, a narrow definition which amputates womankind into merely "Adam's rib."

This reductive categorization serves several patriarchal purposes: 1) It omits women's other contributions to hystory and society; 2) It has the superstructural effect of insuring that women will enter world recorded history only in their roles as they relate to men, as wife and mother and as no other; and 3) It serves patriarchy's social production and reproduction of labor needs,[34] specifically by defining and designing female socialization to supply vast amounts of free labor, wageless work in the roles of wives and mothers.

In *Women's Estate*, Juliet Mitchell writes that "the liberation of women can only be achieved if all four structures in which they are integrated are transformed—Production, Reproduction, Sexuality, and Socialization."[35] Mitchell criticizes both Engels and de Beauvoir for linking women's oppression "after the establishment of her physical inferiority for hard manual work with the advent of private property." Mitchell thinks that female "physical deficiency" relative to males is historically less important than the female's "lesser capacity for violence as well."

Anthropologist Kathleen Gough also points to the element of force, coercion in sexual oppression, positing that a male monopoly of weapons historically maintains male control of women by threat of force.[36]

In *The Second Sex*, Simone de Beauvoir finds Engels' explanation of the "turning point of all history," the transition from communal to private ownership, insufficient.[37] Kate Millett is bothered by much the same problem in *Sexual Politics*, as she criticizes Engels' failure to account for the "patriarchal takeover."[38]

Unless they are socialist feminists, most feminist writers do not think that private property is the sole basis for male supremacy, although they agree that the oppression of women becomes more acute in class society. This position is held by Shulamith Firestone, Juliet Mitchell, Simone de Beauvoir, and feminist anthropologists Karen Sacks, Gayle Rubin, and Kathleen Gough.

Susan Brownmiller criticizes Marx and Engels and their disciples (except August Bebel), for being "strangely silent about rape," and for their failure to grasp rape's "role in the very formulation of class, private property and the means of production."[39] According to Brownmiller in *Against Our Will*:

> Female fear of an open season of rape, and not a natural inclination toward monogamy, motherhood or love, was probably the single causative factor in the original subjugation of woman by man, the most important key to her historic dependence, her domestication by protective mating.[40]

LESBIAN FEMINIST CRITICISM OF HETERO-FEMINISTS

These feminist criticisms are generally shared by lesbian feminists. However, feminists have been criticized for failing to present a theory of women's oppression which would apply to many historical epochs. Lesbian feminists attribute this feminist failure of theory to heterosexism.

Heterofeminists fail to reach theoretical clarity regarding male supremacy and the oppression of women, due to a cognitive dissonance about men. In other words, they cannot see the patriarchal forest for the individual male trees with which they have emotional or vegetative relationships! All of the feminist theorists presented here have written their major works within the confines of a heterosexist universe.

Any theory that chops female sexuality down to exclusive heterosexuality will fail to describe the realities of the female world, because it does not have truth behind it from the start. A theory must be based on an accurate perception of the empirical world. Heterofeminist theory fails because it is based on the inaccurate perception that the female world is totally straight. Heterofeminist theory is missing lesbians and other nonheterosexual women.

Academic feminists have yet to question the role of heterosexuality in the maintenance of male supremacy in either marxist or capitalist social systems. Although heterofeminists have written volumes on what amounts to heterosexual relations, they make the heterocentric miscalculation that their analyses apply to all humanity — when, in fact, they apply only to heterosexual humanity. Along with male academics, heterofeminists rarely acknowledge lesbian existence, much less pretend to have studied it, opting usually to omit lesbians from studies of women or humanity altogether.

LESBIAN FEMINIST THEORY ON WOMEN'S OPPRESSIONS

Lesbian feminists begin analysis of patriarchy in this way: Heterosexuality is a "primary cornerstone of male supremacy."[41] In "Taking the Bullshit by the Horns," Barbara Solomon writes: "Heterosexuality insures male supremacy."[42]

Charlotte Bunch criticizes both "men who rule and male leftists who seek to rule" for attempting to "depoliticize sex and the relations between men and women in order to prevent us from acting to end our oppression and challenging their power."[43] Bunch also writes:

...The original imperialism was male over female; the male claiming the female body and her service as his territory (or property)... Although there have been numerous battles over class, race and nation during the past 3,000 years, none has brought the liberation of women. While these forms of oppression must be ended, there is no reason to believe that our liberation will come from the smashing of capitalism, racism or imperialism today. Women will be free only when we concentrate on fighting male supremacy.[44]

Purple September, a lesbian feminist newspaper in Holland, differentiates clearly between a personal decision in favor of heterosexuality and "The Normative Status of Heterosexuality":

As long as feminism is out to abolish the existing power relationship between the sexes it cannot ignore the normative status of heterosexuality... We live in a culture which sanctions only heterosexuality. As a result you cannot convince anyone that you are straight by choice... The women of *Purple September*...reject the normative status of heterosexuality but not heterosexuality as one type of relationship among other possible types. We do not doubt that there are straight relationships that derive their meaning and content from the people involved and not from the norm alone. But even in those relationships the male partner always has the option of falling back on 'masculine' behavior in the sense of his conditioning, thereby forcing his partner to fall back on 'feminine' acceptance in the sense of her conditioning. He has that option because the oppression of women by men has the status of a universal axiom: No one is surprised by 'axiomatic' behavior, but this is precisely how everyone confirms it. That is why the important thing is not that there are men who do not exercise the option they have. The important thing is that the option exists whether or not it is exercised. [45]

Heterofeminists generally ignore or fail to see the institution of heterosexuality itself, writing only about its oppressive symptoms. To a lesbian feminist, an *analysis of patriarchy is inseparable from an analysis of the power structure of the hetero-sexual world*. Rita Mae Brown dissects heterosexuality from the mainline movement perspective that the "personal is political":

...'Personal' life is political. Relationships between men and women involve power, dominance, role play and opression. A man has the entire system of male privilege to back him up. Another woman has nothing but her own self... If women still give primary commitment and energy to the oppressors how can we build a strong movement to free ourselves? Did the Chinese love and support the capitalists? Do the [Vietnamese National Liberation Front fighters] cook supper for the Yankees? Are Blacks supposed to disperse their communities and each live in a white home? The answer, again, is obvious†
...You do not free yourself by polishing your chains, yet that is what heterosexual women do... Heterosexuality keeps women

---

†Rita Mae Brown's analogy between social separation for women and social separation for urban blacks is, in my opinion, false and misleading. Martin Luther King, Jr. was profoundly correct in his struggle for the complete integration of black people into North American society, as the road to equality between the races—although Dr. King was rightfully criticized by more radical black political thinkers and leaders (most notably, Malcolm X) for preaching unconditional nonviolence on the part of the black masses, in the face of murderous attacks by the racist oppressors. In 1967 King, while holding fast to his democratic integrationism, boldly rejected the program of *integrating black people into the U.S. imperialist political structure*, by publicly denouncing the U.S. war against Vietnam, and declaring his solidarity with the revolutionary peoples of the third world. This set him on a collision course with the U.S. ruling class, which ended in his assassination.

[continued at bottom of next page]

separated from each other. Heterosexuality ties each woman to a man. Heterosexuality exhausts women because they struggle with their man—to get him to stop oppressing them—leaving them little energy for anything else. For this destruction of women's communities, for this betrayal of other women, women indeed get privileges from men: legitimacy (you are a real woman if you are with a man—a sexual definition again), prestige, money, social acceptance, and in some token cases political acceptance.[46]

Feminism questions the power relations between men and women, but it does not question the basic mode of relations, heterosexuality, which male supremacist power assumes on the everyday, taken-for-granted level.[47] Feminists have consistently pointed to the need for theory in the area of sexuality relevant to the oppression of women. Yet feminist discussions of sexuality are circumscribed by heterosexist "limits of debate," limited to female sexuality only as it applies to men, which is in several senses oppressive. To be heterosexually monogamous or not to be—appears to be the limit of the heterosexual conceptual universe.

Sociologically, there is a difference between heterosexuality and the wide expanse of human sexuality. Lesbian feminists regard heterosexists as sociologists regard the classic religious believer who has no conception that his/her world view *is* religious, and not "THE TRUTH." Psychologists routinely report that one is never terribly conscious of being in a delusion when one is in a delusion. Heterofeminists represent society's in-group compared to the marginal, lesbian out-group which sees that there is life for women after social death, after the patriarchal family. The eyes of the marginal have always been highly valued in sociology.

If the marxist viewpoint is correct, the complete and equal integration of all peoples of color into multinational urban society in the context of a socialist revolution, opening the way to widespread interracial marriage, will eventually eliminate all distinctions between the races. But obviously, this will not eliminate the distinction between the sexes. So women's liberation, including the prospects of social separation to the extent that patriarchal relations continue to oppress women, will still be on the agenda in socialist and communist society.

In this light, it is worth noting that the most principled *reactionaries*, the Ku Klux Klan and other fascists, stand for complete *segregation*—in fact, extermination—of nonwhites, but complete *"integration"* of (white) women into the patriarchal family. —*Editor.*

Linda Gordon's *Woman's Body, Woman's Right* is an exceptional academic feminist book, in that Gordon takes account of
the lesbian feminist movement, as well as the relation of heterosexism to women's oppression. Gordon thinks that the development of "sexual equality in heterosexual intercourse" will take
generations to accomplish. She writes:

> The modern women's liberation movement has reaffirmed
> both celibacy and multiple sexual partners for women. The
> modern movement has also given birth to a lesbian-liberation
> movement, possibly the most important contribution to a
> future sexual liberation. It is not that feminism has produced
> more lesbians. There have always been many lesbians, despite
> high levels of repression; and most lesbians experience their
> sexual preference as innate, nonvoluntary. What the women's
> liberation movement has created is a gay-liberation movement
> that politically challenges male supremacy in one of its most
> deeply institutionalized aspects—the tyranny of heterosexual-
> ity. The political power of lesbianism is a power that can be
> shared by all women who choose to recognize and use it; the
> power of an alternative, a possibility that makes male sexual
> tyranny escapable and rejectable.[48]

One of the more exciting economic analyses of lesbianism
coes from the radical grassroots organization, "Wages for
Housework." The "Wages Due Collective, Toronto, Canada"
views the existence of lesbianism and prostitution as evidence
that "sex is work." "Wages Due" sees lesbianism as "worker's
control" of female sexuality, "a refusal to sexually service
men." According to "Wages Due," lesbianism exposes the fact
that "heterosexuality is not in our genes, but in our training for
the work" that women are socialized to do in patriarchy.
"Wages Due Toronto" argues that:

> All women, women who are called lesbians and women who
> are called straight, are existing under capitalism for the same
> purpose—to serve capital through serving the family and
> men. This is what we mean when we say that all women are
> straight. Lesbians are part of women's struggle against capi-
> tal. NO WOMAN WANTS HER SEXUALITY TO BE SUB-
> JUGATED TO THE NEEDS OF THE STATE—TO THE
> NEEDS OF CAPITAL. This is what we mean when we say
> that all women are lesbians.[49]

Lesbian feminists do not regard male supremacy and heterosexism as purely economically[50] determined phenomena—

although the "political economy" of both are identified. Male supremacy and heterosexism, while rampant under capitalism, are not purely or originally capitalist phenomena, either. Both are phenomena of patriarchy, which is older than capitalism. A lesbian feminist approach is that men make patriarchy.   Even if we accept the patriarchist's patriarchal history, i.e., the male side of the male coin, one cannot rationally accept that ape-man climbed out of the trees into a ready-made patriarchy, from ape to *King* Kong, unless the ultimate ideolgical cop-out is invoked —that god created patriarchy.

Patriarchy is as man-made as gynosociety, when it exists, is woman-made. Patriarchy is the male's "social construction of reality." Of course, after patriarchy is made by men, it begins to make men also. That is, after Frankenstein creates his monster, the exchange between the two is dialectical. A key difference between lesbian feminism and heterofeminism can be discerned here.

Heterofeminists tend to pinpoint patriarchal socialization as *the source* of male supremacy, mistaking the result for the cause. This is ahistorical. Heterofeminists mistake the monster for the creator Frankenstein.

For lesbian feminists, patriarchy does not have an ideal existence apart from men. There would be no male supremacist systems without actual, historical male supremacists.

Heterofeminists anxiously try not to target individual men for fear of dividing the human race into two sexes (not recognizing that the human race is already divided into two sexes), and thus make the mistake of seeing the system as having a life apart from historical male supremacists—as if no men manned it, maintained, and profited from the systematic oppression of women. Heterofeminists, of course, have to target the system in order not to target individual males. Lesbian feminists blame both.

Lesbian feminists contend that the system of patriarchy is the collective result of the supremacy of individual men. We do not deny the existence and weight of the patriarchal system in the oppression of women; but, simultaneously, hold that individual men are the historical creators, heirs and profiteering instruments of applied male supremacist systems. Men are both the chicken and the sperm of patriarchy.

Chapter 2

Lesbian Origins

If there is a single dot of social time which fascinates social scientists most, it is society's point of origin. This chapter is a theoretical search for several social beginnings: the original shape of human society, with its female sexualities and sex ratios; the origin of the incest taboo, patriarchy, and heterosexist supremacy, with its oppression of women and especially lesbians.

SEX THEORY OF SOCIAL ORIGIN

I begin with the theory that the origin of human society is characterized by: a predominantly female adult population, a high degree of horizontal sex segregation, chronic incest, and a year-round prevalence of female asexuality, bisex, and homosex compared to the relative infrequency of exclusive heterosex.

Female adults greatly outnumber male adults at the origin of human society. Social relations between adult females form the original and continuing base of society. Homosocial relations between biological female kin of all ages form the original and continuing core of the human family.

These first two chapters are related by a thread of sex theory which seeks to explain the regression from the origin of society to the origin of women's oppression. The political point of studying the genesis of polisex oppression is to understand the future genesis of women's liberation. —*Author*

40

Beginning at adolescence, the majority of males born into original society are horizontally segregated outside the perimeters of the female community, whereas the majority of females born live inside their community of origin. I assume that the high-female/low-male adult population of early society is the result of extreme social and physical separation of the sexes beginning at adolescence, rather than being the result of a high-female/low-male live birth rate.

Extreme separation of the sexes characterizes human social origin. Asexuality, bisexuality, and homosexuality are freely permitted year round. Heterosexuality is practiced for reproductive purposes only, and thus may be rarer than other sexualities at origin.

The prevalence of homosexuality occurs in two separate spaces in relation to the sexually segregated community of origin. Lesbianism occurs *within* the perimeters of the female community, while male homosexuality is a prevalent feature of male life *outside* female society.

Exclusive heterosexuality may be present at origin, as I expect *all* sexualities spontaneously are. Yet, exclusive heterosex is not the numerical "norm" of human sex origin, as patriscientists tend to assume. I expect that bisex is more frequent than exclusive heterosex.

An important point here is that from the beginning, female society is equivalent to society itself. Society is always at core a gynosociety. Female homosocial relations are critical to the formation and maintenance of the family, community, and society. Due to both sexism and heterosexism, patrisociologists miss this point and falsely assume that society is sex neutral. Internal social organization at origin consists of the cooperation between adult females in defense of offspring and in food sharing.

This theory suggests that original human social organization may resemble the predominantly female horde of non-human living primates in the wilds. Although offspring of both sexes are present, there is a wealth of data regarding the numerical preponderance of adult females among such primates (cf. Carpenter, 1963; Sahlins, 1960; Zuckerman, 1932; Gough, 1975; Leibowitz, 1975). This point will be discussed in greater detail in chapter 4, "Sex Ratio Theory."

No one to date has empirically answered the human sexuality question of origin, as to which came first: asexuality (celibacy), bisexuality, homosexuality, or heterosexuality? Or are all sexualities spontaneously present at origin?

Is the first sexual relation the first social relation, and *vice versa*? This is a highly theoretical question, since no one has conclusive or empirical proof of either the first social or sexual relationship. Keep in mind that this leaves us largely in the realm of theory and ideology.

Patriscientists who claim heterosexist origin, i.e., assuming that no lesbians, bisexuals, or asexuals exist originally and insisting that only exclusive heterosexuals populate the original world, are in no empirical position to substantiate their heterosexist ideology.

Patriscientists have never produced a shred of evidence to prove that lesbians are not present at social origin. My position is that patriscientists must prove that all prehistoric women were straight, before it can be concluded that no lesbian, celibate, or bisexual females exist in early society.

Perhaps the most interesting point to be grasped in any theory of sex and society is that *until the actual incidence of lesbianism, asexuality, bisexuality, and male homosexuality is known, the actual incidence of heterosexuality remains unknown.* This is true of either prehistoric or historic society. Heterosexist scientists miss the point entirely by omitting or underreporting lesbian and gay phenomena. In other words, sociologists will never know how many straight people there actually are, until they know how many non-straights exist. The total sexuality per society of any historical epoch is equal to the sum of these four relative frequencies: homosexuality, asexuality, bisexuality, and heterosexuality. Obviously, the value of heterosex cannot be solved without knowing the other values, since each is only a ratio of total societal sexuality.

Heterosexists assume that the first social relationship is male/female, and thus view the first sexual relation as heterosexual. This is a hypothesis which has yet to be proven. I will argue from the other side of the ideological coin, that the first enduring social relation may be the female/female relation, e.g., mother/daughter, sisters, or cooperation between non-kin mothers for protection of young and/or food sharing. This is a hypothesis which also has yet to be proven. Nevertheless, if the first social relation is the female homosocial relation, then its corresponding sexual relation is lesbianism.

In traditional sociology, society requires by definition some form of cooperation. Lesbianism may be functional to early female-centered society, because lesbianism requires and fosters some form of physical cooperation between adult females. Since I regard the adult female homosocial relation as the major functional prerequisite of society itself, I postulate that lesbianism, the female homosexual relation, may be traced to the origin of society. Later, in part II of this book, I will present empirical data to indirectly support this theory using both hunter/-gatherer and nonhuman living primate societies where lesbianism has been observed and recorded by patriscientists in English. This evidence indirectly supports the theory that lesbianism is prehistoric—since in the social sciences, the methodological literatures on hunter/gatherers and living nonhuman primates in the wilds are two traditional indirect measures of early prehistoric human society.

The heterosexist universe has made it custom, and sometimes law, to omit lesbian sexuality from recorded historical society. Here, it is important to mention that lesbianism is recorded in even the earliest written histories of western civilization.

LESBIANISM IN EARLIEST RECORDED HISTORY

It is ironic that heterosexists omit lesbians from discussions of early society, since the earliest recorded history, art, and literature of western society documents the existence of lesbians: Ruth and Naomi[1] among the Hebrews (pre-800 B.C.) in the bible; Sappho's poetry on Lesbos[2] (c. 600 B.C.); Aristotle and Plutarch describe female homosexuality in Sparta[3] (c. 400 B.C.); Aristotle also describes homosexuality sanctioned by the Cretan[4] constitution and among the Celts[5]; lesbianism has been reported in Athens[6] (450 B.C.), and in Rome[7] (A.D. 100).

Plato, a homosexual himself, invents an origin myth of homosexuality in the *Symposium*, but speaks through Aristophanes. I have excerpted only the lesbian passage from the Plato/-Aristophanes story:

> ...for the original human nature was not like the present, but different. In the first place, the sexes were originally three in number, not two as they are now; there was man, woman, and the union of the two, having a name corresponding to this

double nature; this once had a real existence, but is now lost, and the name only is preserved as a term of reproach... Men who are a section of that double nature which was once called Androgynous are lascivious; adulterers are generally of this breed, and also adulterous and lascivious women; the women who are a section of the woman don't care for men, but have female attachments; the female companions are of this sort.[8]

While Plato's fable may appear fantastic, it does historically place the knowledge of lesbianism in Plato's time, which is important from a sociology of knowledge perspective. Sarah Pomeroy compares the "female homoerotic attachments" of Sparta and Lesbos:

In contrast to the personal poetry of the aristocratic Sappho, there are some songs surviving that were performed by choirs of maidens and women. Judging from the extant fragments and remarks of ancient authors, these songs ran the full range from the informal folksongs of spinners and weavers to performance by professionals at festivals. Apart from dirges, already mentioned, there were maiden songs, *partheneia*, which were formal choral hymns sung by unmarried girls to the accompaniment of the flute. A large fragment of one of these maiden songs, written by the poet Alcman in Sparta, has been preserved... The choir names most of the girls in it, and singles out some for special praise. Girls are compared to the sun, their hair to gold, their ankles are lovely, and they run swiftly like fillies. They say of their leader, 'Hagesichora exhausts me.' We may choose to interpret this phrase as 'exhausts me' with praising her, or with trying to win at a festival, or sexually and emotionally. The last interpretation is supported by our knowledge that erotic attachments between older women and young girls were encouraged at Sparta. It is likely that in the female atmosphere of the girls' choir lesbian relationships flourished. The most important factor, both at Sparta and at Lesbos, in fostering female homoerotic attachments was that women in both societies were highly valued. They were admired and loved by both men and women... Women did not, as has been suggested, turn to other women in desperation, due to men's disparagement of them. Rather, it appears that they could love other women in milieux where the entire society cherished women, educated them comparably to men of their class, and allowed them to carry over into maturity the attachments they had formed in the all-female social and educational context of youth.[9]

In another comparison of Spartan and Lesbian society, the early historian Bethe challenges the assumption that Spartan and Lesbian homosexual relationships arose from the total segregation of the sexes. Bethe wrote: "...In Sparta and Lesbos, where we know most about this boy-love and girl-love, the sexes to the best of our knowledge, mixed with each other more freely than in other Greek States."[10]

There are probably other classical references to lesbianism of which I am unaware, but the early historical records of lesbianism here are enough to establish that lesbianism has been reported in society since western society has been recorded.

NON-HETEROSEXUAL ORIGIN MYTHS

A fascinating area rich for cross-cultural study is nonheterosexual original myths. These origin myths place lesbians, gay males, transvestites, hermaphrodites, celibates, bisexuals, androgynes, and other intersexes at "the beginning of all things." The field is much too vast to elaborate here; however, I want to pay brief attention to some of this data for its sociology of knowledge value.

Carolyn Niethammer explores two nonheterosexual origin myths among North American Indians, the Navajo and the Mohave, in her book, *Daughters of the Earth: The Lives and Legends of American Indian Women*. Of the Navajos, Niethammer writes:

A Navajo lesbian was considered an asset by both her family and community. In one of the tribal myths about the beginning of all things, homosexuals are described as being wealthy and as having control of all wealth. Consequently, they were usually put in charge of the household and controlled the disposal of all property.[11]

In the *Female of the Species*, Martin and Voorhies (1975) recount George Devereaux's original report from an old Mohave informant that:

...'homosexuals' and 'transvestites' have been present since the beginning of the world. The Mohave also believe that in the early periods of the mythical era sexes were undifferentiated. This is particularly significant in view of the fact that 'it is a basic principle of the Mohave philosophy of life that everything on earth happens in accordance with rules and precedents dating back to the time of creation.' (Devereaux 1961:12)[12]

Mohave lesbians are called *hwame*. Niethammer writes that:

> The Mohaves, who lived along the Colorado River, also believed that from the very beginning of the world it was intended that there should be homosexuals. They thought that sometimes a baby would dream about becoming a transvestite while still in the womb.[13]

In *Gay American History*,[14] Jonathan Katz summarizes Edward Winslow Gifford's primary report on a Kamia "origin story" which Gifford published in 1931 in the *Bureau of American Ethnology Bulletin*:

> The Kamia ancestors camped on the eastern side of Salton Sea, from which place they later scattered... The dispersal of the people from their camping place at Salton Sea was due to fear created by the appearance from the north of a female transvestite (Warharmi) and two male twins called Madkwahomai. They were the introducers of Kamia culture... The transvestites and the twins...were the bearers of the seeds of cultivated plants.[15]

Twins are associated with parthenogenesis. Thus the Kamia story incorporates two major nonheterosexual elements of origin myths, the female transvestite with her parthenogenetic twins, into one powerful tribal origin myth.

These origin myths are not confined to North American Indian tribal societies. In the *Human Relations Area File*, Belo reports a nonheterosexual Balinese origin myth:

> The crossing of sex roles (there are in Bali both male and female transvestites) is one of the possibilities afforded by culture. There is a definite high valuation placed upon the godly figure which combines the characteristics of both sexes, Sang Hyang Toengyal, the Solitary, or Tjintija, who preceded the separation of male and female in Balinese cosmology. He is, in time, before all the gods, before Siva, Brahman, and Vishnu.[16]

Of course, Greek mythology contains a number of intersex origin myths. In the "Orphic Creation Myths," according to Robert Graves, "Eros was double-sexed."[17]

This brief review of nonheterosexual origin myths does not do justice to the cross-cultural material. I use these nonheterosexual cosmologies only to illustrate that the sociology of knowledge of societies more ancient than our own patriarchal U.S. society is not closed to the idea that lesbianism may trace back to the origin of human society itself.

'Lesbian ignition' in Germany, roughly 475 years ago: This rendition of three excited witches, attributed to Hans Baldung Gruen and dated 1514, was designed as a new year's greeting card.

LESBIANISM AND HUMAN ORIGIN
TABOOED IN PATRIARCHY

Why do patriarchal taboos surround the question of human origin and pre-State sex? In the same vein, why is the question of matriarchy or gynosociety as well as lesbian society and Amazonism tabooed in patriarchal society?

A sociological phenomenon that is positively sanctioned in gynosociety will be negatively sanctioned in patriarchy, and *vice versa*. In Eliade's terms, whatever is sacred to gynosociety is profane to patriarchy; what is sacred to patriarchy is profane to gynosociety.

For example, lesbianism, illegitimacy, spinsterhood, celibacy, bisexuality, male homosexuality, the mother/child household, Amazonism for defense of gynosociety, mostly-female sex ratios, matrilocality, matrilineage, and sororal polygyny are ideologically charged positive and respected by gynosociety, the society of origin. Precisely these same variables are charged negative in patriarchy and are viewed with disdain, sometimes horror.

I hypothesize that what phenomenon is charged positive in original society is charged negative in later patriarchy. To use the coin toss analogy I invoked earlier, original society equals gynosociety, the female side of the female coin—while patriarchy, a later historical occurrence, is the male side of the male coin. They are opposite, not parallel phenomena.

Thus, patriscientists are methodologically off in the wrong field arguing that matriarchy never existed† because they can-

---

†The notion that "matriarchy never existed" would have come as news to the prophet Isaiah, who exerted himself to denounce remnants and/or reassertions of matriarchal relations within the heart of patriarchal Jewish society, around 750 BC: "...As for my people, children are their oppressors, and women rule over them. O my people, they who lead thee cause thee to err, and destroy the way of thy paths." (Isaiah, 3.12). "...Moreover the Lord saith,...the daughters of Zion are haughty, and walk with stretched forth necks and deceitful eyes, walking and prancing as they go, and making a tinkling with their feet. Therefore the Lord will smite with a scab the crown of the head of the daughters of Zion, and the Lord will lay bare their secret parts." (3.16-17). Isaiah also railed against those foreign societies where women held power and influence: "Come down and sit in the dust, O virgin daughter of Babylon, sit on the ground: There is no throne, O daughter of the Chaldeans; for thou shalt no more be called tender and delicate... Thy nakedness shall be uncovered, yes, thy shame shall be seen: I will take vengeance.. Sit thou silent, and get thee into darkness, O daughter of the Chaldeans: for thou shalt no more be called the lady of kingdoms." (47.1,3,5). —*Editor*

not find gynosocial variables such as matrilocality or matri-lineage normally present in patriarchal societies today.

Of course patriscientists will not find matrilineage normal in patrilineal society, because matrilineage is abnormal in patri-archy as patrilineage is abnormal in gynosocieties. Obviously, patrilineage could not be normal if matrilineage prevailed. Pat-riarchal thought along these lines in the social sciences is absurd and illogical. The *patrilinear* notion of progress does not permit patriscientists to reason clearly about sexual devolution. Patrilinearity, as a schematic rationalization of male events, is historically inaccurate.

Discussion of gynosociety, original sexual society, and lesbi-anism is patriarchal taboo. Patriscientists treat lesbianism, gynosociety, and Amazonism as if they never existed, generally. Why? One reason lesbianism is patriarchal taboo is becauase lesbianism is the sexuality mode that matches the material rela-tions of the sexes, displaying the condition that men are unneces-sary to women sexually. This is not a popular display of sexual form in patriarchy.

Patriarchists correctly perceive lesbianism as a contagious revolt against misogynist society and the patriarchal exploita-tion of female sexuality. *Female self-hate and female dislike of other females are necessary for the maintenance of patriarchal sexploitation.* By definition, lesbians love women, not men. In patriarchy, women-loving-women are considered "criminal," "sick," "abnormal," "deviant," "degenerate," or "perverse."

Lesbians are the least likely of all women to internalize patri-archy's irrational contempt for women. Sherry Ortner thinks that those women who accept male society's devaluation of themselves and other women, who try to integrate into male society by vicarious participation through their heterosexual relations with males, are considered by patriarchists as capable of male "transcendence."[18] This means capable of transcending their unwanted femaleness. While I agree with Ortner that this process occurs, I believe that those women who are considered capable of male "transcendence" are exclusively heterosexual women. Straight women, by virtue of patriarchal socialization, undergo a mental transsexual operation in a sense that lesbians general-ly do not. Exclusively heterosexual women are domesticated women in patriarchy.

The sexuality variable cuts neatly across the female population to predict which women in patriarchy can "pass" as men by transcending their femaleness through heterosexual relations. This patriarchal split between exclusively heterosexual women and lesbians is synonymous in many respects with the classic split Helen Diner describes between "Mothers and Amazons." However, this title is slightly misleading. It would be more accurate to say the split between heterosexual mothers and lesbian mothers.

In patriarchy, lesbians are untamed, undomesticated women who try to function outside of male control. Due to their female resistance, they are the most devalued women in patriarchy.

Lesbians are valued in gynosociety, as are celibate women and spinsters. Again, what is devalued in patriarchy is valued in gynosociety, and *vice versa*. What is worshipped in gynosociety is defiled in patriarchy.

I suggest that this inverted ideological charge between patriarchal and gynosocial societies is the major reason that lesbianism, Amazonism, and original sexual relations are looked upon with horror and disgust in patriarchy.

Does the oppression of lesbians begin with the advent of patriarchy? How is lesbianism theoretically tied to the questions of women's oppression and women's liberation?

THEORY ON THE ORIGIN OF WOMEN'S OPPRESSION

I begin with the assumption that women were not originally oppressed by social structure, because original society is gynosociety. Original gynosociety is characterized by: high-female/-low-male societal sex ratios, horizontal sex segregation, and a free range of female sexuality.

Women's oppression begins in the late hystorical transition from gynosociety to patriarchy. The patriarchal transition, the beginning of women's oppression, is characterized by: *a mass societal shift from the original high-female/low-male sex ratios to the historical high-male/low-female sex ratios of early patriarchy,* then later to the *near equal sex ratios of established and late patriarchy.* The transition is accomplished through *gynocide* and female infanticide, accompanied by decreasing-female/increasing-male social space through the mass heterosex integration of all adolescent and adult males into female society.

The epoch of chronic rape, i.e., forced female heterosex, takes hold, marking the start of the male "energy capture" of female sexuality, and thus of reproduction. The mass heterosexualization of women simultaneously ushers in the persecution of nonheterosexual women—i.e., lesbians, spinsters, celibates—as well as nonmonogamous heterosexual women such as prostitutes and so-called "frigid" heterosexual women. This is one critical reason why the oppression/liberation of women is tied to the oppression/liberation of lesbians.

The oppression of women is marked by male societal attempts to limit female sexuality to exclusive heterosexuality for the mass production of fathers and sons.[†] Another critical method of oppressing women is the assimilation of adult males into female society, first by invasion, then by the establishment of male dominance hierarchies superimposed on female society.

The establishment of paternity, the male exploitation of female products, and the separation of daughters from their mothers (patrilocality) are requisite conditions for the establishment of patriarchy. Matrilineage and matrilocality have to be destroyed for patriarchy to exist at all. Matrilineage and matrilocality are the first gynosocial variables to go at patriarchal transition. The construction of patriarchy is based on the destruction of gynosociety.

[†]This raises the question of the origin of *clitoridectomy*, which continues to be widely practiced in Africa, the Middle East and southern Asia, victimizing some 70 million girls and women altogether. The practices of clitoridectomy range from the mildest type, in which only the tip of the prepuce of the clitoris is removed (analogous to male circumcision), to the most extreme form, "infibulation," which involves the complete removal of the clitoris, along with the labia minora and labia majora—with the resulting wound being stitched or bound in such a way as to leave a small hole for penetration. This extreme form of sexual mutilation, depriving the afflicted females of practically all sexual pleasure for the rest of their lives, molds them into tame objects of heterosexual intercourse, from which only the man can derive pleasure. Clitoridectomy is practiced among many muslim peoples, but also among certain christian and jewish peoples as well. It was practiced in the ancient Egyptian civilization, as evidenced by female mummies dating 200 B.C. (See these books, all published by Zed Press, London: Asma El Dareer, *Woman, Why Do You Weep?: Circumcision and its Consequences*, 1982; Raqiya Haji Dualeh Abdalla, *Sisters in Affliction: Circumcision and Infibulation of Women in Africa*, 1982; and Maria Rosa Cutrufelli, *Women of Africa: Roots of Oppression*, 1983, pp. 136-8).

How did clitoridectomy arise historically? It seems likely that it was imposed upon women after their societies were overthrown by patriarchy, as a violent method of repressing female sexuality — above all, lesbian sexuality. —*Editor*

The 'male capture of female energy' through the institution of monogamous marriage: plinth frieze at the Gupta temple in Deogarh, India. Note that the man at left brandishes a dagger, no doubt to secure his recent conquest. (from Joanna Gottfried Williams, *The Art of Gupta India*, Princeton University Press, 1982)

Patriscientific searches for equivalent female structures of oppression, i.e., reverse patriarchies, are diversionary because gynosociety and patriarchy are opposites—not similar in function, principle, or structure. A matriarchy comparable to patriarchy will never be found, and I consider it a waste of time to look. The patriscientific focus, in an effort to disprove gynosocial origin, has been on the *minority* of matrilineal societies today, compared to the majority of patrilineal societies. This approach borders on stupidity, because matrilineage and matrilocality modally had to be destroyed at patriarchal transition in order for patriarchy to be established.

For patriarchists in the 19th and 20th centuries to expect to find world modal matrilineage and matrilocality as their criteria to prove or disprove gynosociety's existence—then of course not to find them in late patriarchy and conclude that gynosociety never existed—is something of a rigged election.

Any fair attempt at reconstruction of original gynosociety would recognize that modal matrilineage and matrilocality may be the first gyno-building blocks to fall at patriarchal transition, when father-right is globally established. The last gyno-variable to go is the high female productivity contributed to the maintenance of society. There is a reason for the endurance of female productivity throughout patriarchy. Once men develop patrilineage and ownership, females can still perform the bulk of social labor without controlling the products of their labor—to the benefit of males.

Once patriarchy is *established*, Engels' account of the establishment of the heterosexual monogamian family, private property, and the state is correct. Engels describes the economic *institutionalization* of women's oppression in already established patriarchal society—not the sexual *preconditions* that make its establishment possible, except for his discussion of patrilineage/matrilineage. Patrilineage is a property relation, but matrilineage is a sexual relation.

The preconditions of patriarchy are: 1) high-male/low-female societal sex ratios in either the total or adult population; 2) the male appropriation of female sexuality through the mode of exclusive heterosexuality (which is a precondition for the establishment of the heterosexual monogamian family), and the oppression of nonheterosexual women such as lesbians, celibate women, even bisexual women. The oppression of male homosexuals is used to straighten out as many men as possible to be patriarchal fathers. 3) A high degree of heterosex integration is necessary for the advent of patriarchy. In other words, the horizontal physical separation of adolescent and mature males from female society breaks down. Males must control uterine society to control society itself. The female body forms the body politic.

Female reproduction and production are the twin bases of society. Marxists usually sacrifice sexual variables for economic variables, viewing male opression of women as only a property relation, when it is also a sexual relation. Sex oppression cannot be understood without sex variables. In this study, I focus on three neglected sex variables—female sexuality, societal sex ratios, and sex separation—to understand the nature of women's oppression and liberation. More research into the role heterosexual incest plays in the development of the patriarchal family should prove extremely relevant to the origin of women's oppression.

INCEST THEORY

The development of the patriarchal family and heterosexual monogamian marriage may be traced back to rape, "marriage by capture," and heterosexual incest. I suggest that the first enduring heterosexual relation is the mother/son relation. My theory is that the first father is the son. Patriarchal biologic maintains that the husband becomes the father who creates the son. My sociologic reverse this sequence. I suggest that *the son is the first male to reside with mother as lover.* The son becomes the first residential and social father, who creates the role of residential husband. Morgan, Marx, and Engels noted that probably the first heterosexual marriages are incestuous.

The first father is the son. When the first incest taboo banning mother/son incest obtains, the brother/sister incest relation replaces it. The father becomes the brother. When the next incest taboo bans brother/sister heterosex, the brother is no longer the biological father. In matrilineal societies extant in the 19th and 20th centuries, the brother remains the *social* father. Patriscientists have puzzled over why the mother's brother would have so much sexual and political power in matrilineal societies, instead of the mothers themselves. I posit that the reason why the mother's brother is regarded as the social father of his sister's children in matrilineal systems surviving into patriarchy is due to the brother's prior biological paternity of his sister's children in the earlier forms of matrilineal sytems.

Using the language of Mary Daly, the ultimate "patriarchal reversal" is that the son becomes the father of patriarchy, when they were one and the same. Engels thought that the primal patriarchal urge comes from the desire of the fathers to pass property on to their biological children. Since I think that the first residential fathers are lovers of their mothers—or in street language, "motherfuckers"—the primal patriarchal urge is more likely to be located in the son's desire for his mother's power.

Incest is a complicated area which needs deeper research by women. This much is clear to me: The effect of the incest taboo on mother/son and sister/brother relations is critical to an understanding of how patriarchal transition and the mass heterosex integration of non-kin adult males into female society may have occurred. Feminist scientists would learn more about women's oppression by studying the effect of heterosexual incest on the family, than by fixating on matrilineage, as patriarchists do.

The incest taboo may have effected patriarchal transition in that the ban on mother/son, then later brother/sister heterosex[†] alters original social organization in at least two ways: 1) These two earliest heterosex incest taboos *may cause the entrance of non-kin adult males into a predominantly female society*, which had previously only allowed select adult male kin in positions of close physical proximity to females; 2) If previously sons and brothers were originally the fathers, and then are replaced by non-kin male strangers, both the biological and social power of mother's sons and brothers are usurped. If this is true, oedipal jealousy may have an historical, reproductive base, rather than just being a mythical or psychological drama in Freudian analysis.

[†]For an elaborate detailing of the incest taboos among the ancient Jews following their liberation from Egypt (around 1490 B.C), see the biblical book of Leviticus, chapters 18 and 20. Interestingly, the first incest taboo listed in chapter 18 is: "The nakedness of thy father, or the nakedness of thy mother, shalt thou not uncover: She is thy mother; thou shalt not uncover her nakedness." (Leviticus 18.7). Next we read, "The nakedness of thy father's wife shalt thou not uncover: It is thy father's nakedness." (18.8). The term, "thy father's wife," in contrast to "thy mother," seems to imply a polygynous family structure. And then: "The nakedness of thy sister, the daughter of thy father, or daughter of thy mother, whether she be born at home or abroad, even their nakedness thou shalt not uncover." (18.9). —*Editor*

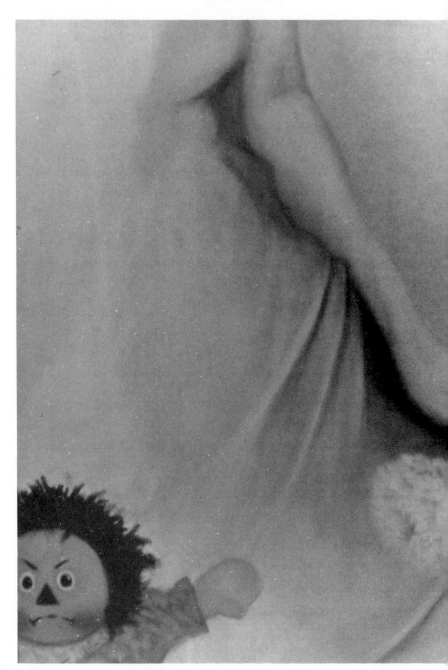

'Raggedy Ann', by Janet Yacht.

It is my theoretical intuition that, given human sexual variation, all forms of incest may appear in any historical epoch.
However, certain incest relations may correspond to certain
social structures normally, and are thus more prevalent under
the ideological regime of those social structures. For example, I
expect that father/daughter incest is more frequent under patriarchal structure (i.e.,, patriarchal family, patrilineage, patrilocality, patriarchal economy) than mother/daughter and sister/-
sister incest.*

While incest is generally viewed as dysfunctional for the
family—and this is true of heterosex incest—I will argue that
*at origin, homosex incest plays a functional role in the develop-
ment of the family.* I delineate between two major forms of
incest in this book: homosex and heterosex incest.

Homosex incest describes the emotional and/or sexual relations between biological kin of the same sex. Heterosex incest
describes the emotional and/or sexual relations between biological kin of the opposite sexes.**

---

*This theory is, in part, supported by mounting evidence compiled by the
burgeoning Incest Survivor movement as well as police/state statistics
concerning contemporary U.S. patriarchy, which reveal that 97% of all
victims of sexual abuse are young girls abused by adult males. (Toni A.H.
McNaron and Yarrow Morgan, eds. *Voices in the Night: Women Speaking
About Incest* (Minneapolis, MN: Cleis Press, POB 8281, 1982), pp. 14-16.
McNaron and Morgan also point to the statistic that "one out of every
three girl children experiences sexual abuse in her family" in the U.S.—
where the victimizer is usually a male member of the family. Now,
although my theory is general and extends beyond U.S. patriarchy to world
patriarchy, these U.S. findings certainly do not disprove my theory—even
though they do not statistically pinpoint the father, only male relatives.
—*Author*

**Here, I purposefully expand the patriarchal Webster's dictionary defini-
tion of incest from merely "sexual intercourse between persons so closely
related that they are forbidden by law to marry" (7th New Collegiate Edi-
tion, 1963, p. 423), to include emotional intercourse, for several reasons.
The old Webster's definition does not even take into account sexual
molestation—much less, the damaging emotional abuse that accompanies
sexual abuse. Incest victims are not only physically violated, but emotionally violated as well. Daughters who are emotionally treated as if they are
their father's lover, mistress, wife or mother are denied their childhood,
their trust in parental figures, which sometimes extends to loss of trust of
the world at large; sometimes they lose trust in themselves as well. When
sexual boundaries blur in a family, emotional confusion abounds and
requires treatment.

Thanks to the Incest Survivor movement (which includes the consciousness raising work of Valerie Heller, Florence Rush and New York Radical
Feminists' speak-outs on incest, Kathleen Brady and many other brave

Homosex incest reveals a different relation and result from heterosex incest. In the first place, homosex incest produces no progeny, so no genetic repercussions result. Aside from this difference, the social bonds and family formation of roles derived from same-sex incest and opposite-sex incest are illustrated on Table 2 on the next page.

Female emotional homosex incest develops these critical family relations: mother/daughter, sisters, aunt/niece, female cousins, grandmother/granddaughter. (See box 1, Table 2).

Male homosex incest denotes these relations: father/son, brothers, uncle/nephew, male cousins, grandfather/grandson. (See box 3 in Table 2).

Matri-heterosex incest develops these family relations: mother/son, sister/brother, aunt/nephew, grandmother/grandson, maternal uncle/nieces. (See box 2 in Table 2).

Patri-heterosex incest describes these family relations: father/daughter, brother/sister, uncle/niece, grandfather/granddaughter, male/female cousins, paternal aunt/nephews. (See box 4).

It is my theory that emotional female incest develops the original core of the human family. This theory presupposes that the family as we now know it in its patriarchal form, is the product of historical development; rather than being ready-made, static,

women who have dared to speak out), we now have more accurate information on the pervasiveness of incest. I trust the Incest Survivors movement's broader definition of incest more than I trust the narrower definition espoused by patriarchal dictionaries, patriarchal judges, social workers and psychiatrists who remain in denial of the reality facing daughters in patriarchy. This denial of the female version of events maintains patriarchy's oppression of women. Toni McNaron and Yarrow Morgan, editors of *Voices in the Night*, point out:

"Instead of looking at incest as an aberration from the norm, we need to question its place and purpose within that norm. We believe that there is not a taboo against incest; merely against speaking about it. And the reason for that taboo, once examined, is clear: If we begin to speak of incest, we may realize its place as a training ground for female children to regard themselves as inferior objects to be used by men, as training that females cannot trust other females (our mothers usually didn't stop the behaviors and often passively acquiesced). Incest is an early and very effective behavioral training in powerlessness and subservience." (p. 15).

Aside from these considerations, I believe that emotional incest (emotional intercourse) is the basis of all family social ties—and without it, family social roles (such as mother/son, father/daughter, brother/sister) would not have historically developed into the rigid role sets we see today. Thus certain forms of emotional incest are healthy and functional for family life, while others are dysfunctional and damaging. —*Author*

TABLE 2. Incest and Sexuality		
SEXUALITY	**Matri-Incest**	**Patri-Incest**
HOMOSEX	**1** Mother/Daughter Sisters Aunt/Niece Female Cousins Grandmother/- Granddaughter	**3** Father/Son Brothers Uncle/Nephew Male Cousins Grandfather/- Grandson
HETEROSEX	**2** Mother/Son Sister/Brother Female/Male Cousins Maternal Uncle/Nieces Grandmother/- Grandson	**4** Father/Daughter Brother/Sister Male/Female Cousins Paternal Aunt/Nephews Grandfather/- Granddaughter

and prepackaged by patriarchal gods for Adam and Eve! The patriarchal family as a norm is a rather late historical development. Its existence has only been recorded over the last 3,000 to 5,000 years—compared to the *millions* of unknown years humans may have lived in society without written record.

I theorize that the family develops its sexuality relations into stable social structure at varying historical stages—although probably all sexualities are present in society across time. Since it is my assumption that gynosociety historically precedes patriarchy, I posit that female (gynosocial) relations precede the mass development of male (patrisocial) relations in the family.

In terms of Table 2, this means that boxes 1 and 2 may historically precede boxes 3 and 4, theoretically. Table 2 assumes that the establishment of maternity precedes the establishment of paternity in the history of the family and accompanying social structures.

Theoretically, I argue that not all family relationships were developed at once into stable social structure. The family develops its varous relationships at different historical periods in this theoretical order: from 1) the original female homosex relations, which subsequently form the base of all families and socities, to 2) matri-heterosex incest relations which normally characterize the beginning of the end of gynosociety and signal the coming transition to patriarchy; 3) the patri-homosex relations of pat-riarchal transition and early patriarchy; 4) the patri-heterosex incest relations of established and late patriarchy.

Female homosex social relations may normally precede the development of heterosex social relations in the human family. Although the mother/son relation is the first enduring heterosex relation to develop, it is the brother/sister relation which is the transitional link from gynosociety to patriarchy. For in Table 2, it is the brother/sister relation and that of male/female cousins which are the only family relations to cross the incest of gyno-society with the incest of patriarchy — making these relations pivotal at patriarchal transition, theoretically.

One of the more interesting historical incest triangles is that where the son, father and brother are all one person — which is reminiscent of the patriarchal christian mystical concept of the holy trinity, three in one, one in three. This situation obtains when a female is inseminated by an unkown male whom she never encounters again, but bears a son, who later inseminates his mother, who bears a daughter, whom the brother/father inseminates.

Although all forms of incest may obtain in any epoch, certain incest forms normally correspond to a certain supportive social structure. I theorize that mother/son incest, the original hetero-sexual relation, is normally associated with gynosociety; sister/brother incest with patriarchal transition and patriarchal structure; and father/daughter incest is normally characteristic of established and late patriarchy. These are theoretical specu-lations which require further research.

I regard the mother/son and sister/brother incest relations as the portals, the windows through which adolescent and adult males impose patriarchy upon female society. The non-kin husband/wife relation is not strong enough to destroy the female homosex bonds of gynosociety. Even patri-anthropolo-gists generally consider the non-kin husband/wife unit to be the weakest biological link in the human family. It is the mother/son relationship which is the strongest heterosex link in the family, followed by the brother/sister. The mother/son and brother/sister relations are critical to an understanding of how patriar-chal heterosex integration occurs in original female society.

Besides incest, other major sex variables which require femi-nist attention are: 1) sexual dimorphism; 2) societal sex ratios;

'*Mosaic Gold Madonna*', by Jean Lois Greggs.
(watercolor, 9" x 12")

3) gender identity; 4) sexual selection; 5) sexual preference or orientation; 6) resistance to marriage; 7) marriage forms, both homosexual and heterosexual; 8) division of labor by sex; 9) homosex segregation/heterosex integration patterns, both horizontally and vertically; 10) reproductivity; 11) sexual practice; 12) sexual norms, taboos and values; 13) matrilocality vs. patrilocality; 14) matrilineage vs. patrilineage; 15) transvestism; 16) sex role crossovers. These sex variables should be studied in a cross-cultural context in relation to the question of women's oppression/liberation.

CONCLUSION

The origin of lesbianism may trace back to human origin. In chapter 6, "Cross-Cultural Lesbianism," I will argue that, since lesbianism obtains among hunters and gatherers, nonhuman living primates, and in the earliest recorded histories of western society, lesbianism probably obtains at human origin.

It appears to gynoscientists that the relationship between adult females and their young is the original family relation. It appears to me that the origin of community relations, society past the family, is based on the homosocial relations between adult females. Society is dependent upon the female homosocial relationship for its very existence. Female society is the constant in all equations of society. If this is true, then lesbianism is functional for society, because it fosters cooperation between females.

Chapter 3

Amazon
Origin Theories

The earliest human female societies reported in cross-cultural recorded history, myth, literature, tribal oral history, cosmology, ethnology, and the arts are *Amazon societies*, by which I mean all-female societies. From a sex ratio perspective, Amazon society represents the theoretical ultimate, the highest female/ lowest male sex ratio. Under these conditions, the societal population is approximately 90% to 100% female.

This concept of all-female societal origin is cross-culturally widespread across the five continents of Africa, Asia, Europe, South America, and North America.[1] In particular, Amazon societies are reported originally in the prehistoric old world: first in "Libya," then in southern Scythia, Anatolia, Asia Minor, eastern Scythia (between the Caspian and Black Seas), Thrace, western Scythia, India, and central Asia.

CLASSICAL AMAZONS OF THE OLD WORLD

These are generally considered the "classical Amazons" of the Old World. The "Libyan Amazons" are commonly thought, by Amazon scholars, to be the original Amazons.[2] Prehistoric "Libya" in the ancient world meant northwestern Africa.[3] The "Libyan Amazons" are said, in Greek prehistory, to have conquered northwestern Africa, Libya, Algeria, Egypt, Syria and Lesbos.[4]

63

The Amazons reported to exist in Scythia, Anatolia, around the Black Sea, Asia Minor, India, and central Asia are termed the "classical Asiatic Amazons." The Greeks, in their sociology of knowledge, have never forgotten the Asiatic Amazons, since it was the Scythian Amazons who are famous in Greek prehistory for having attacked Athens and fought a four-month battle over the city with Theseus.[5]

Bronze statuette of a horsewoman. From Dodona, Carapanos (northwest Greece), c. 550 B.C.
Athens, National Archaeological Museum

The contemporary political states reported to have a prehistoric cultural hystory of Amazons within their geographic borders are: modern Libya, Algeria, Egypt, Syria, Lesbos, Turkey, Georgian Soviet Socialist Republic (SSR), Armenian SSR, Azerbaijan SSR, Crimea, northern Greece, Bulgaria, Rumania, India, China, and Mongolia.

Prehistory, however, is not the only time the appearance of Amazon societies has been noted cross-culturally. Amazon societal sightings are an especially recurrent theme in the journals and official papers of state of the new world explorers in the 16th through 19th centuries, and even later.[6]

AFRICAN AMAZONS

In recorded history, African Amazons have been reported in Dahomey (1591-1860)[7]; in a neighboring state of Katsina south of Zaria in Nigeria[8]; in Sierra Leone[9]; in 16th century Angola[10]; on Zanzibar and Socotra, islands off eastern Africa in the Indian Ocean (16th century)[11]; and in Malawi in A.D. 1964, as "a corps of 5,000 'Amazons' in the army of Dr. Hastings Banda, founder and first premier of Malawi."[12]

AMERICAN AMAZONS

South American Amazons and Amazon societies are reported both by natives and by the Spanish *conquistadores* in the 16th century in: the state of Amazonas, Brazil[13]; Guiana; west Incasic Peru; Colombia; Nicaragua; and in the west Antilles.[14] Mexican Amazons have been reported in North America in the regions of Sinaloa, Colima, Baja California Sur, and on the *"Isla de Mujeres"* (Island of Women) off the Yucatán peninsula. North American Amazons were also reported in California, which is now part of the United States.[15]

Magellan's chronicler, Filippo Pigafetta, reported New World Amazons on Magellan's circumnavigation, "on an island called Acoloro which lies below Java Major," in *Relatione del reame di Congo e della circonvicine per Filippo Pigafetta.*[16]

NEGATION OF THE AMAZON THEORIES
Patriscientists Tear out their Beards over the Amazon Phenomenon

There are perhaps few subjects of inquiry which excite the patriscientific stamp of denial as quickly as the mention of

Amazons. Some patriscientists argue that wherever Amazons are thought to exist, they are instead "beardless male warriors" mistaken for women.[17] A global case of mistaken sexual identity, is it possible?

That negation of the Amazons theory might explain away one or two or three historical sightings of these peculiar UFO's (unidentified fighting objects), but certainly not all. Acceptance of this negative argument would require acceptance of the precarious notion that no one on five continents can distinguish the sex of a person or an army. That seems doubtful.

In *The Glory of Hera: Greek Mythology and the Greek Family*, Philip Slater offers a familiar psychological explanation for the proliferation of Amazons in Greek myth:

> There is a little too much ethnographic and circumstantial detail about the Amazons and the Amazon war to dismiss the entire episode as pure myth.[18] Yet it seems likely that the Victory Over The Women, so conspicuous in Athenian lore, primarily describes an event in the emotional life of each male child.[19]

Now this is a much more interesting, complex denial of the hystorical existence of the Amazons than the aforementioned "beardless" theory. The "Victory Over the Women" festivals have been littered throughout the ethnographic world, as have the male-defeat-of-the-female-sex themes so prevalent in the *origin mythology* of not only the Greeks, but many South American and African tribal societies as well. I agree with Slater that this cultural theme describes a critical psychosexual socialization process "in the emotional life of each male child" *born into patriarchal society*. Slater's analysis displays a beautiful grasp of one dialectic at play between the individual male and patriarchy, between the psychological and the social, between male psyche and male culture. Unfortunately, Slater does not say anything further on the subject.

I would also argue theoretically that the specific societies which celebrate festivals commemorating the defeat of the Amazons or the male victory over the women, are societies which have experienced the historical *transition from gynosociety at origin to patriarchy, in their own geo-cultural evolution*. This statement in no way excludes Slater's psychological explanation. It simply connects in theory the psychological, mythological, and ideological socialization process to a historical base, to material reality.

I would also argue that societies which do not celebrate these victory over the women festivals did not historically experience a transition from gynosociety to patrisociety within the border of their own geo-cultural evolution. Due to the current shakiness of prehistoric methodologies, the existence of Amazons has yet to be disproved by patriscientists, or proved by gynoscientists.[20] The argument still is fascinating; in religion, it is like asking which came first: god or the concept of god? Did the Amazons exist before the concept of Amazons existed?

In *The Amazons: A Marxian Study*, Emanuel Kanter criticizes the "bourgeois" limits of debate over the Amazons for this very reason. He thinks that the question of whether Amazons are hystorically real or mythical fails "utterly to comprehend the importance of the Amazons in primitive history."[21] Kanter thinks that this results from yet another "bourgeois failure" — not to accept the discoveries of Marx and Morgan. However, I could find no Amazons in Marx's work.[22] From my perspective, bourgeois history is a form of patriarchal history, and modern patriarchal history omits Amazons because *patriarchal society is founded on the defeat of Amazons, the defeat of women.*

The origin of western civilization or patriarchy is built on the defeat of Amazons in the cosmological origin myths of western civilization, as also in some African and many South American societies. Some societies institutionalize these origin stories of the male defeat of the women or Amazons in their histories, ritualistic ceremonies, and socialization processes. Other societies carefully guard this information from the female population, for fear of hystoric revenge.

More attention to Slater's negation of the Amazon theory is needed here. His argument that the defeat of the Amazons is "primarily" a psychological event in the emotional life of male children, and not material reality, interests me. If Amazons have no material reality, why then is the *defeat* of nonexistent Amazons such an important socialization ritual in patriarchies? If Amazons are a historical "nothing," what then is it that men are celebrating in these cross-cultural defeat-of-the-Amazons festivals? Their great defeat of nothing? That is an interesting proposition.

I wonder if Slater and other patriscientists who accept his interpretation of the Amazons as a ritualistic psychological event in male life, would argue that generally misogyny in literature, patriarchal myth and religion describe merely a psychological event in the life of males, and not history or material reality. I do not think that misogynist ideology can be separated from misogynist economy and social structure. The misogynist stereotypes of women which saturate patriarchal literature, myth, and religion (ideology) do not live in theoretical isolation from the real world of men. If that were so, women would not be oppressed, except in literature—which is hardly true.

Another common negation of the Amazon's hystorical being is typified by Irving A. Leonard's approach to "Conquerors and Amazons in Mexico."[23] Leonard contends that the extensive reporting of Amazons by Spanish *conquistadores* in the 16th century stems from the "fictional romances of chivalry" produced by Seville publishing houses. Seville is the city from which most of the *conquistadores* embarked for the new world.

Double Standard of the Patriscientists

Patriscientists usually argue that gynoscientists must not extrapolate hystory from literature, myth, goddess worship, or art in any reconstruction of prehistory. Yet here Leonard stands history on its head by claiming that literature caused this 16th century history of the Amazons to be written. Patriscientists cannot have it both ways. They cannot hold that Amazons are not to be deduced from literature, art, religion, or myth—and then turn around to deduce the hystorical nonexistence of Amazons from literature. Perhaps this point will come clearer if Leonard's writings of the New World Amazons are examined. Leonard writes:

> Many were the myths which haunted the minds of the Spanish conquerors and their contemporaries as they adventured in the New World...but the one which perhaps most persistently possessed these heroes was the legend of the warlike Amazon women... The instructions issued to the Spanish leaders and the contractual agreements between the conquistadores and their financial backers—for the conquest of the New World was largely a private enterprise, capitalistic in character (cf. Silvio Zavala, *Las instituciones jurídicas en la conquista de América*, Madrid, 1935)—frequently included clauses requiring a search for these mythical women. Again and again the chronicles and documents of the period contain references to the alleged existence or actual discoveries of such female tribes, and similar reports continued well into the 18th century. Beginning with

Columbus' account of his voyages and in the writings of Peter
Martyr, the first of the historians of the New World, and of his
successors, Oviedo and Herrera, as well as in those of first-
hand chroniclers such as Pigafetta of Magellan's voyage, and
particularly Carvajal, who recorded the famous odyssey of
Orellana... And many other explorers and adventurers of the
16th century and later, including Sir Walter Raleigh, have left
testimony of their varying shades of conviction concerning the
existence of the Amazons... The story persisted through the
Middle Ages, gaining force as such travelers as Marco Polo,
Sir John Mandeville, Pedro Tafur...publicized their journey-
ings into remote parts. These female warriors were also
reputed to be found in Africa, their island home lying in a
marsh not far from the boundaries of the inhabited world, and
also on the west coast near Sierra Leone. But in all accounts
the location of the Amazons is...vague. The older writers
placed them anywhere between Finland and India, but with
Asia Minor, however, continuing to receive the most votes... It
was Columbus himself who aroused such hopes by asserting
that a number of these Amazons hid in caves on some islands
of the Caribbean from which strong winds prevented his
approach. And he was certain that still others of this race
could be reached on the continental mainland by passing
through cannibal country.[24]

Leonard then suggests that the literature of the time of the
Spanish conquest of the new world, especially Garcirodriguez
de Montalvo's *Sergas de Esplandian* (1510—*Deeds of Esplandian*), carried away the imaginations of the *conquistadores* into
romantic searches for the Amazons. Ludovico Ariosto's *Orlando
furioso*, the Italian epic poem which describes an encounter
with the Amazons, also appeared in 1516.[25]

Leonard suggests that Montalvo probably used Columbus'
report of the New World in his romantic novel of "Califia, Queen
of the Amazons," but changed "the name of her island abode
from the ugly Matinino of Columbus' journal" to California.
California, once Spanish territory but now U.S. territory, was
named after the Amazon queen, "Califia," by the Spanish
conquistadores.[26]

The reader must remember that Columbus' historical account
of the Amazons in the Caribbean precedes Montalvo's fictional
novel, which was written in 1510, then later reprinted in Seville
between 1521-26. Thus, Leonard's argument that the Amazon

clauses which proliferate in the official state and financial documents of exchange between the Spanish, Portuguese, and Italian explorers and their kings, queens, and bankers derive from
Spanish and Italian literature of the period—cannot possibly
apply to Columbus' account of the Amazons. In other words,
Leonard's argument is ahistorical. The fact that Leonard
admits that Montalvo borrowed some of his story from Columbus' voyage demonstrates that Spanish history of the New
World Amazons *precedes* Spanish fiction of the New World
Amazons—and not the other way around.

To conclude this survey of negative theories of the Amazons, I
think that Helen Diner's introduction to the Amazons in *Mothers and Amazons* is appropriate:

> The uncontroverted testimony of all of Greek antiquity regard-
> ing the Amazon expedition against Athens has met with a
> certain surly resistance on the part of scholars down to our
> own times. It is reminiscent of that curious verdict in a biog-
> raphy of Goethe, in which the poet's confession that, of all his
> women, he loved Lily most is 'corrected' by his biographer
> with the words: 'Goethe is mistaken here, for that was rather
> the case with Friederike.' Were the Greeks mistaken when they
> asserted the reality of the Amazons, with whom they fought
> overseas as well as in their own country, and when they called
> this life-and-death struggle more fateful even than the Persian
> Wars?[27]

In sum, patriscientists have argued that the Amazons are
mythical, not historical, on these various grounds: 1) Reporters
have mistaken "beardless male warriors" for women; 2) The
defeat of the Amazons is essentially a psychological event in the
life of male children; 3) Romantic literature on the Amazons
caused the explorers of the New World to hallucinate Amazons
in official papers of state; 4) Amazons are purely the inventions
of the ancient poets and historians; and 5) The "Amazonian
tradition was based on vague historical events that could no
longer be definitely determined."[28]

THEORIES ON THE SIGNIFICANCE
OF AMAZON SOCIETIES

Let us now turn to positive theories regarding Amazon
phenomena.

Minerva, the Roman goddess of wisdom (associated with the Greek goddess Athena). In the epoch of life-and-death struggle between matriarchy and patriarchy, it was wise for a woman to be a warrior.
Alinari, Vatican Museum.

Bachofen was the first theorist of the modern era to pay serious attention to Amazon society. Although his work and views on the onward and upward evolutionary progression from the lower stages of hetaerism and matriarchy to the higher and morally superior stage of patriarchy have been aptly criticized by feminists, I think his thesis that Amazon society is original society deserves more attention.

My research shows that one of Bachofen's conclusions regarding Amazon phenomena is empirically well founded. It is: "First, Amazonism is a universal phenomenon... Amazonian phenomena are interwoven with the origins of all peoples."[29] I would alter his statement to read that Amazonism is "interwoven with the origins" of *many* peoples across five continents, ranging in time from prehistory to the Old World exploration of the New World.

In Bachofen's theory, Amazon society or what he terms the "Amazonian extreme of matriarchy" is "closely bound up with hetaerism."[30] Hetaerism characterizes original society; "the Amazonian form of life is an earlier manifestation than conjugal matriarchy, and is in fact a preparation for it."[31]

Bachofen's Amazonian matriarchy theory of social origin was "accepted pretty generally among sociologists until about the beginning of the 20th century."[32] Westermarck attacked it in 1891. In the 20th century of social science, Bachofen is not taken seriously, and for many solid reasons. He is, however, the only male theorist I have read who posits that Amazon society is original society. If this is true, it fits my theory that original society is characterized by the highest-female/lowest-male sex ratios of both hystory and history.

Bachofen does not confine Amazons to original society, historically or theoretically; the Amazons arise in periods of male abuse of women, particularly at patriarchal transition. Emanuel Kanter thinks the Amazons are historical, but theoretically limits them to only one appearance in history, in the transition from matriarchy to patriarchy. Kanter favors the Scythian Amazons as the only real and historical Amazons.

Kanter quarrels with Bachofen's usage of the term Amazon for identifying Amazons with woman warriors of any period of social evolution. He thinks that the Scythian Amazons of antiquity "have played an important part in the evolution of man from barbarism to civilization."[33] He believes that Amazons arose in the pairing family:

The Amazons in the true sense of the word, do not appear until barbarism is firmly established as a system. For it is from the disruption of primitive communist tribes which are on the point of becoming patriarchal in character, either through external or internal economic and military pressure, that they arise. So that women warriors must appear under special conditions for them to be considered as Amazons; else Joan of Arc or the female battalions of death in the hate war would have to be classifed under that head, which is absolutely inadmissible.[34]

Kanter admits that not every Amazonian group proves his theory, especially not the South American Amazons, but the classical Scythian Amazons do fit his model: "that the women in order to avoid slavery were compelled to resist the encroachments of the male by establishing a woman's state."[35]

According to Alexander Chamberlain's translations, Friederici (1910) explains the genesis of South American Amazon legends with these five possibilities: "1) from the notably warlike character of women of many primitive communities in America; 2) from the fact of women having in a few tribes (for economic, religious, etc. reasons) power or influence that seemed strange and extraordinary to the mass of the surrounding population; 3) from rumors of the barbaric splendor of the Empire of the Incas, which had penetrated the wildernesses to the East†; 4) from reports of a certain unusual sexual relation[36] of Indian

---

†In fact, the Inca empire was patriarchal—its god of creation was a bearded god named Cons—and, in the course of its military expansions, it subjugated many gynosocieties and/or matriarchies in the region now called Peru. But while these women's societies were forced to pay annual tribute to the Inca imperial clique, they likely were able to maintain their gynosocial structures more or less intact, along with their traditions of goddess worship. Thus they no doubt continued to practice lesbian sexuality freely, and perhaps engaged in repeated armed rebellions against Inca imperial domination. This *pre-*and *anti-*Inca sexual and sociopolitical dynamic was likely the source of Friederici's rather confusing connection of Amazon legends with "rumors of the barbaric splendor of the empire of the Incas."

Among the Indian peoples, and especially the Indian women of Peru today, goddess worship—overlaid with worship of the Inca gods and of the Jesus/Mary duality of Roman catholicism—continues to play an important part in psychological and religious life. In fact, matriarchal communities still exist in Peru, but they are in the process of being liquidated through land expropriation by the bourgeois government in Lima. (See interview between Kim Womantree and Andrea Gabriel, "Becoming Powerful: Peruvian Women Taking Action and Refusing Shame," *Big Mama Rag*, Denver, November 1981, pp. 14-18, 21; and Andrea Gabriel, "The Survival of Female Power in Peru," *Big Mama Rag*, April 1982, p. 9). —*Editor*

women appearing astonishing and remarkable in contrast to the usual state of affairs; 5) from tales of Amazons due to native reports misunderstood by the Spaniards, or from such tales intentionally spread by the latter."[37]

Chamberlain summarizes the analyses of several other German theorists regarding the origin of Amazon legends in South America. For example, Lasch's 1910 theory that "the Amazon-legend is only a somewhat idealized picture of the dual division of primitive society," refers to the division of labor by sex.[38] In the "Myths and Legends of the Primitive Peoples of South America," Paul Ehrenreich (1905) presents a different perspective. Ehrenreich views these legends as serving to explain patriarchal institutions, as "seeking to legitimize the union of the males over against the aspirations of the women."[39] Ehrenreich cites the Caraya legend, "The Jakare and the Revolt of the Women," where the women are depicted as rising up against the men, killing them and leaving the country. Similar legends have been reported by Brett in Guiana (the legend of Toeyza), from the Rio Jamunda region of Brazil by Barboza Rodriguez, along with the Tupi legends of the Yurupari (wood-demon), according to Chamberlain, Ehrenreich, and others.

In *The Amazons in Antiquity and Modern Times*, G.C. Rothery (1910) classified Amazon legends in this way: "1) women living apart in colonies, but having occasional communications with the outside world on a peaceful footing; 2) women banded together as a fighting organization; 3) nations ruled over by queens, and mainly, or to a considerable extent, governed by women."[40]

It is my theory that whenever and wherever Amazons are reported, this is an indirect measure of the presence of extremely high-female/low-male sex ratios or all-female/no-male sex ratios.[41] This is not to say that Amazon phenomena do not also indicate other sociological conditions in the relations between the sexes — but rather, that one element clothed within a societal reporting of Amazons is the perception that males are missing entirely, or outnumbered greatly by a community of females who are not led or controlled by men.

Sociologically, the term *Amazon* is a social code word, or ideological "buzz word,"[42] connoting one or more of several social conditions: 1) high-to-all-female/low-to-no-male sex ratios in social organization; 2) a group of man-hating females;

3) a community of rebellious females functioning outside of patriarchal control; 4) a group of warlike or militant females who live without men; 5) a community of women who together perform tasks that are viewed in patriarchal society as stereotypical male pursuits—defense, war, hunting, handling weapons, and wearing and handling the accoutrements of war (which in some epochs is associated with riding horses and carrying weapons); 6) a tight community of militant females where heterosexual virginity is a code of ethics, religion or politics, and where man-hating is normal; 7) a community of women who are considered "mannish" in dress, manner, and sexuality due to their lesbian relations with other women.

A LESBIAN FEMINIST
ANALYSIS OF AMAZONS

The last connotation of Amazon coincides with another major vector of this work, lesbianism. Amazons are often described cross-culturally as "mannish" in dress or appearance or activity. Some patriscientists go so far as to conclude that Amazons are mistaken for "beardless" men. Where else in patriarchal literature and ideology are women historically described as "masculine" in appearance, dress or activity? The answer is, of course, in the patriarchal literature on lesbians.

I could not help but note in my research on cross-cultural lesbianism, that most anthropological sources on either lesbianism or "woman-marriage" describe the phenomena as "masculine" female behavior. This is not only due to the anthropologist's outsider's observation; the culture under study *itself* typically defines lesbian or Amazon phenomena as a female acting like a male. For example, Oscar Lewis' description of "woman-marriage" among the North Piegan of Canada—as the Piegan call it, "manly-hearted women."[43]

One of the most fascinating pieces of data which hystorically establishes a connection between Amazonism, lesbianism, and "woman-marriage" is Pero de Magalhaes' 1576 account of Indian women at the time of Orellana's expedition down the Amazon River, in *The Histories of Brazil*:

> There are some Indian women who determined to remain chaste: these have no commerce with men in any manner, nor would they consent to it even if refusal meant death. They give up all their duties of women and imitate men, and follow men's

pursuits as if they were not women. They wear the hair cut in the same way as the men, and go to war with bows and arrows and pursue game, always in company with men; each has a woman to serve her, to whom she says she is married and they treat each other and speak with each other as man and wife.[44]

The Tapuyan tribes, which Orellana encountered along the Amazon River, have been exterminated by the European patriarchists of the 16th and 17th centuries—along with many other gynosocieties. I wonder if all the tribal peoples of the New World who have been destroyed by the imperialism of European patriarchists are now considered by the patriarchal school to be mythical or the imaginative result of our having read too much literature? I doubt it. Why, then, are extinct tribes associated with Amazon phenomena selected out of history by patriscientists and shoved into the dubious category of myth?

The debate over the existence of South American Amazons is complicated by an array of ideological biases in patriarchal scholarship, best described as male supremacy, white supremacy, ethnocentrism, and nationalism. The European patriarchal bias against native American matriarchal society, and the English bias against Spanish historical accounts of the New World, disturb the objectivity of these Amazon accounts.

In fact, since most of the gynosocietal accounts come from the third world, the European white supremacy at play in the 19th and 20th century matriarchy/patriarchy debates is an enormous factor to weigh. The same pattern emerges: European patriarchal imperialism and extermination of third world gynosocieties is complemented by patriscientific scholarship which claims these women's societies never existed anyway.[45]

This ideological form of patriarchal academics is close to heterosexist arguments which omit lesbian existence from recorded history also. The patriscientific standards applied to the patriarchial theories of gynosocietal nonexistence and Amazon nonexistence, are also used to create the heterosexist impression of lesbian nonexistence.

Up until 1969, no one could have easily proved the universal existence of lesbianism from a survey of mainstream patriscientific literature, as it is similarly hard to prove the universality of gynosociety or Amazon society, using the literature of an ideological enemy. It must always be remembered, however, that patriscientists have never empirically disproved the historical existence of the Amazons or Amazon societies. This point is usually overlooked.

AMAZON CONCLUSIONS

This brief study of Amazon phenomena cross-culturally does not do the subject justice, given the vast amount of material, especially in the arts and mythology on Amazons.[46] However, no analysis of female society would be complete without at least theoretical mention of the Amazons.

A major problem which arises immediately in this type of research is recognition of the lack of theoretical clarity regarding even the definition of the term, Amazon. After definition, comes the debate as to whether Amazons are real or mythical. Then comes the question, if Amazons exist, in what period or periods do they appear?

Bachofen holds that Amazon society is original society, but that Amazons reappear at the transition from conjugal matriarchy to patriarchy as well. Kanter rigidly places the Amazons in only one historical period, the transition from "barbarism to civilization"; in Engelian terms, this is the transition from the pairing family to patriarchal heterosexual monogamy. Patriscientists generally place the Amazons in myth, not history. Some political analysts, for example Paul Hofmann, think an "Amazon complex" is contagiously loose today.[47]

I think that Amazons are hystorical, although certainly not all accounts of Amazons are to be trusted. Kanter is correct, I believe, to insist on a strict definition of the term, but wrong to insist that Amazons appear only once in hystory. I agree with Kanter that the Scythian Amazons are hystorical, but I think he abstracts out all other Amazons from hystory only because they do not fit his theory.

Although Bachofen's work is flawed with male supremacist notions about women, his data on the myths of Amazon origins of many societies is valuable. Furthermore, although Bachofen —like most men—despises the idea of Amazonism, he is to be credited for his original insight that Amazon society is original society.

It is my position that *the origin of human society is characterized by extremely high-female/low-male sex ratios* (see ch. 4), *and almost total homosex separation. This theoretically describes the socio-sexual conditions of Amazon society.* However, these conditions also describe lesbian society. There is some rare data to establish an hystorical connection between Amazonism and lesbianism, but not much. At this point in my research, I would generalize that Amazonism and lesbianism are hystorically separate phenomena, although they can coincide in time and space.[48]

This much is clear to me: The origin of human society is gynosociety. The origins of the many forms of gynosociety are either Amazon or lesbian society, or both. The two periods of prehistory which puzzle scholars most are origin and the patriarchal transition. I think that Amazons appear in both. According to Bachofen, Amazons dominate both periods. If it is true that Amazons exist at origin and at the patriarchal takeover, the patriscientific and even marxist[49] refusal to take the Amazons seriously may explain, in part, why these scholars are hazy on these periods.

Although patriscientists will argue that their refusal to take Amazons seriously is based on the historical method, I think other less objective biases are at play here. A survey of the vast amount of literature surrounding both the origin debate and the matriarchy/patriarchy debates in the last two centuries reveals that practically all patriscientists and even all male matriarchists (with the exceptions of Bachofen, Kanter, and Briffault) focus their exclusive attention on heterosexual mothers. The concept of lesbian mothers, bisexual mothers, Amazon mothers, and man-hating mothers has never entered their minds, much less their debate.

I would argue that one critical reason Amazons appear to be imaginary to heterosexist scholars is this: Almost by definition, heterosexists cannot imagine anyone who is not heterosexual. Amazons simply do not fit the heterosexist's imaginary conception of women as the eternal *femme*. Incidentally, a lot of real, historical women do not fit the heterosexist's imaginary mold either. Amazons are clearly *butch*. In the heterosexist mind, only men can play the butch.

Amazons not only break across patriarchal sex lines, theoretically and actually, but Veblen's analysis of the "leisure class" male pursuits of war, hunting, sports, the use of weapons, and religion reveals that Amazons and witches (religion) break across male class lines also. That is, Amazons and witches, both despised in patriarchy, almost by definition break the

Amazons going into battle.
Greek vase, Metropolitan Museum of Art

critical patriarchal taboo of females participating in either the military, religious, social or economic pursuits that are reserved for first males, then "leisure class" males.

Scholarship on the Amazons is ideologically tangled by male supremacy and heterosexism. The debate over whether Amazons have one breast or two seems strange in patriarchal literature, especially since patriarchists claim that Amazons do not really exist. I do not know the word for this obsession, but it is beyond necrophilia. Only females know how many breasts they wear, and for what occasion.[50]

Chapter 4

Sex Ratio Theory

The derivation of a theory is always interesting. The roots of my sex ratio theory in theoretical sociology trace back to Georg Simmel's classic work on *numerical sociation.* I first began to think of the societal sex ratio as an important women's oppression/liberation variable after reading Simmel's theories on numerical social relations. Simmel's work on "the quantitative determination of the group," the effect that "the mere number of [as]sociated individuals" has upon microscopic and macroscopic social life, led me to explore the relationship between sex ratios and social organization.[1]

To my knowledge, Simmel did not address himself to sex ratios.[2] I merely injected the sex variable into Simmel's numerical variable, "the mere number of sociated individuals," cutting social relations into two sexes, male and female relations, to obtain the sex ratio of society. Theoretically, I am working from the same base that Simmel formulated regarding:

> This quantitative determination of the group, as it may be called, has a twofold function. Negatively speaking, certain developments, which are necessary or at least possible as far as the contents or conditions of life are concerned, can be realized only below or above a particular number of elements. Positively,

---

Simmel is the source of my first theoretical glimmer regarding the importance of the sex ratio to society, to women's oppression and liberation. After thinking about Simmel's numerical theories of social forms since 1971,[3] by 1976 I began to apply his quantitative analysis to the social relations of the sexes. It became clearer and clearer to me that societal sex ratios are a critical sociological variable which had not been analyzed in relation to the origin debate or the women's oppression/liberation debate—except by Marvin Harris in *Cannibals and Kings.*[4] For this reason, I made the following theoretical exploration. —*Author*

certain other developments are imposed upon the group by certain purely quantitative modifications. Yet not even those developments emerge automatically, for they also depend on other than numerical characteristics. The decisive point, however, is that they are not the result of those characteristics alone, for they emerge only under certain numerical conditions.[5]

ORIGINAL SEX RATIO THEORY

Following Simmel, I theorize generally that certain sex ratios are historically attached to certain social forms, and that certain social forms have a numerical affinity with certain sex ratios. Although I expect to find a range of sex ratio variation within any historical epoch, I suggest that at origin the modal sex ratio is extremely high-female/low-male.* Further, high-female/low-male sex ratios correlate with gynosociety.

High-female/low-male sex ratios characterize prehistory until patriarchal transition, which gynarchists place between 10,000 B.C. and 1,000 B.C. This means that nearly the entire time span of human existence has been characterized by high female sex ratios.

High-female/low-male societal sex ratios in either total or adult population modally characterize pre-patriarchal sex ratios.

I theorize that *high-male/low-female* societal sex ratios** characterize patriarchal transition, 10,000 to 1,000 B.C. This massive shift in societal sex ratios from the original high-female/low-male to high-male/low-female at patriarchal transition is accomplished by *gynocide*, particularly female infanticide. The patriarchal takeover, reconstructed by gynarchists, is a bloody affair.

*Near equal sex ratios*** characterize established, stable, and late patriarchy. Near equal societal sex ratios are a relatively late historical achievement, although patriarchal ideology falsely teaches that near equal sex ratios are the human norm. Near equal sex ratios are simply a normal condition of *patriarchy*.

High-female/low-male sex ratios are operationally defined as: 54% or more of the societal population is female, while 46% or less of the societal population is male. This definition applies to both total and adult societal populations. The *adult population* in the world samples I later analyze in chapter 5 is defined as *15 years of age or over.* —*Author*

**High-male/low-female sex ratios* are operationally defined as: 54% or more of the societal population is male, while 46% or less of the societal population is female. —*Author*

***Near equal societal sex ratios* are operationally defined as: Both sexes number over 46% and under 54% of the population. —*Author*

Gynocide in 17th century Britain: Four 'witches' are hung to death, while three more are led to the scaffold, hands bound by their executioners. The witchhunter at right (under 'D') gets paid handsomely for rounding up his latest batch of female victims. Note also the women in prison at upper left. (from Rossell H. Robbins, The Encyclopedia of Witchcraft and Demonology, New York: Crown Publishers, 1959)

Patriarchal sex ratios correspond to high-male/low-female and/or near equal sex ratios. The gynosocial sex ratio is high-female/low-male.

Rape Culture = High-Male/Low-Female Sex Ratios

I theorize that rape conditions are created and maintained in human society by the patriarchal societal sex ratios of high-male/low-female and/or near equal sex ratios. I think that the reason rape does not occur among primates in the wilds is due to the high-female/low-male sex ratio which predominates.[6]

As yet there is no conclusive evidence on prehistoric sex ratios. Social scientists have not even systematically recorded all extant societies in the 19th and 20th centuries. Thus, ignorance of prehistoric sex ratios is accompanied by a gross ignorance of many historic societal sex ratios as well. Proof or disproof of my sex ratio theories cannot be established until further empirical research of prehistorical skeletal remains yields more comprehensive data on early human sex ratios. However, I do present relevant empirical data on world sex ratios in chapter 5.

I theorize that near equal sex ratios are generally dysfunctional for females and functional for males. Generally, high-female/low-male sex ratios are functional for both sexes and for society, while high-male/low-female sex ratios are usually dysfunctional for both sexes.* Societies with no adult males, all-female societies, are highly functional for females and highly dysfunctional for males. These are hypothetical Amazon or actual lesbian societies.

The overthrow of mother-right by father-right and the mass development of monogamy cannot occur until the original social organization based on high-female/low-male sex ratios is altered to high-male/low-female and/or near equal societal sex ratios. I regard this massive shift in sex ratios as a prerequisite for the institutionalization of heterosexual monogamian marriage and the patriarchal family.

If gynosociety is located in prehistory, then I expect gynosocial sex ratios to differ dramatically from patriarchal sex ratios. If they are the same, then sex ratios would be unimportant. However, if the sex ratios of prehistoric society differ from those of historical society, or if the sex ratios of gynosociety differ from those of patriarchy, then the sex ratio is a critical variable which may effect women's oppression/liberation.†

The empirical question then is: Are prehistorical sex ratios the same as, or different from historical sex ratios? Are gynosocietal sex ratios the same as, or different from patriarchal sex ratios? It is my theoretical intuition that they are quite differ-

---

*The only historical exceptions to my theory regarding the nonviability of mostly-male sex ratios are a handful of primitive Asian societies which have successfully adapted to this rare sex ratio over centuries. —*Author*

---

†Surprising, if indirect, support for Dr. Cavin's sex ratio theory comes from the first book of Kings in the old testament: According to this biblical tract, which is dated around 1,000 BC, king Solomon had 700 wives and 300 concubines, many of them "strange" (i.e., nonjewish) women. "...And his wives turned away his heart." (1 Kings, 11.1, 11.3). To the intense irritation of the jewish, one and only god, "Solomon went after Ashtoreth, the goddess of the Zidonians," (11.5), and began worshipping the many gods and goddesses of his diverse wives generally. Even such a wiseacre as Solomon could not hold out against a 1,000-to-1 female-to-male sex ratio. —*Editor*

'Remembrance of an Open Wound', by Frida Kahlo (1938)

ent. When the evidence is all in, I expect that prehistoric human sex ratios will correspond to the high-female/low-male sex ratios widely reported in the literature on living nonhuman primates in the wilds. The study of prehistoric sex ratios is critical to a grasp of the origin of society and particularly the origin of women's oppression.

Speaking of nonhuman living primate sex ratios, Evelyn Reed's acount of the "London Zoo catastrophe" convinced me of the importance of the sex ratio as a major sociological variable heretofore unnoticed in the origin debates.

REVIEW OF RELEVANT
SEX RATIO LITERATURE

London Zoo Catastrophe

In *Woman's Evolution: From Matriarchal Clan to Patriarchal Family*, Evelyn Reed describes the "London Zoo catastrophe" in this way:

An experiment was conducted by the London Zoological Society upon a colony of about a hundred Hamadryas baboons in a rockwork enclosure called 'Monkey Hill.' Originally, the colony was all male, but it was decided to introduce females to the Hill to cohabit with the males, thus furnishing an opportunity to study their behavior. The experiment, conducted over a five-year period beginning in 1925, was reported by Solly Zuckerman in *The Social Life of Monkeys and Apes*. Despite what seemed to be optimum conditions, a 'natural' environment with food and care provided, the results were disastrous. There were continuous fights among the males for possession of the females to the point of the virtual extermination of the females and young. The greatest number of deaths occurred in 1925 and 1927 when the main consignments of females were introduced. In the latter year 15 of the 30 females were killed within a month. In 1928, 15 more females were killed in one month. In the fights over females, males were also killed. By 1930 there were 39 males and 9 females left, and only one young baboon surviving of all those bred on the Hill. The injuries were of all degrees of severity. Limb bones, ribs, and skulls were fractured; wounds penetrated chest or abdomen, and many animals showed extensive lacerations in the ano-genital region. At least four of the females killed were immatures; two adult females died after miscarriages precipitated by the fighting. In one case four males fought over a single female. 14 of the 15 baboons born on Monkey Hill perished. In most cases death occurred within six months of birth. One nursing mother dropped her baby in a fight; it was seized by a male who made off with it, and it died. Another death was caused by a male who transferred his attentions from the female to her baby, injuring it severely in the loins. The sexual fights often went on for days, with a female mounted by every male that could gain access to her. During these periods she suffered continuous physical torment and was unable to get food. After death the fights often continued over her dead body, with males still treating her as a sexual object. So protracted and repellent was the last fight that by 1930, when the experiment was declared a failure, the five remaining females were removed and Monkey Hill once again became an all-male colony.[7]

This sadistic experiment typifies patriscientific "objectivity" toward female and animal life. Reed's account cracked the case in my mind regarding the importance of the sex ratio in relation to women's historic oppression. Reed understood that the worst mistake made "was to introduce a small number of females into an overwhelmingly male enclosure. In the wild this ratio is just the reverse, giving females the advantages of numbers."[8] Reed alone pinpoints the cause of the catastrophe to sex ratio reversal of the natural order. The male scientists involved in the case wrote the "freak" occurrence off to: captivity, depravity of those particular apes, no exit from the enclosure when in danger. They missed the sex ratio point.

Unfortunately, Reed did not take her precious insight into natural primate sex ratios and the disaster of reversing them, beyond what is rendered here. She did not take her sex ratio realization into an analysis of human origin and evolution/ devolution.

Sex Ratios of Nonhuman Primates in the Wild

Kathleen Gough describes which of the apes are our closest relatives:

> Within the primate order, humans are most closely related to the anthropoid apes (African chimpanzee and gorilla and Southeast Asian orangutan and gibbon); and of these, to the chimpanzee and the gorilla. More distantly related are the Old and then the New World monkeys and finally the lemurs, tarsiers and tree shrews.[9]

According to Lila Leibowitz in the "Evolution of Sex Differences," patriscientists selectively use studies of those primate societies which mirror human patriarchal relations:

> A number of theorists have revived the view that sexual dimorphism among humans is tied to sex-role patterns that are current or idealized in our own culture. New data on nonhuman primate behavior has provided source materials for such theories: without too much difficulty, theorists have been able to find one or another population of nonhuman primates that conforms to their cultural model of how things were, are, or ought to be. Unfortunately for such theories, humans and nonhuman primates utilize a variety of social forms in which females and males play a variety of roles.[10†]

Baboons are particularly popular in patriarchy, because they are the only apes that strictly live in heterosexual nuclear families; Leibowitz points out, however, that baboons are not our closest relatives. Among mountain gorillas of Uganda, langurs of south India, and hamadryas baboons of Ethiopia, "a single, fully mature male mates with several females."[11] Among east and south African baboons, rhesus macaques, and South American woolly monkeys, the troop usually numbers up to 200. Gough writes that these troops contain "a number of adult males and a much larger number of females."[12] Some macaques

---

†Traditional paleontology since Darwin has held that human beings evolved directly from higher primates, developing upright posture and tool making ability in the course of moving from a forest environment to the savannah, and eventually to the plains. However, a Welsh anthropologist, Elaine Morgan, has advanced a new theory of human evolution from the apes. This theory, originally proposed in 1960 by the English marine biologist Alister Hardy, holds that a group of higher primates (ultimately descended from fishes) *returned* to the sea during the Pliocene drought epoch to become aquatic mammals, underwent a dramatic physical development in the sea environment, and then returned again to land, where they developed into human beings. The Hardy/Morgan theory offers a far more powerful explanation of the physical contrasts between humans and our primate "cousins"—including our upright gait, furless exterior, even distribution of subcutaneous fat about our bodies, our diving ability and sophisticated breath control, our ability to weep, our peculiarly shaped noses, and our "ventral/ventral" mating posture, generally unique among primates—than does the traditional evolutionary scenario. Morgan, bringing a feminist perspective to her insights on human/animal behavior and evolution, has advanced an ingenious and provocative hypothesis on the origin of male sexual violence in the human species. See Elaine Morgan, *The Descent of Woman*, New York: Stein and Day, 1972. Her theory has been met with a kind of conspiracy of silence by the anthropological and biological science establishment. —*Editor*

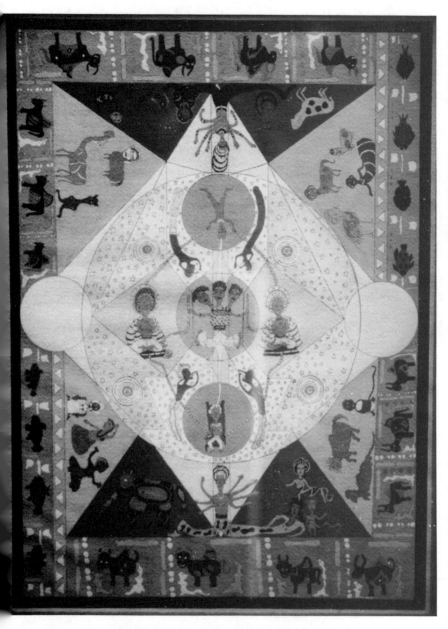

'Transition', by Jean Lois Greggs
(watercolor, 18" x 24")

expel from the troop a proportion of the young males, who then form "bachelor troops." The males that travel on the border of the group have little access to females. Leibowitz describes the social organization of orangutans in this way:

> An orang female and her young occupy a stable range which may overlap that of another female and her young. Where mothers and daughters with young live in adjacent areas, they sometimes join together to make a multi-female group. Adult males travel alone, moving back and forth across a wider area that cuts across the ranges of several females groups. [13]

Leibowitz notes that among gorillas, one of our very close relatives, adult females always live in female groups with one or two silver backed males. Male adolescents are found outside the group. Finally, Gough writes of our closest relatives, the chimpanzee, that:

> Chimpanzees, and also South American howler monkeys, live in loosely structured groups, again (as in most monkey and ape societies), with a preponderance of females. The mother-child unit is the only stable group. [14]

Marshall Sahlins and Carpenter both present evidence regarding the numerical preponderance of females relative to males in primate society. [15]

The assumption behind my sex ratio hypotheses is that it is to the females' safety and advantage to outnumber the male, while it is physically dangerous for females and offsprings to be outnumbered by adult males; approximate numerical equality of the sexes favors the male (as is evident in patriarchy).

Across all mammalian species, it is deadly for the female to live continuously outnumbered by males. Females know this instinctively, although male scientists regard polyandry as the *sine qua non* of female power and prestige. This male interpretation of polyandry is, of course, ideological.

Classical Marxists' Work on Sex Ratios

With the exceptions of Engels, Bebel, and Reed, the classical marxist debate over origin is missing sex ratio analysis. Engels mentions sex ratios on a tangent, but reveals critical insight. In *Origin of the Family...*, he writes:

> In this ever widening exclusion of blood relatives from marriage, natural selection also continues to have its effect... Thus,

the evolution of the family in prehistoric times consisted in the continual narrowing of the circle—originally embracing the whole tribe—within which marital community between the two sexes prevailed. By the successive exclusion, first of closer, then of ever remoter relatives, and finally even of those merely related by marriage; every kind of group marriage was ultimately rendered practically impossible; and in the end there remained only the one, for the moment still loosely united, couple, the molecule with whose dissolution marriage itself completely ceases. This fact alone shows how little individual sex love, in the modern sense of the word, had to do with the origin of monogamy. The practice of all peoples in this stage affords still proof of this. *Whereas under previous forms of the family men were never in want of women but, on the contrary, had a surfeit of them, women now became scarce and were sought after.* [my italics]. Consequently, with pairing marriage begins the abduction and purchase of women—widespread *symptoms* [his italics], but nothing more, of a much more deeply rooted change that had set in.[16]

The "previous forms of the family" to which Engels refers are the "consanguine family," the "punaluan family" and group marriage, which was preceded by promiscuity in Engels' scenario. According to Engels, there was a "surfeit" of women prior to the development of the "pairing family," out of which monogamy developed next. In Engelian time, women outnumber men prior to the development of agriculture. Thus, my theory of high-female/low-male sex ratios at origin is not at odds with Engels' perception of numerical sex relations in prehistory.

Now consider August Bebel's treatment of sex ratios in his classic work, *Women Under Socialism.*[17] Bebel wrote more about societal sex ratios than any other marxist I have read. He is to be credited for that, and for his political support of women, lesbians, and gay men in the *Reichstag* (German parliament). But his personal views of women and lesbians are in many ways crude and heterosexist.

For example, Bebel blamed capitalism for the fact that not all women married in his day, a fact he noticed in his sex ratio computations of world census reports between 1860-1891. Bebel thought that all women should marry, and if they did not, something drastically wrong had happend to society. If women were "unmarried," "celibate," "lesbian," "spinsters" or "old maids," "barren," or "prostitutes" — to Bebel, they were "sick" and "depraved." He fell back on the old patriarchal cure for all women's problems: heterosexual marriage. At least Engels saw clearly that heterosexual monogamian marriage was a major cause of all women's pain!

Nevertheless, Bebel saw the relationship of near equal sex ratios to monogamy in this way:

> The almost equal number of the two sexes, prevalent under normal conditions, points everywhere to monogamy.[18]

I would agree with Bebel if the phrase "prevalent under normal conditions" were omitted. Due to heterosexism, Bebel's work on sex ratios is flawed, but his empirical world sex ratio calculations between 1860-1891 are interesting.[19] Furthermore, Bebel's critical, yet semiconscious realization that sex ratios, birth rates, the "rate of illegitimacy," sexuality, and rates of unmarried females to males are important variables in any discussion of the emancipation of women, is noteworthy—no matter how much his heterosexist interpretations twist these variables.

Anthropology and Sex Ratios

Next consider Marvin Harris' recent work on sex ratios in *Cannibals and Kings*. Harris relates sex ratios to male supremacy and women's oppression, which is correct. Yet his argument tells a great deal more about his own justification of male supremacy than about its historical genesis. Harris' major argument is:

> Far from being arbitrary or conspiratorial, male chauvinism arose during prehistory to counter a basic threat to human survival—the threat of overpopulation and the depletion of resources. Furthermore, my research has convinced me that the patterns of early human sexism cannot be understood without investigating the origin of another scourge—warfare. My theory holds that male supremacy and prehistorical warfare together constituted the core of a primordial system for avoiding the misery and annihilation latent in the reproductive power of the human female.[20]

This is a new twist to the mass psychosis of male supremacy. Harris tells us that male supremacy is really a humanitarian effort to save the world from womb power. His blend of misogyny with "science" is a prime example of patriscience. His argument that man kills woman to save the world is reminiscent of those laughable, but insanely contradictory arguments such as "man fights this war for peace."

Nevertheless, if Harris' figures can be trusted on the numerical relations between the sexes, they are quite interesting regarding the incidence of female infanticide in patriarchy:

> Recent studies by William Divale of City University of New York have revealed that war-making band and village societies often killed their infant daughters and that they did so far more frequently than they killed infant sons. The more intense the warfare, the greater the difference between the number of boys and girls reared to adulthood. Among those band and village societies whose population was known prior to the suppression of warfare, there is an average discrepancy of 128 boys under 14 to 100 girls. In contrast to an expected ratio of 105 to 100 at birth, some groups have as many as 200 boys for each 100 girls. That means that at least half of the girls born were artificially deprived of the chance to grow up... Infanticide continued, not being confined to prehistoric bands, flourishing as well in 'civilized' societies as a principal means of family planning, despite admonitions of church and state. In India and China, as has long been known, female infanticide was common, and the practice survived well into the present century. During the last 100 years, the British were horrified to discover that the ratio of male children to female children in parts of northern India was as high as 233 to 100.† Anthropologist Mildred Dickman contends that some castes destroyed *all* their female babies. In China, in regions such as Amoy and Fukien, 30% of female babies were killed, and in some villages it went as high as 80%. In England between 1250 and 1358 and then again between 1430 and 1545, the sex ratio of male children to female children was 133 to 100. In Italy it stood at 125 to 100 among the wealthy families of Florence during the 15th century.[21]

Harris is also aware that large numbers of men are unnecessary for reproduction. The only variable that raises or lowers the reproductivity rate under any form of social organization is the addition or subtraction of females.[22]

In *The Elementary Structures of Kinship*, Levi-Strauss writes an interesting passage on the relation between sex ratios, polygyny, polyandry, and homosexuality. I have excerpted only the

†On the other hand, the British colonialists were somewhat less than horrified at their own mass slaughters, rape and torture of the peoples of India. —*Editor*

parts which are not blatantly sexist, since Levi-Strauss wanders off into his own opinions about the "scarcity" of "desirable women." He writes:

> Let us first examine the feature of growing scarcity. There is a biological equilibrium between male and female births. Consequently, except in societies where this equilibrium is modified by customs, every male should have a very good chance of obtaining a wife. In such circumstances, is it possible to speak of women as a scarce commodity requiring collective intervention for its distribution?... Consequently, to our eyes monogamy is not a positive institution, but merely embodies the limit of polygamy in societies where, for highly varied reasons, economic and sexual competition reaches an acute form. The Nambikwara, semi-nomads of western Brazil, who live for most of the year by collecting and gathering, sanction polygamy for their headmen and sorcerers. The securing of two, three or four wives by one or two important persons in a band of sometimes less than 20 people necessarily obliges their companions to be celibate. This privilege by itself is sufficient to upset the natural equilibrium of the sexes, since male adolescents occasionally can no longer find wives available from among the women of their own generation. Whatever the solution given to the problem—homosexuality among the Nambikwara, fraternal polyandry among their northern neighbors, the Tupi-Cawahib —the growing scarcity of wives does not appear less serious a problem in a society however predominantly monogamous it might be... This deep polygynous tendency, which exists among all men, always makes the number of available women seem insufficient... Homosexuality in some groups, polyandry and wife-lending in others, and finally, almost everywhere, the extreme freedom of premarital relations would prevent adolescents from experiencing any discomfort while waiting for a wife...[23]

Levi-Strauss demonstrates that unequal sex ratios in society are not always the work of nature, but of societal manipulation. The Nambikwara stratification system stimulates the practice and preference for polygyny, instead of a numerical preponderance of women.

Elman Service, on the other hand, read the Jivaro practice of polygyny as a direct result of a "numerical predominance of women in Jivaro society," caused by "constant warfare."[24] Anthropologists do not agree on which way to draw the causal arrows between sex ratio and social organization. Most intuit a

TABLE 21. Hunting and Gathering by Sex Ratios (Total Population)

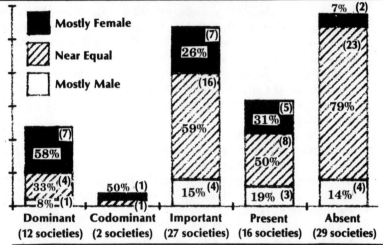

	Dominant (12 societies)	Codominant (2 societies)	Important (27 societies)	Present (16 societies)	Absent (29 societies)
Mostly Female	58% (7)		26% (7)	31% (5)	7% (2)
Near Equal	33% (4)	50% (1)	59% (16)	50% (8)	79% (23)
Mostly Male	8% (1)	(1)	15% (4)	19% (3)	14% (4)

[see page 201 for an examination of the same data from a different angle]

relationship between sex ratios and marriage forms, but the precise relationship between the two has not been delineated.

A direct reading between sex ratios and marriage forms is not always advisable. For example, polyandry may be the result of a disturbed balance of the sexes, or it may obtain under near equal sex ratios. Furthermore, George Peter Murdock's 1957 data on the world distribution of "plural marriages" should *not* be read to mean that 75% of the world same has high female sex ratios, although

> ...we learn that monogamy is characteristic of about 24% of the world's societies, polyandry of 1%, and polygyny of 75%, and that general polygyny is particularly prevalent in Africa, monogamy in the Circum-Mediterranean, limited polygyny in the Insular Pacific, and sororal polygyny in North America.[25]

Women do not outnumber men in 75% of Murdock's world sample, although polygyny is the preference. The dialectic between societal sex ratios and marriage forms is complicated. Both variables are capable of effecting change in the other. However, I do propose that near equal sex ratios are modally characteristic of societies where monogamian marriage prevails. This theory will be tested in the next chapter.

THEORETICAL CONCLUSIONS
REGARDING SEX RATIOS

Simmel's numerical sociology[26] led me to posit that social forms are directly influenced by the number of females relative to males, per society or social unit. I theorize that high-female/low-male sex ratios characterize original society and the bulk of prehistory. High-male/low-female sex ratios characterize the patriarchal transition and early patriarchy. Near equal sex ratios correspond to the sex ratios of established and late patriarchy.

Further, I hypothesize that sororal polygyny is an ancient institution characteristic of gynosociety. I expect that high-female/low-male societal sex ratios correspond to the sex ratios of women's liberation, while near equal and high-male/low-female societal sex ratios correspond to the times and spaces of women's oppression.

There is enough evidence in the next chapter to show that near equal sex ratios predominate in the patriarchal regions of the world today, while high-female/low-male sex ratios survive in regions of the world associated with "matriarchal" variables such as matrilineage, matrilocality, horticulture, and others.

This concludes the theoretical Part I of this book. Now consider empirical data on sex ratios, female sexuality, and homosex-segregation/heterosex-integration cross-culturally, in Part II.

Part II

Cross-Cultural Sex Data

Chapter 5

High Female Societies

by Pierre Auguste Renoir

The data presented in this chapter is unique in that, with the exception of Marvin Harris' work on sex ratios, no other summaries of world sex ratio patterns are available in the literature surrounding the debate over the origin of human society and of women's oppression. It is from this theoretical perspective that I examine the sex ratio data presented here. — *Author*

Now, I turn from the realm of theory to test the following sex ratio hypotheses in the real world, using a subsample of 100 societies[1]:

SEX RATIO HYPOTHESES

1) Total population sex ratios are not always equal in human societies.
2) Adult population sex ratios are not always equal in human societies.
3) Generally, sex ratios correlate with modes of subsistence.
4) High-female/low-male total populations correlate with polygynous marriages.
5) High-female/low-male sex ratios generally obtain in societies where the extended family, mother/child or communal household prevails.
6) High-female/low-male sex ratios generally occur in matrilocal societies.
7) Equal sex ratios correlate with monogamous marriages.
8) Equal sex ratios exist in societies where the independent, nuclear household/family normally prevails.
9) Equal sex ratios generally are found in patrilocal societies.
10) High-female/low-male sex ratios and equal sex ratios display distinct regional patterns.

SEX RATIOS IN THE REAL WORLD: SAMPLE DESCRIPTION

The earliest societal sex ratio found among the 100 societies examined was for the Callinago of the Caribbean in 1647, among whom "a multitude of women" was reported by the Spanish. The Callinago, who displayed a high-female/low-male sex ratio, are now extinct. The only other societal sex ratio I could trace back to the 17th century was that of the numerically equal Lapps of northwest Europe in 1694 and 1772.

The only sex ratio I found in the 18th century was the high female Abipon of the Gran Chaco in South America (1784). Most of my 100 society sample is historically set in the 19th and 20th centuries.

The earliest high-male/low-female sex ratio in the sample is the Miao of east Asia in the 1850's: 60.8% male and 39.2% female (total population).

The historical time range of my sample is: 1647 to 1971, spanning 324 years. I looked for earlier sex ratios in the *Human Resources Area File* (HRAF) *Source Bibliography*, but no information was available on the Babylonians, the Hebrews (800 B.C.), classical Greeks, or imperial Romans, regarding their sex ratios. Scholars still quarrel over whether Rome housed a population of one or four million persons; they are not in a position to know the sex ratio with exactitude when the total population is unknown. Though I would like to have had an earlier historical sample, the information is simply unavailable.

TABLE 3. World Frequency of Adult Population Sex Ratios, 1647-1971*		
ADULT POPULATION SEX RATIOS	**SOCIETIES SURVEYED**	
	Number	**Percentage**
MOSTLY FEMALE (54% and over)	21	35%
EQUAL (both sexes over 46% and under 54%)	32	53%
MOSTLY MALE (54% and over)	7	12%
TOTAL	60	100%

*Most of the data and tables summarizing *adult* sex ratios are located in Appendix C (Tables), e.g., on pages 225-7—while most of the data in this chapter refers to *total* population sex ratios, unless otherwise specified.

TABLE 4. Regional Distribution of Total Population Sex Ratios

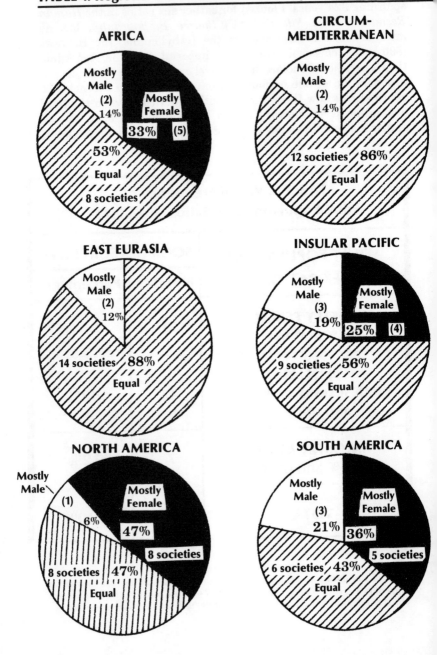

TOTAL

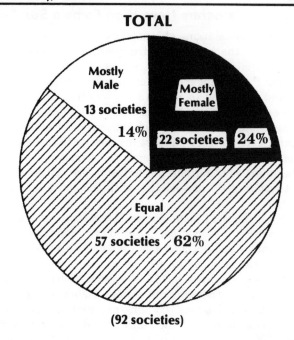

Mostly Male

13 societies

14%

Mostly Female

22 societies 24%

Equal

57 societies 62%

(92 societies)

My total population sex ratio sample of 92 societies is regionally distributed across the world in this way: Africa—15 societies; Circum-Mediterranean—14; East Eurasia—16; Insular Pacific—16; North America—17; South America—14.

HIGH FEMALE SEX RATIOS

Predominantly female populations do not exist in the Circum-Mediterranean or in East Eurasia in the 19th and 20th centuries. However, between 1647 and 1971, predominantly female populations existed in almost half of North American Indian societies, in a third of South America, in a third of Africa, and in a quarter of the Insular Pacific. These findings are significant in view of the fact that patriscientists generally function under the inaccurate assumption that equal sex ratios have always characterized world society, except in times of war or crisis.

In 24% of world society sampled, females outnumber males in the total population. Among *adult* populations, 35% of world society contains more adult females than males.

Hunters and Gatherers Have High Female Sex Ratios

High female populations characterize hunting and gathering society: 58% of the hunting and gathering societies I studied have high-female/low-male sex ratios. From another angle, more than a third of the mostly-female populations I studied are hunting and gathering societies (36%)—while only 10% of societies with equal sex ratios and only 8% of societies with mostly-male populations are hunters and gatherers. These finding are significant, because they support my theory that high-female/low-male sex ratios characterize original society.

Furthermore, hunting and gathering is present as a subsistence activity in 91% of societies with a mostly-female population.[2]

Table 5, on the next page, shows "Dominant Subsistence by Total Population Sex Ratios." (For more information on sex ratios of hunters and gatherers, see pages 95 and 201).

Equal sex ratios occur in: 67% of societies whose dominant subsistence is agriculture; in 71% of animal husbandry societies; in 56% of societies where dominant subsistence is fishing, shell-fishing and marine hunting. By contrast, high-female/low-male sex ratios occur in 58% of the hunting and gathering societies sampled.

This table lends striking support to my theory that high-female/low-male sex ratios characterize original society, since hunters and gatherers are scientifically viewed as the only living human link to prehistoric society. Hunting and gathering subsistence activity is totally *absent* in only 2 of the 22 societies with high-female/low-male sex ratios (9%)—while hunting and gathering is totally absent in 23 of the 52 societies with equal sex ratios (44%), and absent in a third of societies with high male sex ratios.

High Female Sex Ratios Associated with Matrilocality

Table 6, "Marital Residence by Sex Ratios (Total Population)," lends critical support to my theory that high-female/low-male sex ratios highly correlate with the social organization of gynosociety—since matrilocality is theoretically associated with these female social forms in the writings of Engels and classical matriarchists. This table reveals a strong correlation

TABLE 5. Dominant Subsistence by
Total Populations Sex Ratios

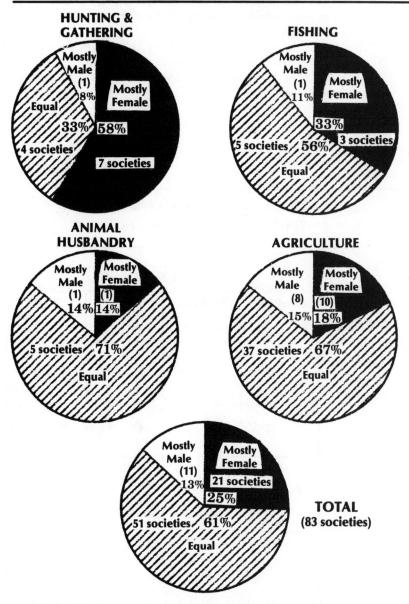

SOURCE: Dominant Subsistence is derived from Columns 2, 3, 4, and 5 in G. P. Murdock's 1975 "World Ethnographic Sample."

between high female total population sex ratios and matrilocality. Matrilocality occurs in 63% of societies with high-female/low-male sex ratios. Interestingly enough, *patri*locality occurs not only in the expected majority (69%) with equal sex ratios, but in 64% of high male societies.

This finding also supports my theory that equal sex ratios and high-male/low-female sex ratios correspond to patriarchal social forms, whereas high-female/low-male ratios characterize gynosocial forms.

TABLE 6. Marital Residence by Total Population Sex Ratios								
	MARITAL RESIDENCE							
Total Population SEX RATIOS	**Matrilocal**		**Patrilocal**		**Bilocal**		**Total**	
	No.	%	No.	%	No.	%	No.	%
MOSTLY FEMALE	12	63%	7	37%	0	0%	19	100%
EQUAL	11	23%	33	69%	4	8%	48	100%
MOSTLY MALE	3	27%	7	64%	1	9%	11	100%

*Egyptian women musicians: wall paintings from a
Theban tomb, 18th dynasty (1580-1350 B.C.)*
Metropolitan Museum of Art, New York City

On the following page, the reader will find a list of societies
with high-female/low-male total population sex ratios—noting
specific historical time, location and exact sex ratio. The average high-female/low-male sex ratio is 58.3% female, relative to
41.7% male. The average year these high female sex ratios
occurred was 1879.

The earliest high female sex ratio reported in this sample is
found among the Callinago in the Caribbean in 1647—followed
by the Abipon of the Grand Chaco in 1784. The latest reported
high female societal sex ratio is that of the Lozi (Central Bantu)
in 1958. However, as the average suggests, most of these high-
female/low-male sex ratios are found in the 19th century. See
also Table 8 on page 109, which gives the regional breakdown of
high-female/low-male total societal populations in this way:
North America—36%; South America—23%; Africa—23%;
Insular Pacific—18%; and none in either the Circum-Mediterranean or East Eurasia.

TABLE 7. Societies with High-Female/Low-Male Total Population Sex Ratios

Society	Location	Time	Percentage of Females
AFRICA			
Lozi	Central Bantu	1958	56.8%
Chagga	Northeast Bantu	1891	62.5%
Fang	Equatorial Bantu	1936-50	54.5%
Mende	Guinea Coast	1921-31	56.3%
Luo	Upper Nile	1900	'female sex predominates'
INSULAR PACIFIC			
Tiwi	Australia	1928-29	60.3%
Murngin	Australia	1946	'more females'
Ifaluk	Micronesia	1905, 1947-48	56.8%
Marshallese	Bikini, Micronesia	1878-1901	54%
NORTH AMERICA			
Alout	American Arctic	1831	54.1%
Klamath	Great Basin & Plateau	1865	68%
Blackfoot	Plains	1896	'preponderance of women'
Gros Ventre	Plains	1847	'preponderance of women'
Mandan	Plains	1870-72	62%
Crow	Plains	1862	'¼ more women than men'
Pawnee	Prairie	1840	56%
Hopi	Southwest	1933	55%
SOUTH AMERICA			
Haiti	Caribbean	1805	60%
Callinago	Caribbean	1647	'multitude of women'
Jivaro	Interior Amazonia	1949	64.6%
Siriono	Interior Amazonia	1950	54%
Abipon	Gran Chaco	1784	'abound more in women'

Mean Year = 1879   Mean Female/Male Sex Ratio = 58.3% to 41.7%

REGION	Number of Societies	Percentage
TABLE 8. Regional Distribution of High-Female/Low-Male Total Population Sex Ratios		
AFRICA	5	**23%**
CIRCUM-MEDITERRANEAN	0	**0%**
EAST EURASIA	0	**0%**
INSULAR PACIFIC	4	**18%**
NORTH AMERICA	8	**36%**
SOUTH AMERICA	5	**23%**
TOTAL	**22**	**100%**

On page 225 in Appendix C, Table 51 presents a list of the societies with high-female/low-male *adult* sex ratios. The average year these ratios occurred is 1895. The average percentage of women in the high female adult populations is slightly higher than the average percentage of females for high female *total* populations presented on page 108: The average sex ratio is 59.7% women compared to 40.3% men, among those high female adult populations. The highest female adult population ratio reported is that of the Jivaro of Interior Amazonia in 1949. The Jivaro had 70.7% women, compared to 29.2% men. Table 52, "Regional Distribution of High-Female/Low-Male *Adult* Sex Ratios" (page 226), shows three such societies in the Circum-Mediterranean—whereas here it has been shown that no high-female/low-male *total* populations existed in the Circum-Mediterranean. East Eurasia holds steady, however: There are no high female sex ratios in either the adult or total populations of East Eurasia. Over half of the societies with high female adult sex ratios are located in Africa and North America.

High Female Conclusions

My study reveals a correlation between high female sex ratios and hunting and gathering subsistence; matrilocality; mother/child household; extended family; polygyny, and particularly sororal polygynous marriage; pre-urban society; and pre-stratified or pre-class society. See Tables 19 through 27 in Appendix C (pages 199-207) for more specific data regarding these conclusions.

This data supports my theory of high female sex ratios at the origin of human society—although more research is needed.

EQUAL SEX RATIOS

Equal sex ratios dominate the Circum-Mediterranean and East Eurasia. Since no high-female/low-male total sex ratios are found in these two patriarchal regions, the only other sex ratios present are a few high male populations. Over half of Africa and the Insular Pacific have equal sex ratios. Less than half of North America (47%) and South America (43%) are characterized by equal sex ratios.

Equal sex ratios clearly characterize late patriarchy. However, there is no evidence to support the patriarchal assumption that equal sex ratios characterize *all* societies—especially not original society. 62% of this world sample of total populations reveal equal sex ratios, while only 53% of the *adult* societies sampled reveal equal sex ratios.

Equal sex ratios in the total population highly correlate with equal adult population sex ratios—although equal sex ratios in one population do not necessarily imply equal sex ratios in the other (see Table 20 on page 200).

Equal total population sex ratios chracterize the majority of societies where agriculture, animal husbandry, or fishing is the dominant mode of subsistence. Equal sex ratios are *not* characteristic of the majority of hunting and gathering societies sampled. Only 8% of the equal societies sampled are mainly hunting and gathering societies—whereas 32% of high female societies are mainly hunter/gatherers.

Notably, 85% of patrilocal societies have either near equal sex ratios (70%) or high male ratios (15%); and 69% of societies with near equal sex ratios are patrilocal.

I found that 77% of monogamous societies contain equal numbers of males and females in the total population. (As stated before, Engels noted the correlation between heterosexual monogamy and patriarchy).

Interestingly enough, equal sex ratios characterize the majority of monogamous and polyandrous societies, as well as limited polygynous societies.

Equal sex ratios are associated with nuclear households, occurring in 68% of all the independent families in this sample. The independent family is thus the normal family for equal total popuation sex ratios. Equal sex ratios describe complexly stratified, urban societies.

In sum, equal sex ratios are normally associated with patrilocality, complex stratification systems, urban societies, monogamous and polyandrous marriages as well as limited polygynous unions, independent families, nuclear households, and societies based on animal husbandry and agriculture.

The average sex ratio is 49% female, relative to 51% male. The average year these ratios occur in 1920. Thus, already a time difference appears between near equal sex ratios, whose mean time is in the 20th century—and high-female/low-male sex ratios, whose mean time is in the 19th century.

This finding lends some support for my theory that high-female/low-male sex ratios historically precede near equal sex ratios—albeit weak and indirect support from the 19th and 20th centuries, regarding prehistory. Still, it is amazing that a quarter of world high-female/low-male societies survived the 19th century, and that it was not until the 20th century that high-female/low-male sex ratios have been almost knocked off the map by patriarchy's equal sex ratios. Female infanticide has chopped away at high female sex ratios in the patriarchal regions of the world, East Eurasia and the Circum-Mediterranean notably—chiseling them to near equal sex ratios for the purposes of the heterosexual monogamian family, for the father/son/brother's power circuit over mother/daughter/sister/female society. In this light, the survival of several high female societies into this century is astounding.

HIGH-MALE/LOW-FEMALE CONCLUSIONS

Only 13 mostly-male societies were located in this world sample. They are the Dorobo, Rundi, Siwans, Georgians (USSR),

Toda, Miao, Lesu (New Ireland), Easter Islanders, Tlingit, Cagaba, Tapirape, Trumai, and Maori. Only one high male society was found in North America; there are between two to three such societies in each of the other world regions. Only 7 of the 60 adult populations sampled had more men than women.

High male sex ratios preclude the possibility of high female ratios within the same society, regarding either total or adult populations.

Agriculture is the dominant subsistence in 73% of the societies studied with high male total populations. Only one hunting and gathering society was found with a high male population: the Dorobo of the upper Nile.

64% of societies with high male populations are patrilocal. This finding corroborates my theory that high-male/low-female sex ratios are patriarchal. One reason I first studied the sex ratio question was my fury over the patriscientific misinterpretation of one female with many males as an example of female profit due to scarcity of female resources—and over the harem approach of seeing one male with many females as a male controlled group. The correlation with patrilocality indicates that high-male/low-female sex ratios are definitely patriarchal in character; they benefit the male, and not the female. Patrilocality does not benefit females, any more than patrilineage does.[3]

Among societies with mostly-male adult populations, 60% prefer to practice monogamy. Among societies with mostly-male *total* populations, however, 58% prefer to practice *polygynous* marriage (71% of these favoring limited polygyny).

Only one polyandrous society was found among those with high male ratios. This was unexpected: I had theoretically associated polyandry with high male sex ratios. As it turns out, the majority of polyandrous societies sampled have *equal* sex ratios.

The lineal family and household characterize high-male/low-female sex ratios. Mostly-male ratios do not occur in large urban populations; instead they are found in societies with fewer than 1,000 inhabitants.

Most frequently, high-male/low-female societies lack stratification systems—although these societies cross all stratification categories.

Table 53 (page 226) lists societies with high-male/low-female sex ratios (total population). The average year these mostly-male societies exist is 1913. Their average sex ratio is 58.2%

males, relative to 41.8% females. Eastern Polynesia contains two high-male/low-female societies—which means that 15% of this high male sample is curiously located there.

The average time of the societies recorded with high male adult sex ratios was 1912. The average adult high male ratio was 59.2% men, compared to 40.8% women in these seven societies: Dorobo, Somali, Toda, Easter Islanders, Maori, Kaska, and Tapirape. The range of their male proportions is between 54.6% and 63% of the adult population.

THEORETICAL INTERPRETATION OF THE DATA

An empirical case can be made for my argument that high-female/low-male sex ratios are correlated with early society, through the indirect observation of hunting and gathering society sex ratios. The information on hunter/gatherer sex ratios is poor, thus decreasing the number of usable hunter/gatherer societal cases to 18 in this study. Nevertheless, 58% of these hunters and gatherers, where information is available, display high female sex ratios in their total population.

Information on *adult* sex ratios among hunters and gatherers is even rarer; only 10 hunter/gatherer societies were located with any information on adult sex ratios. Seven of the ten report high-female/low-male sex ratios; two report near equal; and the Dorobo have a high-male/low-female adult and total population in 1929—among the 226 persons left.

This Dorobo case brings to mind a pertinent problem: the sex ratios of extinction. Hortense Powdermaker discusses an interesting theory of Pitt-Rivers in regard to the sex ratios of extinction:

> The connection of sex ratios with a declining population is also of interest. Pitt-Rivers (G.H.LF. Pitt-Rivers) has drawn attention to the significance of sex ratios by his theory that an increasing masculinity occurs when a people is dying out or declining.[4]

Sex Ratios of Extinction?

Anthropologists in general do not accept Pitt-Rivers' theory, but Powdermaker considers it because high-male/low-female sex

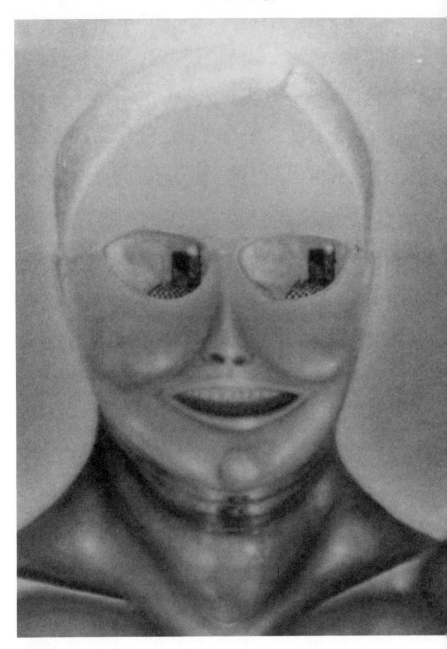

by Janet Yacht

ratios obtained among the Lesu of New Ireland, whom she describes as a "declining people" on the way to extinction in the 1930's. The Lesu are not hunters and gatherers; they are horticulturalists, subsisting on roots and tubers while keeping some pigs. They are classed as a matrilineal society.

I found this theory fascinating in view of the fact that a number of hunter/gatherer societies, as well as matrilineal societies, are already extinct or on their way to extinction. Many were simply murdered by their conquerors or by their conquerors' diseases, physically or psychologically. There is no doubt about it: Patriarchy has dealt death blows to societies with high female sex ratios, matrilineage, matrilocality, and extended mother/child households — both militarily and economically.

But I wonder if low-female/high-male sex ratios are a *cause* or a *symptom* of forthcoming societal extinction, and under what circumstances. As Eleanor Leacock suggests, the evidence on hunters and gatherers shows a great deal of variation.

One hunter/gatherer society I found, the Tasmanians, became extinct in 1876. I did not include them in the sample, because the same source gave conflicting sex ratios which knocked each other out of the sample of 100 usable societies. Nevertheless, the Tasmanians may fit Pitt-Rivers' theory, because in 1817 they numbered around 7,000, yet by 1833 had dwindled to 122. Roth,[5] the primary ethnographer, footnotes this figure:

...It was said at this date that the proportion of males to females was 6 to 1 (Van Diemen's Land Annual, 1834, pp. 79-80).

By 1848, when the Tasmanians were down to a pitiful 38 persons, the sex ratio flipped back to high female: 23 women to 12 men. The last 39 years, there were more females than males left. Roth reports that "the last representative of the race, a female, died in 1876." I thought that was an interesting case study where, when the tendency towards extinction first set in, there was a high-male/low-female sex ratio — but the females endured longer than the males.

Another provocative hunting and gathering society I had to throw out of the sample due to conflicting reports of near equal and high male sex ratios at the same time, are the Semang of southeast Asia, the forest dwarfs. Evans (1935) writes:

Schebesta has made a very interesting suggestion with regard to the decrease in number of the Negritos, which is that it is due in part to lack of women among them—'a great dearth of women is making itself felt in their ranks.' I believe that he is correct in his statement, for one certainly does notice considerably more men and boys about the camp than women and girls. If I remember rightly, this is also one of the causes of depopulation in the South Sea Islands, but I do not know that any satisfactory reason has been advanced for the too great preponderance of males.[6]

WAR AND SEX RATIOS

The sex ratios of extinction are as interesting as the "effects of warfare on population." That is, if high-male/low-female sex ratios are dangerously maladaptive for societal survival, it has been argued by Warner[7] that Murngin warfare is a mechanism to keep the male population in check:

The statistical average of wives to one middle aged man is 3½... The one important effect of warfare on Murngin society is the seasonal slaying of a small proportion of young men who have passed adolescence and are potential or eligible mates... Warfare, then, is one of the mechanisms on which polygyny is based.

The Murngin are hunters and gatherers. Berndt (in *Alien Contact in North Eastern Arnhem Land*) also writes of the Murngin:

Constant feuding over a long period is said to have reduced especially the male population, and brought about the extinction or amalgamation of many clans. This warring propensity led to a surplus of women, and had a direct bearing on sexual behavior. For example, large polygynous families were formed; and these are conventional even today (1946-50).[8]

Evans-Pritchard comments on a fascinating complex of sex variables among the Nuer people—which relates to this discussion:

Wives of female husbands and wives in ghost-marriage are to all intents and purposes in the same legal position as wives in simple legal marriages... The number of widow-concubines and of old women without mates (who are also widows) suggests a very high mortality rate among males. This is partly due to the constant fighting that used to go on, and still to a lesser extent goes on between Nuer. In a number of cases recorded in the village women have been widowed by the violent death of their husbands.[9]

John Brierly, one of the HRAF curators at Yale University, informed me at the onset of this empirical study of sex ratios, that I would find high-female/low-male sex ratios among hunters and gatherers, warring primitive peoples, and polygynous peoples. My research generally supports Brierly's prediction.

The relationship between war and high female sex ratios is a topic for a book in itself—but not this one. I thought it critical to mention, however, since male wars (whether they be on the technological scale of world war 2 and its effects on Russian and European sex ratios, or on the primitive technological level of the headhunting Jivaro of Interior Amazonia, whose adult population is 70.7% female vs. 29.2% male[10]) are one of the classical interpretations of high-female/low-male sex ratios.

I also mention these specific cases of unusable, but fascinating sex ratios of declining hunter/gatherers, as well as other declining matrilineal peoples, because I think some of the most interesting cases are the ones that are thrown out of studies, due to inability to meet strict criteria for hypothesis testing.

CONCLUSIONS

My theory that early society—gynosociety—is characterized by high-female/low-male sex ratios, has never been tested before. This type of explanation of high female sex ratios is unique in the social scientific literature.

The correlations I found between high-female/low-male sex ratios and hunter/gatherer societies, support my contention that, on average, in earlier societies females outnumber males in either total or adult population, sometimes both. The historical evidence I have amassed shows that the mean time of high female sex ratios is in the 19th century, while near equal and high male mean sex ratio time is in the 20th century.

The correlations I found between high female sex ratios and matrilocality, extended mother/child family and household, pre-urban society, and an absence of stratification or class systems, also support my contention that classical concepts of gynosociety or "matriarchy" are empirically associated with high-female/low-male sex ratios.

Further, my evidence demonstrates a strong correlation between near equal sex ratios and the classic constructs of patriarchal society: patrilocality, the heterosexual monogamian family (nuclear/independent), complex stratification systems, plow agriculture subsistence, animal husbandry, and the development of cities.

Chapter 6

Cross-Cultural Lesbianism

*You may forget but
Let me tell you
this: someone in
some future time
will think of us.*

—Sappho (c. 600 BC)
translated by
Mary Barnard

LESBIAN HYPOTHESES

While researching my doctoral dissertation (Rutgers University, political sociology, 1978), I tested the following set of hypotheses on a sub-sample of 30 societies (drawn from Murdock's 1957 "World Ethnographic Sample"), where lesbianism is reported:

1) Lesbianism is geographically widespread across human society.[1]
2) Lesbianism obtains across all major human subsistence types.
3) Lesbianism obtains in societies other than and historically prior to "decadent, bourgeois capitalist society."

The problem of lack of information will plague any researcher who attempts to study cross-cultural lesbianism. Ford and Beach (1952) note the problem that "feminine homosexuality is accorded much less attention than is comparable behavior among males." Ford and Beach found information on lesbianism in only 17 of 185 societies, compared to 76 societies where data on male homosexuality was recorded. The societal "fallout" rate, due to lack of information, is incredibly high around female sexuality compared to male sexuality—whether it be gay or non-gay.

Nevertheless, the data I have gathered on the recorded presence of lesbianism across society reveals more information on pre-industrial world lesbianism than is presently summarized in the social science literature.

4) Lesbianism obtains across all types of human settlement patterns.

5) Lesbianism is not associated with any *one* marriage form, marital residence, family, household type, or marital economic exchange; it crosses all major marriage and family forms.

6) Lesbianism crosses all social stratification systems.

7) If lesbianism obtains in hunting and gathering society, it may obtain in early society and possibly at social origin.

PATRISCIENCE'S OMISSION OF LESBIANISM: UNRECORDED REALITY OR RECORDED UNREALITY

I begin this discussion of cross-cultural lesbianism by underlining the point that I do not regard my small sub-sample of societies reporting lesbianism as numerically representative of the true world societal population of lesbians, because: 1) The sub-sample is largely drawn from western anthropological data (*HRAF*, 1978); 2) Western anthropologists have hardly addressed themselves to the subject of lesbianism seriously; and 3) My studies lead me to conclude that the social sciences are generally ignorant of lesbian phenomena. The smallness of the sub-sample is, I believe, due to the underreporting or omission of lesbianism in the anthropological literature. The widespread patriarchal societal sanctions against lesbians inhibit the free flow of information regarding lesbian phenomena.

The lack of recorded information on either the presence or absence of lesbianism per society in the social science literature forced me to create a rather unique and indirect research methodology to study the scope of pre-Stonewall (pre-1969) world lesbianism.

METHOD

My research case is society, not individual lesbians; specifically, societies where the presence of lesbianism is recorded in the English language in social science literature—primarily anthropology, ethnology, sociology and history. I do not use religious or psychiatric literature on lesbianism in my secondary analysis. My primary source for compiling a list of 64 societies where the existence of lesbianism is recorded in English is the

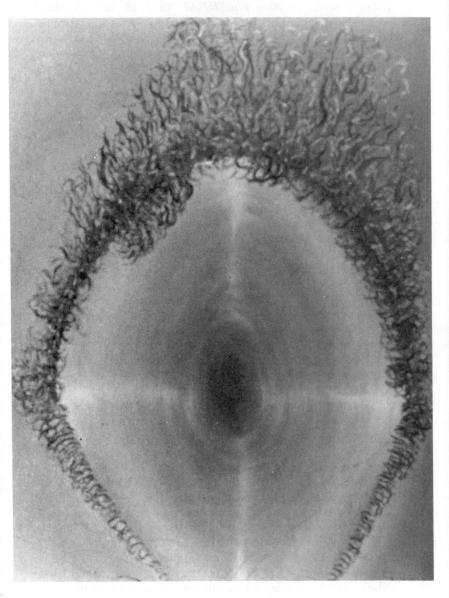

'Cunt Coif', by Janet Yacht

Human Relations Area File (HRAF, 1978) at the City University of New York. This is supplemented by some gay movement historical literature (Katz, 1976), although I tend to stay within the more hostile patriscientific literature to prove an academic point.

64 Societies Where Lesbianism is Reported

The original list of 64 societies where lesbianism is reported include: Amarakaeri, American (New England), Aranda, Argentina, Athenian (450 B.C.), Aymara, Azande, Balinese, Blackfoot, Brazil, Cagaba, Canada, Cantonese, Celt, Chile, Chiracahua (Apache), Chukchee, Cocopa, prehistoric Crete, Crow, Cuba, Dahomey, Denmark, Egypt, England, Eskimo, France, west Germany, Greece, Haiti, Hawaii, Herero, Holland, Hottentot, Ifaluk, ancient India, Ireland, Israel, Italy, Japan, Kaska, Klamath, Kutenai, Lesbos (c. 600 B.C.), Manus, Maricopa, Mayan, Mbundu, Mexico, Navaho, New Zealand, Ojibwa (Chippewa), Puerto Rico, imperial Roman (A.D. 100), Russia, Rwala Bedouin, Samoa, Spain, Sparta (450 B.C.), Sweden, Tapuye (pre-columbian Brazil), Tswana, Yuman, and Zanzibar.

I then cross-checked the original list of 64 societies where lesbianism is reported, against Murdock's 1957 "World Ethnographic Sample" of 565 societies, and immediately lost 34 societies from the sub-samples, due to these reasons: 1) They were not listed in the same way, especially timewise; 2) They were not listed at all in Murdock (1957); 3) The source reporting lesbianism did not appear reliable; 4) Contradictory reports regarding the presence or absence of lesbianism sufficed to exclude a society from my sub-sample; or 5) Not enough specific information existed regarding societal lesbian location and boundaries. For example, I had to throw Westermarck's report of lesbianism in "India" out of the sub-sample because Murdock (1957) lists and codes 23 different Indian societies; there is no one "India" in the *HRAF*. Another rule for exclusion from the sub-sample regards societal overlap. I threw the Yumans and the Kamia out of the sub-sample, because of their cultural and geographical overlap with Maricopan society.

Since I decided early on in the study that I wanted to test my lesbian hypotheses on a large number of societies which were representative of known world society, I selected Murdock's 1957 world sample of 565 societies. Murdock (1957) contains no information on modes of sexuality, but contains a great deal of information on the economic and social structure, family, marriage and inheritance systems of each total society listed therein. Here lies the value of Murdock (1957) for my research purposes. I use Murdock's information on the total society in order to study lesbian sexuality comparatively across society.

Having had to exclude 34 societies (many of which are industrial) for the reasons listed on the previous page, I found that my sub-sample had decreased in size from 64 to 30 societies. It was a trade-off of information. However, I gained more information on 30 total societies which report lesbianisn than I previously had without Murdock's (1957) world data bank.

Lesbian Sample: 30 Societies

Thus, the 30 usable societal cases in my sub-sample are at the same time societies which report lesbianism and which are cross-indexed in Murdock (1957). These societies are listed by world region: AFRICA—Azande, Dahomey, Herero, Hottentot, Mbundu, Tswana; CIRCUM-MEDITERRANEAN—Athenian (450 B.C.), Roman (A.D. 100), Rwala Bedouin; EAST EURASIA—Cantonese and Chukchee; INSULAR PACIFIC—Aranda, Balinese, Ifaluk, Manus, and Samoa; NORTH AMERICA—Americans (New England), Blackfoot, Chiricahua, Cocopa, Crow, Kaska, Klamath, Kutenai, Ojibwa, Maricopa, and Navaho; SOUTH AMERICA—Aymara, Cagaba, and Maya.*

LESBIAN RESULTS

The data supports the first four hypotheses; however, the 5th and 6th hypotheses are not supported.

Lesbianism crosses all world regions. Specific distribution of the sub-sample of societies where lesbianism is reported runs as follows: Africa—six socities (20%); Circum-Mediterranean—four societies (13%); East Eurasia—2 societies (7%); Insular Pacific—five societies (17%); North America—ten (33%); and

---

*These societies form the data base of my hypothesis tests on world lesbianism. I tend to throw out, rather than keep, societies which fall on the borderline of sample criteria acceptability—because I prefer a smaller, more methodologically sound sample to a larger, questionable one. The following data on the recorded presence of lesbianism across society reveals more information than is presently summarized in social science literature on pre-industrial lesbianism. —*Author*

South America—three (10%). Lesbianism crosses all six world regions, although unevenly.[2]

Lesbianism in Pre-Industrial Societies

The data indicates that lesbianism obtains across all pre-industrial economies and subsistence levels, and is not confined to the capitalist mode of production, as has been erroneously assumed by various marxists. Over half of the societies which report lesbianism (16 societies) depend on agriculture for dominant subsistence, while 20% (six societies) depend upon hunting and gathering for principal subsistence; 13% (four societies) depend mainly upon animal husbandry and 13% (four societies) upon fishing.

A closer look at the hunting and gathering activity of this sub-sample reveals that not only is hunting and gathering the principal subsistence for 6 societies (20% of the sample), but it is "important though not the major subsistence activity" for the mode, 11 societies (37%). Hunting and gathering is relatively unimportant, but present among 3 societies (10%), and absent among 10 societies (33%).

A more careful look at agriculture demonstrates that, while it is the dominant subsistence in 16 societies (53% of the sample), and important but not major in only one society, agriculture is absent in 13 societies (43% of the sample).

Lesbianism Occurs Across All Human Settlement Patterns

The data further reveals that lesbianism crosses all types of human settlement patterns distinguished in Murdock (1957): compact villages (11 societies, the mode), nomadic bands (8 societies), compound settlements (4 societies), semi-nomadic communities (3 societies), neighborhoods of dispersed homesteads (2 societies), and clusters of hamlets (1 society). No information was available on the settlement patterns for one of the societies.

Marriage and Family in Societies Reporting Lesbianism

Regarding marital residence, most of the sub-sample is patri-local, which means that the married couple resides in the husband's community. Only five societies are matrilocal (17%), where the married couple resides with the wife's kin. Only one society is bilocal, like U.S. society, where the married couple may live near or with either spouse's parent. Although my subsample of societies reporting lesbianism did cross all major forms of marital residence, it did not cross *all* the exotic categories, particularly avunculocal, where a married couple resides with the maternal uncle of the husband.

My study of the frequency of marriage forms among societies reporting lesbianism reveals that lesbianism obtains across all heterosexual marriage forms except polyandry. Specifically, 22 societies (73%) are polygynous, and only 8 societies (27%) are monogamous.[3] A more detailed examination of these polygynous societies where lesbianism is reported reveals that eight of these prefer limited polygyny, six prefer sororal polygyny, four prefer general polygyny, and three nonsororal polygyny.

Regarding family types in relation to societies reporting lesbianism, the data reveals that lesbianism crosses extended, independent, and lineal family types; but I found no data to support the contention that lesbianism is reported in societies preferring stem families.

An examination of preferred household types in societies reporting lesbianism shows a bimodal distribution in the subsample between mother/child households and nuclear family households. Each type represents 33% of the subsample. That is, ten mother/child households and ten nuclear family households characterize two-thirds of the societies in the subsample.

Over half (53%) of the subsample is characterized by independent families; 37% by extended families; and 10% by lineal families. While no society in the subsample reports a stem family, there is one society with a stem household.

As regards marital economic exchange, societal lesbianism crosses all forms of economic exchange of females in marriage, except "token bride price." The mode or 33% of the subsample prefer bride price, while 30% of these societies are characterized by an absence of any significant material consideration in marriage; 23% practice "bride-service."

Over half of the subsample (56%) requires a substantial payment to the bride's family from the groom, while only two societies require a dowry. One society reciprocally exchanges gifts between the relatives of the bride and groom, while another practices exchange of the groom's sister or another female relative for the bride.

Lesbianism and Class Systems

The final finding concerns the social stratification systems of this subsample of societies which report lesbianism. Societal lesbianism crosses all world stratification systems except "formal age grades only." Over half of the subsample are either nonstratified (30%), or are societies where wealth distinctions, while important, lack definite crystallization into hereditary social classes (30%). Complex stratification systems are found in 23% of the subsample, while 17% of these societies which report lesbianism are hereditary aristocracies.

The subsample size is too small to perform any meaningful statistical tests of significance.

ANALYSIS OF LESBIAN DATA

The unequal regional distribution of the societal lesbian subsample may be the result of several problems inherent in secondary research: 1) unequal reporting of the phenomenon on the level of primary ethnographers; 2) unequal recording of the phenomenon on the secondary academic research and textbook level; 3) the unequal distribution of the Murdock world sample itself. Murdock concedes that his 1957 sample is overrepresented by African and North American societies. So is my lesbian subsample. The same must be said of the high frequency of agricultural societies in the subsample. I do not interpret this data to mean that lesbianism necessarily occurs more frequently in agricultural societies than in others, just because 61% of the societies in Murdock's sample principally depend upon agriculture.

Further research and larger cross-cultural lesbian samples are needed before any general conclusions regarding exact geographical distribution of lesbianism can be calculated. My subsample only establishes that lesbianism is, in fact, geographically and anthropologically widespread. Its exact breadth can only be determined through future research.

The same caution must be advised in the interpretation of all the frequencies reported here due to the smallness of the subsample. However, what we can safely conclude from this data is that *lesbianism does not appear to be peculiar to any one economy, family or household type, marriage form, stratification system or marital residence.* Moreover, the strength of this study lies in its very weakness: Even with a tiny subsample of societies which report lesbianism, we can see clearly from this data how far across society and social categories lesbianism reaches.

Lesbianism Found Among Hunters and Gatherers

In my mind, the most significant of all the results of this study is the finding that 6 societies (20% of the sample) depend upon hunting and gathering for principal subsistence, and that the activity is important, though not major in 11 other societies. This suggests that lesbianism obtains in early society, as hunting and gathering subsistence is methodologically linked to the study of social origin. This study does lend some empirical support to my 7th hypothesis—although the topic of origin is highly speculative.

Lesbianism Found in Pre-Class Society

The 3rd hypothesis is supported by several types of data— e.g., pre-industrial subsistence types and pre-class stratification systems. I included this hypothesis, that lesbianism obtains in societies other than and historically prior to "decadent bourgeois capitalist society," because throughout the 1960's and 1970's various North American, Cuban, Chinese, and Russian marxists[†] have blamed capitalism for homosexuality—which is ignorant and ahistorical. The existence of lesbianism among hunters and gatherers, animal husbandry and fishing societies prior to class formation exposes the erroneous nature of this rhetoric.

---

†The bolshevik revolution, under the leadership of Lenin, Trotsky, and Alexandra Kollontai, immediately struck down the tsarist laws that had banned homosexuality and abortion—declaring as one of its key goals the complete liberation of women from the domestic slavery of the patriarchal family. In the early years of the revolution the Soviet women's organization, despite the desperate material conditions faced by the country, conducted a number of radical experiments in the socialization of housework and child-rearing. But with the consolidation of a parasitic, conservative state bureaucracy which Stalin came to head, the patriarchal values of the old society reasserted themselves. Stalin revived the tsarist ban against homosexuality, and in 1936 banned abortion. Divorce once again became extremely difficult, and women were exhorted to produce babies "for the socialist motherland." In the course of liquidating practically the entire bolshevik leadership, Stalin liquidated the Soviet women's organization as a force for revolutionary change. In the post-Stalin period, abortion and divorce rights were restored to Soviet women, but the ban against homosexuality remains actively in force. —*Editor*

'Unity', by Jean Lois Greggs
(watercolor, 18" x 24")

Aside: The fact that lesbianism obtains across industrial economy, although not studied here, can be easily demonstrated by the hystorical fact that the current wave of lesbian feminist movement in the 1970's and 1980's originated in New York City in 1969 with the Stonewall rebellion and that most all industrial societies—e.g., Britain, France, Germany, the Netherlands, Sweden, Italy, and Japan—have lesbian feminist movements which hold public demonstrations and publish a variety of lesbian feminist literature.

Conclusion

The 5th hypothesis is supported by the data: Lesbianism is not the result of any one marriage form, type of marital residence, family or household type or marital economic exchange. However, lesbianism did not cross certain *rare* categories such as polyandry, the stem family, and token bride price.

In conclusion, this study suggests that lesbianism is far more widespread geo-socially than heterosexist social scientists indicate by their "benign neglect" of the subject.

'WOMAN-MARRIAGE'

To lesbians the term, "woman-marriage," signifies lesbianism. To anthropologists, "woman-marriage" does not necessarily imply lesbianism; instead, it is regarded as a property relation. That is, "woman-marriage" is regarded anthropologically as a way for women to own their own children in patrilineal societies. Because of this definitional discrepancy, I treat "woman-marriage" separately from lesbianism in this chapter.[4]

Kathleen Gough's 1968 definition of marriage conceptually leaves room for the phenomenon of "woman-marriage." Gough defines:

> Marriage is a relationship established between a woman and one or more persons, which provides that a child born to the woman under circumstances not prohibited by the rules of the relationship, is accorded full birth-status rights common to normal members of his society or social stratum.[5]

According to Gough, women are necessary for marriage; men are optional. In *Culture, People, Nature: An Introduction to General Anthropology* (published in 1971—two years after Stonewall), Marvin Harris discusses "woman-marriage" and Gough's general definition of marriage:

> Yet Gough's definition seems oddly at variance with English dictionary and native Western notions of marriage. First of all, there is no reference to rights and duties of sexual access, much less to simple sexual performance. More remarkable, if Gough's definition is accepted, the conclusion drawn would have to be that marriage need not involve a relationship between men and women. She merely signifies that there must be a woman and 'one or more other persons' of undefined sex! What accounts for these omissions?... Gough's reasons for defining marriage as a relationship between a woman and 'persons' rather than between 'a woman and a man' are based on several additional well-known ethnographic facts. It is clear, first of all, that polyandrous marriages involve a relationship between a woman and men, not *a* man. Second, there are several instances among African peoples—the Dahomey case is best known—in which a woman is said to marry one or more women. This is accomplished by having a woman who herself is already married to a man pay brideprice. [Extended families exchange their daughter/sisters for wife/mothers among herder/farmer people of eastern and southern Africa—p. 324]. The female bride-price payer becomes a 'female husband.' She founds a compound of her own by letting her 'wives' become pregnant through relationships with designated males. The offspring of these unions fall under the control of the 'female father' rather than the biological genitors. Yet Gough's definition ignores the equally marriage-like relationships that have no women at all. Some anthropologists would like to include man-man relationships as marriage... It has been suggested that all reference to the sex of the people involved in the relationship should be omitted in the definition of marriage in order to accommodate these additional cases.[6]

It is curious that polyandrous marriage, which Murdock reports is so rare as to comprise only 4 out of 565 societies in his 1957 world sample, is always afforded honorable mention in social science discussions of marriage—while "woman-marriage," which is numerically more frequent around the world than polyandry, is rarely cited in world or societal tables of marriage forms. I attribute this unequal attention to "woman-marriage," which incidentally outnumbers polyandrous unions, to heterosexism in the social sciences.

Woman-Marriage in Africa

In "A Note on 'Woman Marriage' in Dahomey," Herskovits reports that the "phenomenon of 'woman marriage'" is a social institution among not only the Fon in Dahomey, but the Yoruba in southwest Nigeria, the Ibo of southeastern Nigeria, the Dinka and Nuer in the Sudan, and the Bavenda or Venda of the Transvaal (South Africa)—and in other "various parts of the African continent."[7]

Herskovits thinks that these female "matings" in Africa "may represent a pattern having a far wider distribution." That is, he posits that "woman-marriage" may have been transported from Africa to North America during slavery, and that "woman-marriage" survived slavery:

> The 'competent, self-sufficient women' who wish to have no husbands are of especial interest. The social and economic position of women in West Africa is such that on occasion a woman may refuse to relinquish the customary control of her children in favor of her husband, and this gives rise to special types of matings that are recognized in Dahomey and among the Yoruba, and may represent a pattern having a far wider distribution. The phenomenon of a woman 'marrying' a woman which has been reported from various parts of the African continent and is a part of this same complex, testifies to the importance of a family type which might well have had the vitality necessary to make of it a basis for the kind of behavior outlined in the case of the 'self-sufficient' woman who, in the United States, desires children but declines to share them with a husband.[8]

Woman-marriage is not confined to Africa, although most of the cases I have read in research for this work, are. I did not research woman-marriage to the extent that I studied lesbianism cross-culturally; thus, the data presented here is exploratory, and in no way conclusive. I think that woman-marriage is far more common than anthropologists allow, and that the study of this phenomenon should yield significant findings with further research.

Woman-Marriage in the Americas

In *Daughters of the Earth*, Carolyn Niethammer reports five cases of native American women marrying other women—

among the Mohave, Navajo, Eskimo, Yuma, and Cocopa.[9] Oscar Lewis records woman-marriage as a practice among the North Piegan (Blackfoot).[10]

Jonathan Katz, in *Gay American History*, describes a Kutenai woman with a wife.[11] Thus, I am aware of seven societal cases of woman-marriage in North America, seven societal cases in Africa, and one case, reported by Pero de Magalhaes, of the Tapuye in South America,[12] who are now extinct.

Woman-Marriage Prevents 'An Unhappy Old Age'

I have no information on woman-marriage in the Circum-Mediterranean, East Eurasia, or the Insular Pacific. This does not mean that the practice of woman-marriage is unknown in these parts. In Perlman and Moal's "Analytical Bibliography" in *Women of Tropical Africa*, they summarize Taraore's 1941 report of woman-marriage among the Bobo Nieniege in this way:

> Marriage between women practiced by the Bobo Nieniege (Ivory Coast): to avoid an unhappy old age, Nieniege women who have passed child-bearing age without having had any children attempt to assure themselves by indirect means of the services of a fictitious progeny to be attained by *Yaro ha* or marriage between women.[13]

I wonder if this is the anthropologist's interpretation of *Yaro ha*, or if it is the Bobo's explanation of the phenomenon. I think that the general anthropological assumption that woman-marriage is not a lesbian relationship has never been empirically substantiated.

Woman-Marriage and Lesbianism

I do not question the contention that woman-marriage is a mechanism by which women can own their children in patrilineal societies; but this proposition does not exclude the possibility that woman-marriage may also be a lesbian relationship.

In several societies of my lesbian sample, woman-marriage was also observed. In Dahomey, for example, both lesbianism and woman-marriage obtain; this is also true of the Mohave and the Tapuye. This suggests there are hystorical links between lesbianism and woman-marriage.

At any rate, I consider this anthropological assumption that woman-marriage is not a lesbian relationship as valid as the assumption that heterosexual marriage is not a heterosexual relationship, since the latter is definitely a property relation also.

Here, I leave woman-marriage for lack of further data on the subject, and return to a discussion of lesbianism, particularly the estimated incidence of lesbianism in the patri-social scientific literature. The rest of this chapter is confined to lesbian phenomena.

ESTIMATIONS OF LESBIAN INCIDENCE

In McMurtrie's 1914 study, "A Legend of Lesbian Love among the North American Indians," he concludes that:

> Lesbian love, the sexually inverted phenomenon of love relations between women, is found to exist among all peoples regarding whom complete and accurate data concerning the *vita sexualis* is available.[14]

Most male researchers contend that male homosexuality is far more common than lesbianism, across both human and non-human society.[15] I think that lesbianism is far more common than patriscientists imagine or record. Ford and Beach do recognize that "in most other societies, as in our own, feminine homosexuality is accorded much less attention than is comparable behavior among males."[16]

After reading patriscientific literature on lesbianism, I conclude that the true or actual incidence of lesbianism per society or globally is an unknown quantity. Conclusive research has yet to be done. My intent here is to summarize the current scientific estimates on the incidence of lesbianism per society.

Kinsey (1953) estimates that 2% of the United States female population is lesbian.[17] This is the lowest estimate I came across in research. Even Kinsey admits that his lesbian and gay male estimates are lower than probable actuality.

Davis (1929) reports that half of 1200 women sampled have "intense emotional relationships with other women as adults," while some 27% acknowledge "overt lesbian experience."[18] Davis also thinks that lesbianism is more prevalent among unmarried women and employed women than married, unemployed women. About 20% of the unmarried Davis sample stated that their affairs with other women developed into genital contact or mutual masturbation. An additional 78 cases in Davis' study stated that although they had not gone beyond

'Self-Portrait with Cropped Hair', by Frida Kahlo (1940).
The line of lyrics reads:

"When I used to love you, it was for your hair —
but now that you've lost it, my love's just not there."

kissing and hugging another woman physically, their homo-erotic experience had been "recognized at the time as sexual in character."[19]

Shere Hite estimates that 8% of her sexuality sample is les-bian.[20] Hamilton (1929) found that 26 out of 1000 North Ameri-can women studied admitted having "intense emotional rela-tions" with other women, without explicitly stating the progress of their sexual interaction with other females.[21]

Landis and Bolles (1942) report that all but 22 of the 295 females interviewed in their book, *Personality and Sexuality of Physically Handicapped Women*, had crushes on other adoles-cent females.[22]

In their article, "Is Women's Liberation A Lesbian Plot?", Barbara Love and Sydney Abbott suggest that "there are prob-ably more lesbians than male homosexuals."[23] Thus far, these lesbian estimates apply to the United States. Now consider some cross-cultural societal estimates in the literature.

In certain societies, it has been reported that lesbianism is as phenomenally common as male homosexuality. Havelock Ellis describes India in this way.[24] Westermarck (1908) and his prim-ary source, Julius Jacobs (1888), report that female homosexual-ity is almost as common in Bali as male homosexuality, "though it is exercised more secretly."[25] Westermarck is one male researcher who does not think that lesbianism is rarer than male homosexuality. His position is that lesbianism is less noticeable than gay male behavior, and not necessarily rarer in actuality—which is rather perceptive of him. Westermarck writes:

> From Greek antiquity we hear of 'Lesbian' love. The fact that homosexuality has been much more frequently noticed in men than in women does not imply that the latter are less addicted to it. For various reasons the sexual abnormalities [sic] of women have attracted much less attention, and moral opinion has generally taken little notice of them.[26]

Margaret Mead offers no comparative data on female and male homosexuality, but does present some extraordinary data on female homosexual experience in *Coming of Age in Samoa*.[27] Mead found that out of the 25 female adolescents she studied on Samoa, 17 of them had "homosexual experience," while 8 did not. In contrast, only 12 out of 25 girls had "heterosexual experience"; 13 did not. The relative frequencies then are: 68% of Mead's sample had homosexual experience, while only 48% had heterosexual experience.[28] This is a rare finding. It upsets the patriscientific assumption that heterosexuality is the statistical norm and homosexuality the deviant case. Unfortunately, Mead does not elaborate.

In *Keep the River on Your Right*, Schneebaum reports that with the Amarakaeri of eastern Peru, lovemaking is almost exclusively homosexual among women and men—except for heterosexual acts performed two or three time a year at ceremonial rites.[29]

I think that homosexuality is probably present in almost all, if not all, societies; but that its incidence will vary by society. I do not expect there to be a fixed rate of lesbian incidence in all societies at all times, any more than I would expect to find a fixed, unalterable rate of heterosexuality per society, or globally. Like homosexuality, heterosexuality is a variable, which means that it varies. I do not think of either mode of sexuality as an eternal constant in the equation of sex and society.

I have no new evidence on the incidence of lesbianism within societies. I have focused my attention on the societal macrocosm of cross-culturally reported lesbianism. The data I have presented does not indicate the numerical extent of lesbian sexuality per society, only its *reported* presence or absence. Admittedly, this is a crude methodology, but the only one possible given the crude state of social science literature on lesbianism. Hopefully, some future researchers will provide the sorely needed, refined research. There is a small but interesting literature, which I will briefly review, comparing the incidence of lesbian orgasm to heterosexual orgasm among women.

LESBIAN ORGASM

From the data available, there is an orgasmic discrepancy between lesbians and straight women. No orgasm during lesbian sex is exceptional, while *female* orgasm during heterosex acts *is* exceptional.

Ford and Beach utilize G. W. Henry's finding in *Sex Variants*, which report that 95% of the 40 "long-term, active homosexual women" Henry interviewed

...regularly achieved orgasm during homosexual activity. This is a much higher proportion than has been found among women in any married group indulging in heterosexual intercourse or in individuals practicing solitary masturbation.[30]

Shere Hite reports that the "majority" of the 3,000 North American women who answered her questionnaire (although only 1,844 were statistically analyzed) do not achieve orgasm during heterosexual intercourse. Hite concludes:

> Did most of the women in this study orgasm regularly during intercourse (the penis thrusting in the vagina), without additional clitoral stimulation? No. *It was found that only approximately 30% of the women in this study could orgasm regularly from intercourse*—that is, could have an orgasm during intercourse without more direct manual clitoral stimulation being provided at the time of orgasm. In other words, the majority of women do not experience orgasm regularly as a result of intercourse. For most women, orgasming during intercourse as a result of intercourse alone is the exceptional experience, not the usual one.[31]

Yet, according to Henry's data, orgasm among lesbians is the usual experience for 95% of the sample: *The Joy of Lesbian Sex*.[32] Now it must be considered that Henry's sample of 40 long-term lesbians is much smaller than Hite's sample. Until further and larger samples of lesbians are drawn and analyzed, numerical generalizations based on these comparisons are uncertain.

Nonetheless, the orgasmic differential among females practicing lesbian sex, solitary sex, or heterosex is statistically significant at this stage of study, and suggests the obvious: Males do not know how to make love to women as well as women can make love to each other.

Chapter 7

Sexual Separation

'Ta Matete' (The Market), by Paul Gauguin: Polynesia, 1892

This chapter is concerned with empirical data on homosex segregation and heterosex integration across society. It contains cross-cultural evidence of female languages, the segregation of adolescent boys, post-partum sex taboos, and the sexual division of labor. The data here is minute, compared to the actual sexual separation of the true world population. I only open the lid. —*Author*

THEORY OF SEXUAL SEPARATION

Homosex segregation is same sex social organization. Heterosex integration is opposite sex organization. Hystorically, the original form of social organization is female society. Female society is the original form of horizontal homosex segregation, as it is the original form of society itself.

Modal heterosex integration does not historically occur until the advent of patriarchy. Heterosex physical integration is a basic property of patriarchy. Without heterosex integration on a physical level, patriarchy cannot exist at all.

Gynosex social organization is characterized more by homosex physical segregation. All societies are at base female, since no society is functional without adult females. The term "society" is essentially a patriscientific neutralizer for female society.

Individual males have little or no relationship to society unless they have some form of relationship to an adult female: mother, sister, wife, aunt, grandmother. If success in reproduction is a measure of survival, as patriarchal theory holds, then males without any heterosexual connection to an adult female, the mean of reproduction, are the least likely to survive well. Heterosexuality is the male's only link to reproduction and to female society—which is, after all, society itself. The only way the majority of males can enter female society is through heterosexual integration, which makes possible the heterosexual relation.

Incest Theory Revisited

The first heterosexual relation is the mother/son relation. Some matriarchists think that the first heterosexual lover consorts of women are their sons. However, the mother/son relation

---

In this chapter, I will explore some of the forms sexual separation takes.[1] For lack of time, I did not summarize all known forms of sexual segregation that have been reported in the ethnographic world. For example, I have no systematic world data on residential sex segregation, where the husband and wife live separately by custom, or where males and females dine in separate quarters, or sleep separately. I have no world data on the preponderance of segregated male and female organizations.[2]

Since it is always best to begin empirical work from a theoretical base, I will first briefly discuss the theoretical context in which I view homosex segregation and heterosex integration, before moving directly into the data. —*Author*

The Cumaean Sibyl (a prominent prophetess in Roman
mythology), by Michelangelo. The "physical inferiority" of
women is a quite recent invention of patriarchy.
(from the Sistine Chapel in the Vatican)

is not the original social relation; it is merely the original *hetero-sexual* relation.

The *mother/daughter* relation is probably the first enduring family relation—as the relation between adult females is the original community relation. In my section on "Incest Theory" in ch. 2 (pages 54-60), I analyze the connection of female homosex relations and the mother/son relation, with original society and its internal sex dynamics.

Transition to Patriarchy

Here I must move into the mechanics of transition to patriarchy and the maintenance of its systems. This originates with the mother/son relation, but then develops more forms of hetero-sex integration as patriarchy develops its exploitative heterosex relations historically.

The sex segregation/integration variable shapes the distribution of the sexes in society; the sex ratio controls the frequency of men and women. Sexual separation/integration and the sex ratio are variable combination locks which shape the form and content of society. Female sexuality is the material content, the womb of social forms, and female sexuality is what turns society on. Men cannot make social forms without a female population base; but women *can* make social forms without a male base.

In order for men to control a societal base at all, they must continually and *physically occupy female society.* The more pleasant modern term for this phenomenon is integration. While certain liberals consider the "integration" of women into patriarchy a solution to women's oppression, I view heterosex integration of females into patriarchy as a major cause of women's oppression.

Women's oppression is not the result of too much separation from men physically.

Women's oppression is directly tied to the mass physical integration of adolescent and adult males into female social networks. Dominance hierarchies are characteristic of most male groupings, but not female, among primates. The entrance of the mass of males into everyday residential contact with female society brings dominance hierarchies into society. In a real sense, these male dominance hierarchies economically, socially, and politically segregate the mass of women from positions of power in society. Vertical social segregation, not horizontal physical segregation, characterizes patriarchal formations. That is, patriarchy is physically integrated and socially segregated sexually, as the North American south is racially.

The eye of the beholder becomes important here. For example, patriscientists routinely see a male-controlled harem when they see a group of females with a lone male. How does the patriscientist know that the females are not controlling the male?

Now let's take a parallax view of sexual separation. Patriscientists—including Marx, Engels, Zaretsky, and others—think that the original source of the sexual division of labor is the heterosexual act. I see the sexual division of labor as the classic form of homosexual segregation. There is little that is heterosexual about it, except the role play. Physically, the sexual division of labor amounts to separation of the opposite sexes by same sex characteristics. There are, to be sure, a few societal cases where women and men are physically integrated, performing the same tasks. However, the majority of the world's sexual divisions of labor are based on the principle of placing people of the same sex together at labor, away from the opposite sex. I call this homosex segregation.

I challenge the notion that the division of labor by sex is originally based on the heterosexual act. No doubt the sex stereotypical occupations assigned to women and men in patriarchal society resemble heterosexual femme/butch roles. I contend that the patriarchal sexual division of labor does not represent the sexual division of labor in original society. The division of labor by sex has more to do with homosex groupings and homosex relations than it does with the heterosexual act of coitus. Heterosexists tend to see the nature of the world in terms of their heterosex acts—literally viewing their sex act as the center of the world. This is a bit grandiose.

FEMALE LANGUAGES

Ernest Crawley's discussion of the relation between sexual separation and the cross-cultural phenomenon of female languages is a fascinating topic that need further research. Crawley reports that the "island Caribs have two distinct vocabularies, one used by men and by women when speaking to men, the other used by women when speaking to each other."[3]

G.P. Murdock identifies the "island Caribs" in *Outline of South American Cultures* as the Callinago.[4] Crawley located these "island Caribs," who needed to know three languages, on Guadeloupe and Dominica. They were first observed by Breton in the middle of the 17th century.[5] Murdock notes that the Callinago were "probably matrilineal." They are now extinct.

Crawley reports that women and men speak almost different languages in some 20 societies. I have selected only a few cases out of Crawley's female language sample for discussion here. These cases are: the "island Carib," the Guaycurus of the Argentine Gran Chaco, the Karaya (Caraya) of Brazil, the Eskimos of the Mackenzie Delta (North America), the Polar Eskimos of Greenland, the Japanese, and the Berbers of the Great Atlas mountains in north Africa.

Westermarck's *History of Human Marriage* is the primary source for this phenomenon among the Berbers.[6] He informs:

> The comparative isolation of women from the outside world undoubtedly accounts for the fact, noticed by myself among the Berbers of the Great Atlas, that the women use the old Berber numerals in cases where the men invariably use Arabic loan-words.[7]

This phenomenon of women speaking an older language than men has been reported by Briffault regarding the Tuareg of the Sahara, who are one of the oldest matrilineal societies in the world; by the Murphys regarding the Mundurucu of the Lower Amazon; and by Ehrenreich regarding the "Karaya" of Brazil.[8] Crawley paraphrases Ehrenreich in this way:

> The Karaya have a special women's dialect, which, it has been suggested, is an older form of the tribal speech, retained by the women.[9]

Further research into this vastly unexplored realm should yield pertinent information on the separate social development of females and males, as well as lend a different perspective to the matriarchy/patriarchy debates. Since this separate sexual evolution of language crosses four world regions—South America, Africa, North America, and East Eurasia—there is some evidence of older female culture manifested in language preceding the patriarchal language-cultures of these continents. In patriscience, similarity in language is frequently used as an indicator of closeness in social genesis. Difference in language implies separate social development.

Japan offers the strongest model of all, due to the fact that the Japanese case is written, whereas the other cases of female language are oral. "...The Japanese alphabet possesses two sets of characters, *katakana* for the use of men and *hiragana* for women."[10]

The Tuareg of the Sahara represent an hystorical link between matrilineage and female language. The Tuareg women keep an older culture and language separate from Tuareg men. Briffault writes of this phenomenon:

> The culture of the Tuareg is almost exclusively confined to the women (the men are entirely illiterate); and it is they alone who preserved knowledge of the ancient Libyan tongue and script, which appears to resemble that of Minoan Crete.[11]

Briffault is not alone in thinking that the Berbers of northwest Africa are "the direct representatives of the race which laid the foundations of Western civilization on the islands and shores of the Mediterranean."[12] The Berber race was known to the Greeks as "Libyans." Any student of Amazon literature has to wonder about the relation between the origins of western civilization and the "Libyan Amazons" of Greek mythology.

With the hope that feminist linguists will study female languages and unearth this critical data, I leave female language in order to describe further empirical data of sexual separation.

ORIGINAL SEX SEPARATION

I do not take the position that all that was present in original society is still present in modern society; but some traces have survived patriarchal disconfiguration, rewired (reweird) for patriarchal purposes. Neither do I think that all that is present in modern society was present in original society, but some features remain the same.

I theorize that human sexual separation can be traced back to late-ape/early-human social organization. Sexual separation is still a prominent feature of the social organization of the predominantly female herd of nonhuman primates living today in the wilds. The segregation of adolescent males from the female community is found in both living ape and human society in sufficient numerical quantities to merit further investigation. It is my yet unverified theory that sexual separation is present in the social organization of the "community of origin." I do not have the empirical evidence to prove this theory at this time, but I do have evidence to support its consideration.

by Pierre Auguste Renoir

SEX SEPARATION HYPOTHESES

I hope to empirically support the following hypotheses:

1) Patriarchal regions of the world display a higher degree of physical heterosexual integration than nonpatriarchal regions.

2) Nonpatriarchal regions display a higher degree of homosex separation (physically) than patriarchal regions.

3) A significant number of societies throughout the world segregate their adolescent boys, partially or totally.

4) Patriarchal societies have either no taboo or a very short post-partum sex taboo. That is, in patriarchal societies, men are not segregated away from women after childbirth.

5) Nonpatriarchal societies have longer post-partum sex taboos than patriarchal societies. That is, more separation of the sexes after childbirth occurs in nonpatriarchal societies.

I begin with the general hypothesis that sexual separation is present in one form or another (at meal times, in sleeping quarters, at labor, in total residence) every day of the year or at certain ceremonial times of the year, or at certain sexual moments (before, during or after childbirth, lactation, sexual intercourse, menopause, the menses, at certain stages of marriage or sexual initiation) or at certain ages (childhood, adolescence, young adult, maturity, old age) as well as in death (funeral burials)—by custom, social institution or law, in most societies. Since some forms of sexual separation similar to human practices are observed in ape society, this makes it possible to wonder if sexual separation is a product of ape nature (wild society) or human society.

I must remind the reader that much of the theory posited regarding sexual separation here is not empirically testable. It is, for the most part, theoretical speculation.

Nevertheless, I will empirically examine the scant data pertaining to sexual separation that is indexed in Murdock (either 1957 or 1967). Obviously, further research is needed on this crucial variable, especially since the further integration of women into patriarchal economies has been offered in the 1970's as a solution to women's oppression. I think this is a misguided direction for feminists to follow, and that further integration of women into patriarchy will only exacerbate women's oppression, rather than alleviate it.

The type of evidence I will use is drawn primarily from Murdock's 1967 *Ethnographic Atlas*, which has information on 862 societies.*

POST-PARTUM SEX TABOOS

Information on post-partum sex taboos is available in Murdock (1967) on only 313 societies.** From this data bank I find that there is only one society which has "no taboo" surrounding the sexes after childbirth. This means that 99% of world societies, where information is available, require "a lactating mother to refrain from sexual intercourse" for at least a short period. Post-partum sex taboos can last anywhere from one month to over two years.

The world breakdown on post-partum taboos against heterosexual intercourse is as follows: 17% of world societies require a short taboo "lasting not more than one month"; 32% have a taboo "lasting more than a month"; 10%, "from more than six months to one year"; 20%, "from more than one year to two

---

*Since Murdock 1957 contains no specific coding categories for sex segregation or integration, except regarding the sexual division of labor, I selected Murdock's 1967 *Ethnographic Atlas* of 862 societies for my sex segregation/integration hypothesis tests.

The *Ethnographic Atlas* contains two coded variables that serve as measures of sexual segregation in this study: "Post-Partum Sex Taboos" and "Segregation of Adolescent Boys." Murdock's world data on these two dimensions of sex separation are the most direct indices readily available to measure the degree of homosex segregation vs. heterosex integration. Thus, Murdock's sample of 862 societies is the sample I utilize to empirically test all hypotheses in chapter 7 not specifically concerned with the sexual division of labor.

Hypotheses specifically related to the "division of labor by sex" are tested separately on the Murdock 1957 sample. Great care is taken never to test the same hypothesis on both the 1957 and 1967 Murdock samples, because of sample overlap.

I assume that *some* degree of heterosexual integration, female homosexual segregation and male homosexual segregation are present in most societies, but that their relative frequencies vary. I hypothesize that on average, the highest degree of physical heterosex integration will be located in societies with equal sex ratios, while the highest degree of female homosex segregation obtains in societies with high female sex ratios.

Again, I use hunters and gatherers as an indirect measure of prehistorical sexual separation. I expect to find that some form of homosexual segregation obtains in all societies, but takes the form of *vertical* social sexual segregation in patriarchal societies. This vertical type involves a stratification system. —*Author*

**This means that I lost 549 societies in the sample due to lack of information. —*Author*

years"; and 20%, for "more than two years."[13] That is, 40% of the world sample taboos post-partum sex for one year or more. Further, 50% of the sample taboos heterosex for lactating mothers anywhere "from more than six months" to "more than two years." The one society which has no taboo is located in East Eurasia.

Africa rates high in sexual separation after childbirth: 71% of the 82 African societies for which information is available taboo post-partum sex for "more than one year" to "more than two years"; while 45% (37 out of 82) of the African sample taboo heterosexual intercourse for "more than two years" after childbirth. Extreme phenomena of this sort are usually reported for nonhuman living primates and other mammals; but little analysis of similar customs among humans has been done. Africa remains interesting throughout this study of sexual separation, especially regarding segregation of adolescent boys, to be discussed later.

Regarding post-partum sex taboos, hunters and gatherers do segregate the sexes after childbirth much more so than at adolescence, according to this exploratory data.

For example, all hunters and gatherers sampled have some sort of post-partum sex taboo. That is, no hunting and gathering society has no taboo at all. 41% of the hunters and gatherers sampled display a long post-partum sex taboo, ranging anywhere from over six months to over two years.

The breakdown is as follows: *no taboo*—0; *taboo for less than one month*—10 societies; *taboo for 1-6 months*—16 societies; *taboo for 6 months to 1 year*—4 societies; *taboo for 1 to 2 years*—9 societies; *taboo for over 2 years*—5 societies. The mode for hunters and gatherers is 1-6 months post-partum sex taboo. This is the same as the world societal mode.

Not only does the post-partum sex taboo evidence indicate homosex segregation after childbirth; but the hunting and gathering sexual division of labor itself is one of the strongest homosex divisions of labor to be found, as compared to other subsistence level divisions of labor.

SEGREGATION OF ADOLESCENT BOYS

Based on a universe of 607 societies[13] I studied, there is a general "absence of segregation of adolescent boys" in the majority of Circum-Mediterranean, East Eurasian, North

TABLE 9. Post-Partum Sex Taboos among Hunting and Gathering Societies		
Post-Partum Sex Taboos	**Hunter/Gatherer Societies**	
	Number	Percentage
No Taboo	0	0%
Less than 1 month	10	23%
1—6 months	16	36%
6 months — 1 year	4	9%
1—2 years	9	21%
Over 2 years	5	11%
TOTAL	**44**	**100%**

American, and South American societies. In other words, adolescent boys resided and slept in the same dwelling as their mothers and sisters in 79% of the Circum-Mediterranean, 78% of East Eurasia, 88% of North America, and 75% of South America, by the 19th and 20th centuries.

In contrast, only 22% of the 142 African societies allow adolescent boys to reside and sleep in the same dwelling as their mothers and sisters. 42% of the African sample partially segregate adolescent boys by allowing them to reside or eat with "their natal families but sleeping apart from them, e.g., in a special hut or in a cattle shed."

Only 10% of the African sample completely segregate adolescent boys from their mothers and sisters by requiring the boys to "go live with relatives outside the nuclear family." No African societies, where information is available, send adolescent boys to go live with nonrelatives. But 26% of African societies where data is available completely segregate adolescent boys in this way: "Boys reside with a group of their own peers, e.g., in bachelor dormitories, military regiments, or age-villages."

Added together, 36% of the African sample completely segregate adolescent boys "at or approaching puberty" from their mothers and sisters.[14]

The Insular Pacific is the other world region where the majority of societies (64% in this region) either partially or completely segregate adolescent boys approaching puberty from the natal female community. 12% of the 97 Insular Pacific societies where data is available partially segregate boys by not letting them sleep in the same dwelling as their mothers and sisters. They are allowed to eat with or reside with their natal families, however. 5% of the Insular Pacific societies completely segregate adolescent boys by sending them to live with relatives outside the nuclear family. 2% completely segregate pubescent boys by sending them to live with nonrelatives as individuals. 44% completely segregate adolescent boys from their native community. The boys reside with a group of their own age-peers, "bachelor dormitories," etc.

I cannot help but note that this Murdockian category reminds me of the "bachelor troops" of adolescent males common among baboons and other nonhuman primates.

In sum, there is an absence of segregation of adolescent boys in 36% of the Insular Pacific societies; 12% of the Insular Pacific partially segregates boys; and 51% (over half) of the Pacific islands practice "complete segregation" of adolescent boys in one form or another. The Insular Pacific appears, then, to be the world region where the highest rate of "complete segregation" of adolescent boys is practiced. Compare the Insular Pacific's 51% of societies practicing "complete segregation" with Africa (36%), Circum-Mediterranean (5%), East Eurasia (20%), North America (4%), and South America (18%).

Africa is the world region where the bulk of "partial segregation" of adolescent boys is practiced. 42% of African societies practice "partial segregation" compared to 16% of Circum-Mediterranean societies; 2% of East Eurasian societies; 12% of Insular Pacific societies; 8% of North American societies, and 7% of South American societies.

In terms of total world incidence, 369 of the 607 societies (61%) are characterized by an "absence of segregation" of adolescent boys. This is to be expected in late patriarchy, for it is my theory that the longer patriarchy exists, the more it overturns the early (i.e., matriarchal) societal practice among both humans and apes of segregating adolescent boys from their mothers, sisters and the rest of the female community.

Still, some 39% (238 out of 607) of Murdock's world sample (1967) either partially or completely segregate adolescent boys. To be precise, 16% of the world sample partially segregates boys, while 23% of the sample completely segregates pubescent boys from their mothers and sisters.

Throughout the world, it is a rare practice for societies to send adolescent boys to live as individuals with nonrelatives. Yet the practice of sending boys to reside with their own age and sexual peers is not rare at all, except in North America and the Circum-Mediterranean. Even in East Eurasia, where the majority of societies tend toward an absence of male adolescent segregation, 16% of the sampled societies send boys to live with their own age and sex peers.

CROSS-TABULATIONS BETWEEN SEGREGATION OF ADOLESCENT BOYS AND POST-PARTUM SEX TABOOS

Table 43 on page 216 presents "Post-Partum Sex Taboos by Segregation of Adolescent Boys." It shows that 61% of the 93 societies which segregate their boys either partially or totally, *also* have a long post-partum sex taboo, lasting anywhere between six months and over two years. Meanwhile, 63% of the 158 societies which do *not* segregate boys at all, have a *short* post-partum sex taboo, lasting less than six months. Thus, there is a correlation between the two variables.*

This evidence suggests that societies which are highly heterosexually integrated on one sexual separation variable are likewise heterosexually integrated in relation to other sex segregation variables. The same may be true of highly homosexually segregated societies. That is, this evidence indicates that societies which integrate boys into society do not physically separate the sexes in adulthood either — while societies which segregate boys from society, also segregate men from women at other critical sexual moments, such as childbirth. This evidence is not conclusive, but it is suggestive.

---

*Unfortunately, the dropout rate due to lack of information on both variables is extremely high. Information is not available on 611 out of the 862 societies indexed in Murdock (1967). —*Author*

Conclusions on Adolescent
and Post-Partum Sexual Separation

1) The majority of world societies (61%) do not segregate their boys from society. Neither do the majority of hunters and gatherers.

2) However, a significant number of world societies (30%) do segregate adolescent boys from society, either partially or totally.

3) Of the African societies sampled, 42% partially segregate adolescent boys, whereas 44% of societies in the Insular Pacific totally segregate boys.

4) The majority of societies in the Circum-Mediterranean, East Eurasia, North America, and South America do not segregate adolescent boys from society.

5) Half of world society (as represented by Murdock 1967) has a long post-partum sex taboo, while the other half has a short taboo.

6) Africa displays the most frequently long post-partum sex taboo of all the world regions: 45% of African societies taboo heterosexual intercourse for over two years after childbirth; 71% of African societies taboo sex anywhere from one to over two years. Africa also displays the highest frequency of *partial* segregation of adolescent boys.

PATRIARCHY IS GEOGRAPHICALLY LIMITED

Africa and the Insular Pacific are the most homosexually segregated of the world regions, regarding post-partum sex taboos and the segregation of adolescent boys. The Circum-Mediterranean and East Eurasia, by contrast, appear to be the most heterosexually integrated in regard to these two sex segregation variables.

From my perspective, when sexual segregation/integration is cross-tabulated with sex ratios, the Circum-Mediterranean and East Eurasia appear to lock in on two patriarchal variables: near equal sex ratios and high heterosexual integration. Further geographical cross-tabulations of sex variables will demonstrate that patriarchy is geographically limited. Patriarchy is not, and never has been a total world phenomenon—even in late patriarchy. Further research is needed to substantiate this contention.

LESBIAN SEPARATIST THEORY OF LIBERATION AND WOMEN'S WORK

Data on the world agricultural division of labor by sex indicates that women perform equal amounts of labor to men in a third of societies where agriculture is the dominant subsistence, and most to all subsistence labor in 23% of world societies.

Furthermore, by combining societies whose dominant subsistence is either agriculture, animal husbandry, or fishing, I find that 282 societies—50% of Murdock's 1957 sample of 565 societies—display sexual divisions of labor where females perform equal, greater, or all subsistence labor relative to males in their societies.

I theorize that females generally perform half, if not more, of the subsistence labor of society, regardless if they are liberated or oppressed. In this sense, women's labor is quite similar to working-class labor, in that the working class generally performs most of the subsistence labor of society, yet the workers are not liberated, because they do not generally control the fruits of their labor. Engels' solution for the liberation of women based on their further entrance into social production is not empirically well founded, since all societies are at all times heavily dependent upon women's productive labor. This is not so much a condition for the liberation of women, as it is a condition for the maintenance of most, if not all, societies.

It is not to the benefit of women to do further work for patriarchal economies. Rather, I suggest the opposite tactic, a lesbian separatist tactic, for women to stop all work for patriarchy. Women can collapse patriarchal economy by refusing to work for patriarchy at all, since all societies, even patriarchies, need the labor power of women to function. I do not mean a temporary strike for higher wages. I mean a permanent female pull-out of both their reproductive and productive labor from patriarchal economy.

Women must work for themselves to recreate gynosocieties, rather than work for men and patriarchal economies. As in all revolutions, it is when the oppressed stop working for their oppressors, and instead begin to work for their own oppressed community, that liberation solutions are actualized. As long as women work in patriarchal economies, they will remain oppressed.

THE SEXUAL DIVISION OF LABOR

The following world data on the division of labor by sex derives from Murdock's 1957 "World Ethnographic Sample." I begin first with the agricultural division of labor by sex. Generally, agriculture is *absent* in 22% of Murdock's 565 societies; *present but relatively unimportant* in 4%; *important though not major* in 5%; *codominant* in 6%; and *dominant* in 62% of this world sample.

On the following page, Table 10, "World Agricultural Subsistence and Sexual Division of Labor," contains information on only 426 societies in Murdock's sample where agriculture obtains. The result is that the modal labor case in Murdock's 1957 sample is: "both sexes participate equally in the activity."[16]

Of the 342 societies where agriculture is dominant, 14% or 47 of them are characterized by this type of division of labor: "both sexes participate, but the female share is appreciably greater." Further, 7% or 23 of these agriculturally dominant societies display this division of labor by sex: "females conduct the activity, male participation being negligible."

This means that in a fifth of these 342 mainly agricultural societies, females perform greater work than men. This figure does not even include the 27 societies where the "standard" sexual division of labor obtains, with men doing the "heavy" work such as load lifting, and women doing the "light" work such as reaping. I do find it strange that, of the 426 societies where information is available on both agricultural subsistence and division of labor by sex, there are only 40 societies where a "standard" sexual division of labor obtains. That is, only 9% of Murdock's sample is "standard."

Numerically, these 40 societies with a standard division of labor by sex are only a few more than the 34 societies where "females conduct the activity, male participation being negligible." This discrepancy illustrates that whatever is considered the "standard" or "norm" in patriarchy and patrisociology is not always a function of numerical incidence, but a function of patriarchal ideology. What patriscientists call the standard sexual division of labor by sex is the most rigidly stereotypical butch/femme role play.

TABLE 10. World Agricultural Subsistence and Sexual Division of Labor

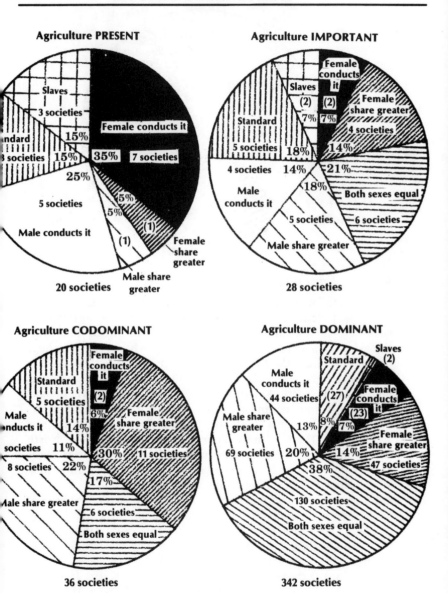

Agriculture PRESENT

Slaves
3 societies
andard
3 societies 15%
15%
25%
5 societies
5%
5%
(1)
(1)
Female conducts it
35% 7 societies
Male conducts it
Female share greater
Male share greater

20 societies

Agriculture IMPORTANT

Slaves
(2)
Female conducts it
(2)
Female share greater
4 societies
Standard
5 societies 18%
7% 7%
14%
4 societies 14%
21%
18%
Both sexes equal
6 societies
Male conducts it
5 societies
Male share greater

28 societies

Agriculture CODOMINANT

Female conducts it
(2)
Standard
5 societies
6%
Female share greater
Male conducts it
14%
30% 11 societies
societies 11%
8 societies 22%
17%
Male share greater
6 societies
Both sexes equal

36 societies

Agriculture DOMINANT

Slaves
(2)
Standard
Male conducts it
44 societies (27)
Female conducts it
(23)
8% 7%
Male share greater
69 societies 13%
20%
14%
Female share greater
47 societies
38%
130 societies
Both sexes equal

342 societies

[For TOTAL, see next page]

TABLE 10, continued

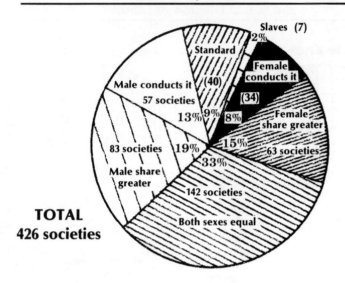

Female Agriculture

The division of labor where "females conduct the activity, male participation being negligible" in mainly agricultural societies, is absent in the Circum-Mediterranean and East Eurasia. Africa contains only one society where female agriculture is dominant: the Kwere. In the Insular Pacific, there are five such societies: Buka, Ifugao, Loyalty Islanders, Mangaians, and Miriam. North America contains ten societies where agriculture is dominant and females conduct it: Creek, Delaware, Fox, Huron, Iroquois, Mandan, Miami, Pawnee, Wichita, and Winnebago. Here it must be remembered that most North American societies are nonagricultural. In South America, there are six dominantly female agricultural societies: Cayapa, Miskito, Taino, Tucano, Tupinamba, and Witoto.

There are 47 societies where agriculture is dominant and "both sexes participate, but the female share is appreciably greater." They are: AFRICA, 16: Bassakomo, Bete, Dahomeans, Hehe, Ibo, Kabre, Kikuyu, Kpe, Mika, Msaw, Safwa, Sukuma, Thonga, Yako, Yao and Wute; CIRCUM-MEDITERRANEAN, 1: Wolof; EAST EURASIA, 2: Aryans (800 B.C.), Kafir; INSULAR PACIFIC, 13: Alfur, Alorese, Atayal, Banaro, Manobo, Mentaweians, New Caledonians, Palauans, Rossell Islanders, Samoans,

Tanimbarese, Ulawans, and Yapese. NORTH AMERICA, 3: Cherokee, Choctaw, and Natchez; SOUTH AMERICA, 12: Apalai, Bacairi, Black Carib, Bush Negroes, Camaracoto, Carib, Cashinawa, Chama, Jivaro, Panare, Trumai, and Wapishana.

Both Sexes Equal

The 130 societies where agriculture is dominant and "both sexes participate approximately equally in the activity" are: AFRICA, 28: Ashanti, Bemba, Bongo, Chagga, Cure, Dera, Dogon, Dilling, Ibibio, Jukun, Kadara, Karekare, Kissi, Koma, Konkomba, Lamba, Lovedu, Luo, Margi, Matakam, Mende, Mesakin, Mumuye, Shilluk, Shona, Tenda, Tiv, and Tullishi; CIRCUM-MEDITERRANEAN, 16: Bulgarians, Cheremis, Czechs, Danes, French, Fur, Georgians, Guanche, Hungarians, Italians, Kabyle, Kanembu, Konso, Kunama, Rumanians, Serbs; EAST EURASIA, 40: Abor, Akha, Ao, Baiga, Bhil, Bondo, Burmese, Burusho, Cambodians, Chakma, Dard, Garo, Gond, Japanese, Kachin, Karen, Khasi, Koreans, Lakher, Lamet, Lepcha, Lolo, Malay, Merina, Miao, Mikir, Minchia, Monguor, Muong, Nepalese, Okinawans, Palaung, Rengma, Santal, Sinhalese, Tanala, Tibetans, Thado, Thai, and Vietnamese; INSULAR PACIFIC, 32: Ambrym, Arapesh, Belu, Bougainville, Chamorro, Dobuans, Dusun, Hanunoo, Iban, Ifaluk, Ili-Mandiri, Javanese, Kapauku, Keraki, Kiwai, Kutubu, Mailu, Malaitans, Malekulans, Minangkabau, Nakanai, Nauruans, Rotinese, Subanun, Tagalog, Tagbanua, Tannese, Tobelorese, Toraja, Trobrianders, Wogeo, and Yami; NORTH AMERICA, 2: Cocopa, Yuchi; SOUTH AMERICA, 12: Apinaye, Araucanians, Aymara, Cagaba, Cayua, Chibcha, Inca, Mundurucu, Paez, Palikur, Sherente, Tenetehara.

This data on the world agricultural division of labor reveals that women do a great deal of the labor in societies where agriculture is the dominant subsistence. Since large-scale agriculture and the surplus it produces are historically associated with the rise of patriarchal states, it would appear that equal participation of women in patriarchal economies does not imply liberation for women. In fact, it can be a condition of oppression. Obviously, further research is needed on the relationship between women's oppression/liberation and the sexual division of labor. This work is only a brief exploration of the mountains of labor performed by women.

(See Appendices A and C for more statistical data).

Part III

Lesbian Feminist Praxis

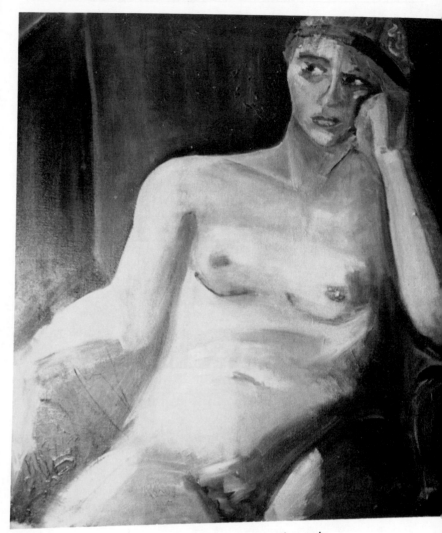

'Lesbian Thinking', by Laura Zeidenstein

Chapter 8

Women's Liberations

While some feminists and lesbian feminists think that the liberations of women depend upon a knowledge of hystory and the *his*tory of women's oppression, others do not think it matters whether women were ever liberated, free, or powerful in the past. The point is that liberations for women are the present necessities, and at the same time, future female visions.

Since I do not think there is only one oppression of women, there is not only one liberation path for women. I refer to the plural oppressions of women which demand plural liberations.

Liberations of women may derive from hystory and female consciousness of it. The various solutions to the problems of women's oppressions can be learned from a reconstruction of past female forms of society: female family, sex socialization, sex ratios, marital residence, inheritance, marriage, marriage resistance[1], homosex segregation, sexuality channels, female space, female art, goddess religions, female social organization, all-female armies, female languages and literature, feminist political struggles, hysteconomy[2], reproduction, sexual selection, and other socio-hystorical variables.

This chapter is the last bridge between the theoretical Part I and the empirical Part II of the book. Consider now the final analysis of the sources of women's oppressions, patriarchal transition, and then back to theoretical women's liberations. The patriarchal takeover is conceived as the theoretical pivot in the devolution from gynosocial women's liberations to patriarchal women's oppressions. Theoretical women's liberations begin the hystorical end of patriarchy. —*Author*

Or the liberations of women can be built upon a new, emerging female consciousness, such as lesbian feminism or lesbian separatism. What is beyond all doubt is the historicity of women's oppressions. Women's oppressions obtain whether or not all women are conscious of their sources — but women's liberations do *not* obtain when all or most women are unconscious of the sources of their oppressions.

THEORY OF WOMEN'S OPPRESSIONS

The historical preconditions for the universal subjugation of women are: 1) near equal or high-male/low-female sex ratios; 2) a high degree of physical heterosex *integration* of the mass of adolescent and adult males into female society — while economically and politically, females are *segregated* down to the bottom of male dominance hierarchies, and the men are segregated upward in relation to women; 3) the male confiscation and "energy capture" of female sexuality by forcing or paying females to practice exclusive heterosexuality for male reproductive purposes.

All three of these are simultaneously the pre-conditions for the mass societal establishment of patrilineage, the heterosexual monogamian family, private property, and the male state, which Engels perceived as the sources of women's oppression. Engels' economic sources of women's oppression are historically preceded by their sexual sources, just cited.

PATRIARCHAL TAKEOVERS

I do not think there is only *one* patriarchal takeover buried in the remote, forever lost prehistoric past. The sexual power of women is overthrown daily, so long as patriarchy exists. Although evidence of the first patriarchal takeover may remain empirically inaccessible, the functional requisites of this male-overthrow-of-female-sex process are re-enacted daily in patriarchy.

Bachofen and Engels knew that monogamy invents paternity. Engels knew that monogamy and paternity are associated with the rise of private property. Father right is, by definition, the male expropriation of someone else's (mother's) labor. Father right is the classic and original form of private property. The development of private property is inseparable from the development of heterosexual monogamy. They not only develop at the same time; their relationship is closer than that.

Engels blames the oppression of women, in the end, on private property instead of father right itself. Since Engels was, after all, a man, he could not bring himself to blame father right for the oppression of women. He mistakes the institutionalized result of father right, i.e., private property, for the source of women's oppression. Because socialists and communists accept Engels' analysis of private property as the source of women's oppression, their subsequent practical attempts to abolish this suffering by abolishing private property have failed because father right, the original source of women's oppression, has not been abolished at the same time.†

---

†In reality, private property is still far from having been eliminated in the existing *workers' states* (Soviet bloc countries, China, Nicaragua, etc.). While they have nationalized the bulk of the largescale means of production and banks, they are still saddled with an enormous—and, in many cases, growing—sector of petty commodity production and exchange through private farming, smallscale industry and commerce—whether legal or not, and whether the leaders of these "socialist" countries want to admit it or not. Since the "old crap" of private property relations continues to assert itself, and since the parasitic bureaucracies heading these states maintain an *unprincipled compromise* between the socialist property of the future and the bourgeois property of the past, it is not surprising that they have failed to abolish father right. Indeed, they have enshrined the patriarchal nuclear family as a centerpiece of their "socialist" ethical and constitutional codes. Despite the considerable social gains which women have made through the victorious workers' and peasants' revolutions that created these states, in many cases a deep patriarchal reaction is setting in.

The most dramatic expressions of this are seen today in China and Rumania. In China, where the Deng Xiaoping regime has opened the floodgates of petty capitalist agriculture, the clock has been turned back in the countryside. The patriarchal nuclear family, which the "great leap forward" had made a spasmodic attempt to overcome, has reasserted itself with a vengeance: The societal preference for boys over girls has again become entrenched. Moreover, the government has taken draconian measures to halt population growth, depriving children after the firstborn in a family of free education and health care, and in some cases forcing women to have abortions once they've already borne one child. The traditional practice of female infanticide has made a big and scandalous comeback in the countryside.

In Rumania, the Nicolae Ceausescu regime, facing a superficially opposite problem of a declining birthrate, has made a different sort of patriarchal crackdown: Declaring that early and stable marriages are to be the patriotic norm, it has effectively banned abortion—enforcing this policy by requiring all young women to have an official gynecological checkup every month. In the spring of 1984, there was a mass arrest of midwives.

And along with the renewed oppression of women has gone the oppression of homosexuals. In China, the regime claims that homosexuals "do not exist"; in Rumania, as in the Soviet Union and Cuba, homosexuality is banned and persecuted. —*Editor*

Can patriarchy exist without father right, the male knowledge of paternity? I think not. How is father right determined? It can only be determined by the strict *female* observance of heterosexual monogamy. What the "father" does is irrelevant; recognition of the precarious existence of fathers depends solely upon the mother's decision to be heterosexually monogamous.

It is not enough that all women be straight for straight men. If women are promiscuous and straight, as Bachofen and Engels thought women were originally, paternity cannot be determined. It must always be remembered, from a sociology of knowledge viewpoint, that the hystorical or legendary period when women are thought to have been *un*oppressed or liberated is the time period Bachofen termed "hetaerism," a time of promiscuity. What this means, translated into female terms, is that women slept with whomever they wanted. I disagree with Engels that Bachofen picked a poor term, hetaerism, to describe the original anarchy.

Scholars have missed a critical point about original promiscuity. Promiscuity is not limited to heterosexual relations. *Webster's New World Dictionary of the American Language* defines *promiscuous* as "characterized by a lack of discrimination; specifically, engaging in sexual intercourse indiscriminately or with many persons."[3] Thus, the original promiscuity can include homosexual relations.

To say that a woman will sleep with anybody does not exclude the possibility that she will sleep with a member of her own sex. I have wondered throughout this research if the promiscuity posited at origins by male matriarchists connotes a sexual period where anything goes—homosex, asex, bisex, and heterosex.

The transition to patriarchy is made possible by the male heterosexualization of women. The sexual mode of patriarchy is the required heterosexual monogamy of the female. In order to straighten out the mass of women—lesbians, celibate women, spinsters, manhaters (Amazons), mother heads of households, and "illegitimate" children (gynosociety's children) must be targeted by straight men as examples of female sin, the acts of sick women, abnormal women, diseased women, insane women, dangerous women—and set up as outcasts, criminals, deviants, marginal exmples of what fate befalls women who do not become heterosexually monogamous. Women refusing to practice heterosexual monogamy must be punished as examples to the rest of the female population.

Even then, the heterosexualization of the mass of women in patriarchy could not be achieved so easily. The early history of heterosexual marriage teaches that even straight women did not desire this relation. Early heterosexual monogamies were accomplished by abduction of females, then payment. Men had to either physically force or buy women to be their wives. Obviously, if even straight women had to be captured, enslaved, or bought and sold into heterosexual monogamy, they did not freely choose to become wives. If man had to force or pay woman to first marry him, then obviously she would not have done so if he had not forced or paid for her to become his wife.

Not only are nonheterosexual women isolated and degraded by the forced heterosexualization of the mass of women; heterosexual women are isolated and degraded too, but in a different way. The nonheterosexual women are locked out of society, exiled to the margins; the heterosexual females are locked *into* a heterosexist male society, isolated from core female society. These two types of isolation serve the same purpose: the male disorganization of female society for the purpose of production of heterosexually monogamous females, to enable men to become "fathers."

Patriarchal social organization is based on the disorganization of female society. More precisely, the isolation and separation of females from each other and from female society makes possible the heterosexist integration of males into society.

And unfortunately, the male overthrow of female society is not just a prehistoric question, far removed from the exigencies of the female present. I suspect that some of the same psychology or egonomics that originally brought fatherhood into existence is still at work every day in patriarchy.

Women do not need to search tirelessly through all of prehistory to find the first rape, dissect it, reconstruct it before we can understand rape.† The same occurrences happen every hour in

---

†The biblical book of Genesis, while by no means chronicling the first rape, provides some interesting material on the prevailing attitudes towards rape in the patiarchal society of the ancient Hebrews. According to chapter 19, the wealthy pastoralist Lot, a nephew of Abraham, had his house surrounded one night by men from the city of Sodom, who demanded to have sexual relations with two male visitors whom Lot was entertaining. Beseeching the men to avoid such "wicked" behavior, Lot instead offered them his two virgin daughters to satisfy their sexual desires (Genesis 19.1-8). So homosexual rape was considered wicked, but heterosexual rape quite acceptable.

[continued at bottom of next page]

patriarchy. We can take our pick of present day rapes and analyze the phenomenon still. The reasons behind rape today are not entirely different from the reasons behind the first rape. It is the same dynamic repeating itself between males and females. In the same vein, we do not need to search back into the primeval past for the first father, in order to understand the dynamics of fatherhood. The same process of re-inventing fathers is re-enacted every day in the life of patriarchy.

For example, one of the most telling tales of artificial fatherhood is found in the 1970's reincarnation of natural childbirth, the LaMaze method, which is progressive for women relative to the brutal alienation of patriarchal hospital methods. Nevertheless, the father, or non-woman,[4] is given a simulated "equal" part to play in natural childbirth, which makes him feel included in a process that does not ordinarily involve his presence. The non-womon goes to classes with the expectant mother; he is given the artificial role of "coach" with a stopwatch! He tells the woman what to do at birth, a subject about which he is experientially ignorant.

The non-womon "coach" (boss) directs the labor of the woman worker, then claims her product (child) as his own. The male egonomic (male-centered) process is probably not that different from the original male invention of the artificial father right.

My point is that the sources of women's oppressions are all very much still with us today. Women are still surrounded by the sources of their oppressions. In this sense, the sources are accessible for the analysis of liberation. The great difference is that the basics of male overthrow of female society are ritualized and institutionalized in established patriarchy, rather than being a premiere performance.

The Hebrew pastoralists considered Lot "the only good man" living in the vicinity of Sodom, and his family was the only one spared when the lord (i.e., the top chief of the Hebrew pastoral clans) totally destroyed Sodom and Gomorrah, with all their inhabitants and crops. But Lot's wife made the fatal mistake of "looking back from behind him" towards the burning cities of Sodom and Gomorrah, where women had no doubt enjoyed far greater social and sexual freedom than among the Hebrew nomadic pastoralists. For her sin, she was turned into a "pillar of salt." (19.26). Lot's daughters, evidently well conditioned by patriarchal ideology, then became terribly concerned that their father's "seed" (i.e., male lineage) be transmitted into posterity. So they got him drunk on wine on two successive nights (or is this story a "wine-wash" of what actually happened?), and both had sex with him—allowing them each to bear him a son (19.30-8). —*Editor*

by Janet Yacht

The mother/daughter bonds are severed daily by patrilocal residence; the imaginary father is recreated daily; the separation of females from female society is achieved daily by the male occupation or heterosex integration of males into female space; the mass of women are still terrorized by rape; there is no public space where females can move freely without male interruption; the punishment of nonheterosexual women and nonmonogamous heterosexual women still goes on; women's sexual, reproductive, and produetive services are either taken or bought; female childbirth is stifled, and female physical growth stunted; female infanticide still goes on.*

An important psychological factor at play in the patriarchal transition is: male jealousy of female reproductive power, or womb envy. This contributes enormously to the problem of women's oppressions. Male jealousy of female reproductive power is also responsible for the "patriarchal reversal"[5] of the natural, material relations of the sexes, where the male is dependent upon woman for his existence, his every social act being a response to his unequal material position.

At patriarchal transition and since, the male has been able to artificially reverse his natural dependence upon woman through the mechanism of male dominance hierarchies superimposed on top of female society. These male dominance hierarchies now make women economically and politically dependent upon their male relatives and other heterosexual relations who have a position in the local, state, and national or international male dominance hierarchies which rule society.

The patriarchal takeover of female energy and service requires further study by a number of women. Here I want to concentrate on the theoretical role that heterosexual incest plays at patriarchal transition and in the development of the heterosexual family, which is closely related to the oppressions of women. I will then discuss several theories of women's liberations, sororal polygyny, and theoretical female power.

---

*See Barbara Ehrenreich and Deirdre English, *Witches, Midwives and Nurses: A History of Women Healers* (Old Westbury, NY: The Feminist Press, 1973); see also Mary Daly, *Gyn/Ecology* (Boston: Beacon Press, 1978); Kathy Berry, *Female Sexual Slavery* (New York: NYU Press, 1984); Ruth Hubbard and Marian Lowe, *Woman's Nature* (Elmsford, NY: Pergamon Press, 1984); and Adrienne Rich, "Compulsory Heterosexuality and Lesbian Existence," *Signs*, vol. 5, summer 1980, pp. 631-660. —*Author*

INCEST

The development of the patriarchal heterosexual family, and heterosexual marriage in general, may be traced back to rape, "marriage by capture," and heterosexual incest. Further gyno-research into this cross-cultural and historical development of the incest taboos will yield important data on the development of the patriarchal family.

As stated in chapter 2, the first enduring heterosexual relation is the mother/son relation. This hetero-relation is followed by brother/sister marriage. Morgan, Marx, and Engels noted that probably the first heterosexual marriages are incestuous.

Although I cannot prove it, I theorize that family relations develop modally in the following historical sequence: from 1) the original female homosex matrilineal relations, which subsequently form the female base of all societies and all families, to 2) the heterosex matrilineal relations which I think characterize the beginning of the end of gynosociety, signalling the coming transition to patriarchy; 3) to the patrilineal male homosex relations of transitional and early patriarchy; 4) to the hetero-sex patrilineal relations of established patriarchy. Not all family relations were developed at one time.

Female homosex social relations may modally precede the development of heterosex social relations of the family. Although the mother/son relation is the first enduring heterosex relationship, it is the brother/sister heterosex relation which is the transitional link from "conjugal matriarchy" or heterosexual matrilineage, to heterosexual patrilineage. (see ch. 2, pp. 54-61).

THEORY OF WOMEN'S LIBERATIONS

There are numerous avenues to the liberations of women. The possibilities outlined here are not the only routes out of patriarchy, but they are each capable of the empirical test. The real empirical test of any liberation solution to the oppressions of women will be conducted by grassroots women themselves, not in an academic paper or social science laboratory.

The several practical solutions I see to the problems of women's oppression are:

1) Open, direct sexual warfare; all-female armies fighting for the military overthrow of patriarchy and for female self- and gyno-defense.

2) Female sexual separation from patriarchy and individual men; individual women can leave men sexually, emotionally, socially, politically, ideologically—thereby refusing to perform wageless services for men—and join all-female collectivities; a mass exodus of females from the highly heterosexually integrated areas of patriarchy to remote regions, to form all-female colonies (supposedly this is an Amazon method of avoiding patriarchy by moving to the outermost borders of male space; in a different sense, not necessarily geographic, this is also the marginal lesbian subculture's method of surviving the hostile environment of patriarchy—by being marginal to it).

3) Collective refusal of women to tell men who is the "father" of their children; this could be accomplished by the simple method of hetero-females never sleeping with only one man for any length of time, but always having two or more male lovers. This method is based on the assumption that massive rates of "illegitimacy" will destroy the patrilineal family, especially its monogamian form. Female abolition of fatherhood.

4) Collective female secession from established, nationalistic male political states to join an international collectivity of women committted to creating new gynosocieties.

5) Collective female reproductive strikes, shutdowns; the refusal of women to bear patriarchy any more sons until female demands are met: the end of male domination of earth space.

6) Female economic sabotage of patriarchy, using the male supremacist sexual division of labor against itself—that is, across sexist divisions of labor, women are economically segregated into food preparation and production, health care, education, child care (socialization production), service sectors, clerical and typing in industrial societies, housework, etc. These are critical areas of societal maintenance, whose disruption would prove problematic for the continuance of patriarchy; indirect or direct female revolts in these sectors should prove interesting.

7) Development of high-female/low-male societal sex ratios at all levels of community size, though the assertion of the female prerogative to retreat when in danger of rape or violence caused by too many males in the same space; I consider patriarchy as a systematic human "London Zoo catastrophe"; near equal sex ratios and high-male/low-female sex ratios which are institutionalized in patriarchy are the source of the dangerously high rape rates, child molestation, and violence against females; the female community must assert itself by closing ranks, and selecting only those men who respect women's liberation to live inside the female community; sororal polygyny may be more liberating for straight women than exclusive monogamy.

'Winged Serpent', by Jean Lois Greggs
(magic marker, 8½" x 11")

8) Mass pull-out of female reproduction and production from patriarchal economies altogether to form new hysteconomies.

9) Development of mass high female consciousness regarding male supremacy and patriarchy, which should lead to a feminist reexamination of the mother/son relation and the development of nonpatriarchal socialization of sons by mothers.

10) Strengthening female social/political/economic organization, female solidarity and social ties, female social networks which disrupt the patriarchal process of isolating women from the female community, and thus reduce the casualties of women lost to patriarchy.

11) Increased rates of female heterosexual frigidity and female celibacy, as well as lesbianism—to decrease the rates of females strictly observing heterosexual monogamy, thus interrupting the mass production of "fathers."

12) Abolition of, and struggle against the patriarchal family, the state, private property, the patriarchal church and male religions.

13) Female political struggle for redistribution of earth space, and the creation of all-female space for women to escape the oppressions of patriarchy; under the principles of majority rule, females have the right to preserve at least 52% of earth space from male exploitation, destruction, and pollution of the female environ.

These are only a few of the possibilities of the female fightback for liberation. There are other ways out, other exits from patriarchy yet to discover and empirically test in the female future. Now briefly consider sororal polygyny.

SORORAL POLYGYNY

Kathleen Gough discusses the empirical relation between sororal polygyny, matrilineal systems, and matrilocal residence in *Matrilineal Kinship*.[6] Gough's work in this area is quite valuable, since the intersection of matrilineage, matrilocality, and sororal polygyny is a triple feature of gynosociety.

I find that 20% of my lesbian societal sample prefer to practice sororal polygyny. Sororal polygyny is the modal form of marriage among societies with high-female/low-male sex ratios in either the total or adult populations. These findings lead me to believe that further study of sororal polygyny is important for the reconstruction of hystorical gynosociety, as well as for the liberation of women.

HIGH FEMALE SEX RATIOS & FEMALE POWER

Why high-female/low-male sex ratios imply power for females must be explained here. First, it must be understood that power for women is not the same as power for men. The first requisites for female power are: female control of the female body ("our bodies, our selves"); female control of female reproductive and productive capacities; and the establishment of female space for the physical safety of females and offspring from rape, child molestation, and other forms of male violence.

While power for men may be cynically defined as the ability to coerce or threaten others into obedience or to do his will, power for women is freedom from male exploitation and coercion. Practically speaking, power for men is offensive—while power for women is defensive. These two opposite forms of sex power are related in this way: Historically, male power is based on both an individual and collective male offense against the female sex for the purpose of "energy capture" of female reproductive and productive capacities—while hystorically, female power is based on both the individual and collective female defense against the male sex, for the purpose of female energy release or female freedom.

Historical male power is based on slavery, -*archy*, exploitation of women, nature, animals, and children. Hystorical female power is based on freedom, anarchy, and defense of women, nature, animals, and children. Thus, the reason that high-female/low-male sex ratios imply power for women is essentially a defensive operation. Practically, the liberation of women is closely bound to the defense of individual females and the collective female community. The watchword of the women's movement is apt: All women will not be free until every woman is free from the threat of rape.

High-female/low-male sex ratios provide defense for women against rape and other male terrorization. Women will grasp this point immediately: The likelihood of a woman being raped is greatly reduced when females outnumber males. Consider this comparison of sex ratios in regard to rape: What are the possibilities of a woman being raped when she is in the company of ten other women and one man? What are the possibilities of a woman being raped when she is alone in the company of ten men? In the former case, rape chances are low; in the latter, chances are high.

High-male/low-female sex ratios are intolerable for women, and generally dysfunctional for society as well. High-female/-low-male sex ratios imply defense and safety from male violence and exploitation. Near equal sex ratios in social organization, on a microcosmic level, enable the individual male to isolate an individual female from the rest of the female community. The isolation of a single female from the female community, which is simultaneously the condition for the development of monogamy, is the quintessential rape condition.

Rape does not generally occur in front of the female community; on the contrary, it occurs when a female or females are isolated away from their network of female connections. The Mundurucus, according to the Murphys, make this point quite clear.[7] Any woman who leaves the female community to walk alone on the outskirts of the village is, by custom, openly considered fair game for any man or boy to rape by tribal right. Most patriarchies are not this honest, but the same custom covertly obtains. The separation of females from female society is the point of danger.

THEORETICAL FEMALE POWER

The problem is: how to define and measure female power? Feminists in the social sciences have criticized male models of power on the grounds that they do not apply to women, nor to other band and tribal peoples.

Rohrlich-Leavitt, Sykes and Weatherford find the male model of political power, i.e., ruling elites, inapplicable to band and tribal cultures, since it is a "projection of Euro-American society."[8] In her article, "Matriarchy: A Vision of Power," Paula Webster summarizes the difficulty in this way:

> The first thing that becomes apparent after reading the literature on the position of women in society (past and present) is the need for sharper, explicit, and cross-culturally applicable definitions of power, authority, influence and status. Our own male-biased socialization as women and as anthropologists has allowed us to accept and use conceptually limited descriptions of social reality. We need to develop new concepts to identify clearly the areas of women's power and the factors that facilitate or obstruct its exercise.[9]

I think lesbian feminists and feminists agree to reject the typical male model of power as the ability to control others, especially through political institutions, force, threat of force, or legal authority. Neither lesbian feminists nor feminists want this as a model for female power.

I also reject any ideal type of power for women that is ahistorical. A social science scale of female power must be empirically, hystorically and cross-culturally based on the actions and traditions of living women, past or present.

I therefore offer an elementary lesbian feminist power gauge based on hystorical and cross-cultural examples of COLLECTIVE FEMALE (not exceptional individual) power lines, or life rights exerted in female social organization.

Essentially, I present lesbian feminist ideas of female power derived from female practices, which are empirically observable and often documented in the anthropological literature. This multi-dimensional scale of female power is introduced to facilitate the comparison of the *relative* power of women cross-culturally, rather than the usual dead-end street of comparing the virtual nonpower of women to the power of men in the same patriarchal society. Consider now 14 dimensions of a lesbian feminist power scale. Each dimension is weighted equally.

LESBIAN FEMINIST POWER SCALE

1) Traditional female community recourse against individual or collective male abuse of women, or rape. For example, the existence of a female collective grievance system, where a woman can make a complaint against a man, and receive some form of help or support from the female community. Female resistance to male abuse can be either realistic or ritualistic. Rituals of resistance include: worship of female deities which protect women from the danger of men, witchcraft spells, etc.

2) Evidence of a hystory of female revolts — e.g., the Aba "war of the women," where over two million women rioted over taxes men put on their trade in the 1920's (also known as the "Aba riots"[10]).

3) Collective female veto power of male decisions which women perceive to be wrong. For example, among the Iroquois the women could and did stop men from going to war by voting against it and withholding food from the warriors. The warriors could not go to war without a food supply, and the war was called off.

4) Evidence of women's economic organizations which look after collective female interests in community affairs.

5) Evidence of women speaking a female language which men cannot understand.

6) Feminist leagues, female solidarity associations, marriage resistance sororities,[11] lesbian organizations, covens, etc.

7) Female self- and collective defense organizations.

8) Female control of the female body; women secretly practice abortion against men's authority; other women conspire to support each other's birth control methods.

9) Women practice herbal medicine, make medicines and narcotics for other women.

10) Women have a strong sense of female achievements and values in their female cultural traditions and hystory; women have some form of feminist consciousness about male supremacy and female sex oppression, and do not consider themselves inferior to men at all.

11) Tradition of women founders of tribe, country, nation, town, district; female governoresses, women holding political power.

12) Women perform half or more of subsistence labor for societal maintenance; women control the distribution of the food supply and/or the products of their labors.

13) Matrilocal residence, the mother-headed household, matri-lineage; women live in homosex separated communal houses.

14) Women have access to, or control over the major technology of society.

SEX AND SOCIETY

Although sex is one of the most basic, empirical sociological variables used on social science questionnaires, the broader theoretical relation between sex and society[12] is still largely an analytical gap. Generally, North American sociologists tend to subsume the study of sex within the heterosexist limits of debate (marriage and family), heterosexist sex roles, and butch/femme sexual divisions of labor.

Up until the 1969 upsurge of the political movement of lesbians and gays, the study of homosexuality and bisexuality was classed under the sociology of deviance in the U.S. These heterosexist biases lodged within the discipline prevent sociologists from accurate observation of the sexual world and the world in general — which is, after all, the point of sociological analysis.

In this study, I have attempted to present evidence from the other side, to redress this bias, and provide a new theoretical framework (lesbian feminism) for the analysis of sex and society.

Lesbian feminism has come out of society's closet as one of the most revolutionary political and intellectual movements in the 20th century, and can no longer be ignored by sociologists and society.

'Goddess with a Thousand Breasts': Diana of Ephesus (west Asia Minor, now part of Turkey), A.D. 125-175.

Cross-Tabulations of Sex Ratios, Sexuality, and Sex Segregation/Integration

Throughout this book, I have studied three sex variables—sex ratios, female sexuality, and homosex segregation vs. heterosex integration—as separate, dependent variables. Here, I empirically examine the correlations among these three sex variables. The first hypothesis to test is whether or not sex ratios, sexuality, and sex segregation/integration correlate at all. I believe they do.

The cross-tabulations are divided into three major sections: sex ratios and sex segregation; sexuality and sex segregation; and sex ratios and sexuality. Methodologically, I cross-tabulate my sex ratio sample, drawn from CUNY-*HRAF*, with my lesbian sample, which is cross-indexed in Murdock's 1957 "World Ethnographic Sample"; I then cross-tabulate both lesbian and sex ratio samples with Murdock's 1967 sex segregation/integration sample from the *Ethnographic Atlas*.

The sample size of these cross-tabulations varies according to the samples used. Sample size can range from 30 societies to 346 societies, depending upon which variables are being cross-tabulated. Now consider the relationship between sex ratios and sexual segregation/integration.

SEX RATIOS AND SEXUAL SEGREGATION/INTEGRATION

Table 11, "Segregation of Adolescent Boys by Sex Ratios (Total Population)," on the next page, shows no correlation between high female sex ratios and segregation of boys—and no correlation between high male sex ratios and the segregation of boys.

Table 11 does reveal a correlation between *no* segregation of boys and equal sex ratios. This finding supports my hypothesis that these two variables, which are both separately characteristic of patriarchy, are interrelated in patriarchy. Some 68% of societies with equal sex ratios do not segregate adolescent boys. Only 32% of societies with equal sex ratios partially or totally segregate their boys.

TABLE 11. Segregation of Adolescent Boys
by Sex Ratios (Total Population)

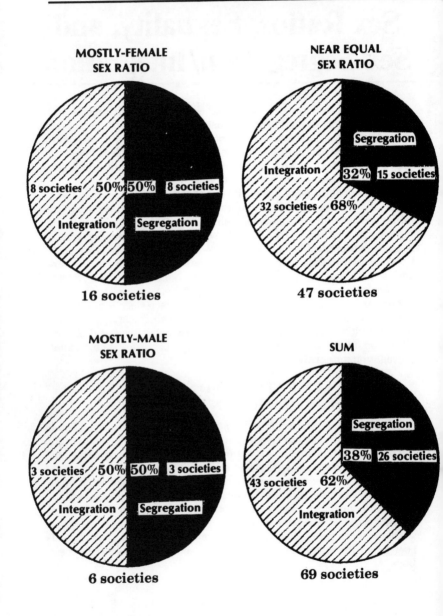

MOSTLY-FEMALE SEX RATIO

8 societies 50% 50% 8 societies

Integration Segregation

16 societies

NEAR EQUAL SEX RATIO

Segregation

Integration 32% 15 societies

32 societies 68%

47 societies

MOSTLY-MALE SEX RATIO

3 societies 50% 50% 3 societies

Integration Segregation

6 societies

SUM

Segregation

38% 26 societies

43 societies 62%

Integration

69 societies

TABLE 12. Post-Partum Sex Taboos by Sex Ratios

(Sex ratios are for the total populations involved)

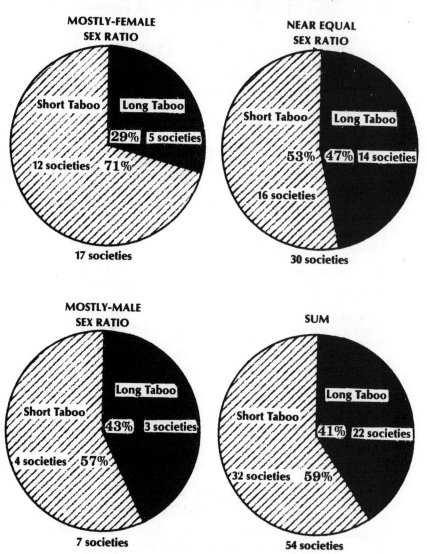

MOSTLY-FEMALE SEX RATIO
Short Taboo — 12 societies — 71%
Long Taboo — 5 societies — 29%
17 societies

NEAR EQUAL SEX RATIO
Short Taboo — 16 societies — 53%
Long Taboo — 14 societies — 47%
30 societies

MOSTLY-MALE SEX RATIO
Short Taboo — 4 societies — 57%
Long Taboo — 3 societies — 43%
7 societies

SUM
Short Taboo — 32 societies — 59%
Long Taboo — 22 societies — 41%
54 societies

Short Taboo = post-partum sex taboo shorter than 6 months
Long Taboo = post-partum sex taboo between six months and over 2 years

Table 12 (page 181) shows that 71% of societies with high-female/-low-male sex ratios (total population) have a short post-partum sex taboo, lasting less than six months—while only 29% of these high female societies have a long taboo, lasting anywhere from six months to over two years.

Of the equal sex ratio societies sampled, 53% have a short taboo, while 47% have a long taboo. Regarding high-male/low-female sex ratios, the breakdown is similar to equal sex ratios: 57% of high male societies display a short taboo, while 43% have a long taboo.

This means that *equal and high male sex ratios (total population) characterize societies with a longer post-partum sex taboo than societies with high female sex ratios.* This finding was unexpected. I expected to find longer taboos more frequently in societies with high-female/low-male sex ratios.

It could be argued that societies with high-female/low-male sex ratios have less numerical need to segregate males from women after childbirth, than societies with equal or high male ratios. However, I did not originally see the relation between these two sex variables in this way.

To conclude this section, I will briefly review the most significant results. Table 11 shows a correlation between *absence* of segregation of adolescent boys and equal (total population) sex ratios. Operationally in this study, the absence of homosex segregation is synonymous with heterosex integration. This finding supports my earlier contention that equal sex ratios correlate with heterosex integration. I have postulated that both of these properties are characteristic of patriarchy. However, this finding restricts the age range of heterosex integration to adolescence. More precisely, then, it can at least be shown in this work that *equal sex ratios (total population) correlate with heterosexual integration of males at adolescence.*

Less than a third of societies with equal sex ratios (total population) segregate their boys either partially or totally—compared to 50% of societies with either high male or high female sex ratios who segregate their boys.

Table 12 reveals that high-female/low-male sex ratios (total population) have short post-partum sex taboos.

SEXUALITY AND SEX
SEGREGATION/INTEGRATION

Table 13, "Segregation of Adolescent Boys by Premarital Heterosex" (next page) shows a strong correlation between these two variables. Of societies which do not segregate boys at adolescence, 61% prohibit premarital heterosex—while 60% of societies which partially or totally segregate boys allow premarital heterosex.

TABLE 13. Segregation of Adolescent Boys
by Premarital Heterosex

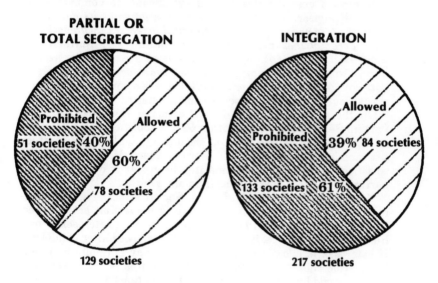

**PARTIAL OR
TOTAL SEGREGATION**

Prohibited
51 societies 40%

Allowed
60%
78 societies

129 societies

INTEGRATION

Allowed
Prohibited 39% 84 societies
133 societies 61%

217 societies

Allowed = premarital heterosex allowed
Prohibited = premarital heterosex prohibited

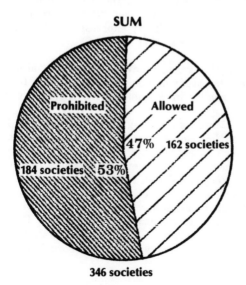

SUM

Prohibited Allowed
47% 162 societies
184 societies 53%

346 societies

Premarital heterosex is prohibited in only 40% of those societies which partially or totally segregate boys from girls; yet premarital heterosex is prohibited in 61% of those societies which *do not* segregate boys. I consider this finding significant. In common sense terms, it appears that *the more society segregates its adolescent boys, the less need to prohibit premarital heterosex. Segregation of boys accomplishes prohibition of premarital sex.* Furthermore, *societies which do not segregate boys at all are in greater need of norms prohibiting premarital heterosex than societies which segregate boys (either partially or totally).* There is a correlation between sexual segregation at adolescence and premarital heterosex norms.

On the next page, Table 14, "Premarital Heterosex by Post-Partum Sex Taboos," reveals that 56% of societies where premarital heterosex is allowed have, at the same time, long post-partum sex taboos: from six months to over two years. Meanwhile, 62% of societies which prohibit premarital heterosex have short post-partum sex taboos, lasting less than six months.

My interpretation of this data is: Societies must regulate heterosex for their own survival. Society is a juggling act between homosex separation and heterosex regulation. If heterosex is prohibited at adolescence, it will normally be allowed after childbirth. If heterosex is allowed at adolescence, it may normally be prohibited after childbirth—although certainly this is not always the case. It would be interesting to study the relations between prohibitions of homosex and heterosex at varying age levels. I suspect that in societies where heterosex is prohibited at adolescence, homosex may be allowed in its stead. Further research is needed before the precise trade-off relations between heterosex regulation and homosex segregation can be clearly expressed. Still it is interesting to speculate while interpretating Table 14.

Throughout this work, I have concentrated almost entirely on lesbianism in my study of sexuality. Here I wish to briefly discuss male homosexuality in relation to the segregation of adolescent boys.

Table 15, "Murdock's Segregation of Adolescent Boys by Ford and Beach's Homosex Sample" (page 186), reveals that 62% of societies which do not segregate boys at all regard homosexuality as "socially acceptable for certain members of the community," according to Ford and Beach's evidence.

Furthermore, 75% of societies which partially segregate adolescent boys find homosexuality acceptable for certain members of the community. The reader will recall that most of Ford and Beach's evidence on homosexuality actually concerns male homosexuality, although their evidence includes some lesbian data.

TABLE 14. Premarital Heterosex by Post-Partum Sex Taboos

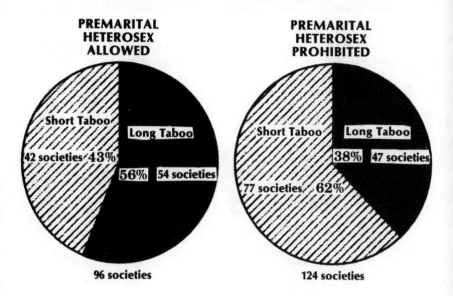

PREMARITAL HETEROSEX ALLOWED

Short Taboo
42 societies 43%

Long Taboo
56% 54 societies

96 societies

PREMARITAL HETEROSEX PROHIBITED

Short Taboo
38%

Long Taboo
47 societies

77 societies 62%

124 societies

Short Taboo = less than 6 months
Long Taboo = from 6 months to over 2 years

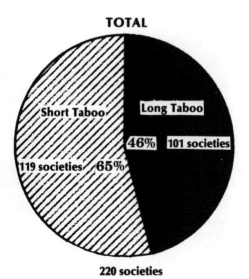

TOTAL

Short Taboo
46%

Long Taboo
101 societies

119 societies 65%

220 societies

TABLE 15. Murdock's Segregation of Adolescent Boys by Ford and Beach's Homosex Sample

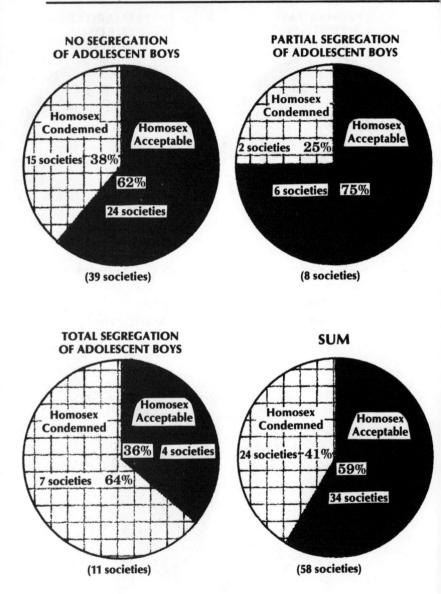

NO SEGREGATION
OF ADOLESCENT BOYS

Homosex Condemned
15 societies 38%

Homosex Acceptable
62%
24 societies

(39 societies)

PARTIAL SEGREGATION
OF ADOLESCENT BOYS

Homosex Condemned
2 societies 25%

Homosex Acceptable
6 societies 75%

(8 societies)

TOTAL SEGREGATION
OF ADOLESCENT BOYS

Homosex Condemned
7 societies 64%

Homosex Acceptable
36% 4 societies

(11 societies)

SUM

Homosex Condemned
24 societies 41%

Homosex Acceptable
59%
34 societies

(58 societies)

In contrast, only 36% of societies which totally segregate boys regard homosexuality as acceptable for certain members of the community. That is, 64% of societies which totally segregate boys regard homosexuality as "absent, rare, or carried on only in secrecy" because it is "condemned."

What this implies is that *the greater the segregation of adolescent boys in society, the more that society condemns homosexuality— whereas the less segregated a society is, the more homosexuality is considered acceptable.* This is an interesting twist I had not anticipated. I must caution that further research is necessary to empirically support these interpretations before the interrelationships between sexuality and sex segregation/integration can become comprehensible. Nevertheless, my evidence does show that these two sex variables are correlated.

SEX RATIOS AND SEXUALITY

This section yields one of the most important findings in this book. I have taken Ford and Beach's sample of societies which approve or condemn homosexuality, and cross-tabulated it with my adult sex ratio sample in Table 16 (next page).

Information is available on only 19 out of Ford and Beach's 76 societies. Table 16 supports my contention that sex ratios are correlated with sexuality, specifically that *high-female/low-male sex ratios characterize societies which are not heterosexist. That is, they approve homosexuality.* The reader will remember that high-female/low-male sex ratios represent, in my theory, a prominent characteristic of gynosociety—while equal sex ratios are modal in patriarchy.

Table 16 reveals that 80% of societies with high-female/low-male adult sex ratios approve homosex relations for at least certain members of the community. Information is available on only one society with a high-male/low-female sex ratio; it approves homosex.

The correlation between high female adult sex ratios and approval of homosexuality, as well as the correlation between equal adult sex ratios and condemnation of homosexuality, is one of the most significant findings of this study. However, larger samples are needed to corroborate this evidence before it can be regarded as conclusive. Nevertheless, Table 16 raises a provocative question: *Are high female sex ratios important not only for the liberation of women, but for the liberation of lesbians and gay men as well?*

Next, consider the relationship between sex ratios (total population) and premarital hetersex norms. I find that *67% of societies with high-female/low-male sex ratios prohibit premarital heterosex, while 53% of societies with equal sex ratios allow it.* No significant

TABLE 16. Adult Sex Ratios by Homosex Norms

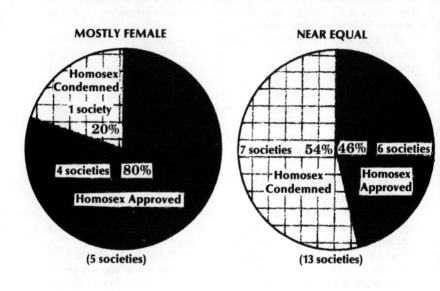

MOSTLY FEMALE

Homosex Condemned 1 society 20%

4 societies 80% Homosex Approved

(5 societies)

NEAR EQUAL

7 societies 54% 46% 6 societies

Homosex Condemned Homosex Approved

(13 societies)

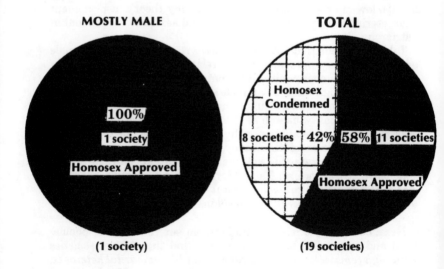

MOSTLY MALE

100% 1 society Homosex Approved

(1 society)

TOTAL

Homosex Condemned 8 societies 42% 58% 11 societies

Homosex Approved

(19 societies)

relationship between high-male/low-female sex ratios and premarital heterosex norms can be established from this data. These results are expressed in Table 17 below:

TABLE 17. Premarital Heterosex Norms by Total Sex Ratios

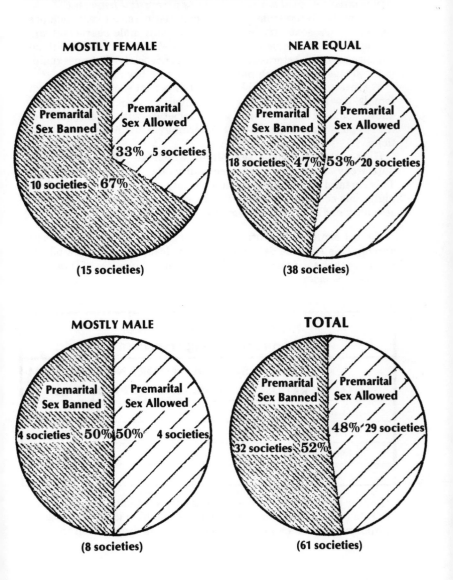

MOSTLY FEMALE

Premarital Sex Banned · Premarital Sex Allowed · 33% 5 societies · 10 societies 67%

(15 societies)

NEAR EQUAL

Premarital Sex Banned · Premarital Sex Allowed · 18 societies 47% 53% 20 societies

(38 societies)

MOSTLY MALE

Premarital Sex Banned · Premarital Sex Allowed · 4 societies 50% 50% 4 societies

(8 societies)

TOTAL

Premarital Sex Banned · Premarital Sex Allowed · 48% 29 societies · 32 societies 52%

(61 societies)

The correlation found here may not be the one expected, given the widespread dissemination of *vulgar feminism*, which erroneously implies that the liberation of women is synonymous with unlimited heterosexual intercourse. If, as I posit, high-female/low-male sex ratios characterize gynosociety, then Table 17 shows that *gynosociety prohibits premarital heterosex normally—while patriarchy, represented by equal sex ratios, allows premarital heterosex.*

This makes sense from a lesbian feminist perspective, which posits that heterosexuality is the basis of both male supremacy and patriarchy. Lesbian feminists expect patriarchy to allow, if not encourage, more heterosex than does gynosociety. Heterosexuality is the sexuality on which patriarchy runs its business.

My interpretation of Tables 16 and 17 is that societies with high-female/low-male sex ratios (numerical gynosocieties) normally allow homosexual relations, while societies with near equal sex ratios (consolidated patriarchies) normally allow heterosexual relations.

High-male/low-female sex ratios, which are also sex ratios of patriarchy, allow both heterosexuality and male homosexuality. This certainly describes Athenian society around 450 B.C., with its high male sex ratios combined with allowance of both male homosexuality and oppressive heterosexuality.

Next, I examine sex ratios (total population) in relation to lesbianism. This exercise demonstrates that lesbianism crosses all sex ratio categories, unevenly. Table 18 below gives the "Total Sex Ratios of Societies Reporting Lesbianism."

TABLE 18. Total Sex Ratios of Societies Reporting Lesbianism

	SOCIETIES REPORTING LESBIANISM	
TOTAL SEX RATIOS	**Number**	**Percentage**
Mostly Female	4	27%
Near Equal	10	67%
Mostly Male	1	6%
TOTAL	**15**	**100%**

Larger samples are needed to verify these results, since the fall-out rate of societies from the sample was so high (50%) due to lack of information. Since my sex ratios sample is drawn from the last

300 years, I interpret these findings to mean that in the *late* patriarchal epoch, lesbianism is reported more often among societies with equal sex ratios, simply because such societies are the most numerous and widespread in late patriarchy.

The sex ratio breakdown of my world sample is as follows: High-female/low-male sex ratios obtain in 22 out of 92 societies (24%); near equal sex ratios obtain in 57 out of 92 societies (62%); and high-male/low-female sex ratios obtain in 13 out of 92 societies (14%). Comparing these world frequencies of total population sex ratios to the societal frequency of reported lesbianism cross-tabulated with total sex ratios, much the same percentages arise. Societies with high-female/low-male sex ratios that report lesbianism comprise 27% of the sample; near equal sex ratios comprise 67% of the lesbian sample; and high-male/low-female sex ratios comprise 6% of the lesbian sample. The only difference is the drop in the reporting of lesbianism in high-male/low-female societies. I would not expect lesbianism to be as frequent in high male total populations, due to the careful hoarding of women in societies where women are scarce.

In conclusion, the evidence shows a correlation between sex ratios and sexuality. This sexual nexus is a ripe field for study, both politically and sociologically. The tables presented in this sex section indicate that sex ratios (total population) directly effect the allowance or prohibition of premarital heterosexuality, and that adult sex ratios directly effect the approval or condemnation of homosexuality in various societies. Larger samples of world sex ratios and world incidence of homosexuality are necessary to satisfy patriscientific standards of hypothesis testing, however.

High-female (total population) sex ratios are characteristic of societies which tend to prohibit premarital heterosex more than societies with equal or high male sex ratios. High female adult population sex ratios characterize societies which normally approve homosexual relations for at least certain members of the community. Societies with equal adult sex ratios tend to condemn homosexuality more frequently than they approve of it. I interpret this data as support for my theory that homosexuality is accepted in gynosociety, while it is repressed, suppressed, and depressed in patriarchy (societies with equal sex ratios).

This concludes my cross-tabulations of the three sex variables of this study.

The Little Snake Goddess
Crete, Heraclion Museum

Methodology

I will describe the methods I used to study sex. In chapter 5, I tested a set of sex ratio hypotheses on a regionally representative world sample of 100 societies drawn from the *Human Relations Area Files (HRAF)*. Following that, I tested a set of lesbian hypotheses in chapter 6, "Cross-Cultural Lesbianism," using a small world sample of 30 societies where lesbianism is reported.

In chapter 7, "Sexual Separation," I tested a set of homosex-segregation/heterosex-integration hypotheses on Murdock's 1967 sample of 862 societies where information is available in *Ethnographic Atlas*.

Chapters 5, 6, and 7 of this work test hypotheses in the empirical world, which is indirectly measured here by G.P. Murdock's 1957 and 1967 world samples of known society, and the *Human Relations Area Files*.

GENERAL SEX RESEARCH DESIGN

I decided at the onset of this study to use only secondary data to test my hypotheses. The decision was made for these reasons: 1) I wanted the largest cross-cultural sample of societies of varying historical periods in order to generalize my findings. 2) Since the study of early society is no longer subject to first-hand observation (unlike the study of current society), secondary analysis is the only option open to most researchers of prehistory anyway. 3) Due to the global scope of the study, it would require a vast amount of time and finances to begin primary analysis on sex ratios, sexuality, and sexual separation; furthermore, an enormous amount of cross-cultural and historical data on sex variables had already been gathered by social scientists. Thus, it was both economical and logical to test my hypotheses on available world data.

There are, however, serious and well known research limitations to the procedure of secondary analysis. First the re-use of completed studies, which generally consist of summary reports rather than unprocessed data, leaves the secondary analyst vulnerable to the biases of the primary research design, as well as her own — thus compounding design biases. A researcher is also forced to interpret the generalizations of the primary ethnographer. The information sought in secondary analysis may not be the information found, emphasized, or included in primary reports by others.

Morris Zelditch's cross-cultural study of Talcott Parson's theory on instrumental and expressive sex roles in the nuclear family demonstrates some of the methodological problems and procedures I encounter and employ. Although Zelditch's hypotheses are ideologically at odds with mine, his research design is a model for my study. Zelditch's two hypotheses are essentially a test of Parson's bio-social determinist theory regarding sex roles.*

Regardless of the ideological differential, my study is methodologically similar to Zelditch's in these ways: 1) Both are secondary sociological analyses of cross-cultural data, primarily gathered and summarized by anthropologists and other social scientists. 2) Both rely empirically on George Peter Murdock's cross-cultural data. 3) Both studies use the total society as the research case: While Zelditch uses the whole society to comparatively study the nuclear family, I use the total society to study the incidental reporting of lesbianism, sex ratio variation and homosex segregation. 4) Both studies posit universal hypotheses regarding sex and society which require empirical testing in a wide variety of societies.

Zelditch and I both utilize findings about different total societies at different periods of time. Similarly, I share some of Zelditch's methodological problems.

METHODOLOGICAL PROBLEMS

The problem of "indirect indices" of prehistorical society's sex relations is a major problem for women's liberationists in general,

---

*They are:
  1) If the nuclear family constitutes a social system stable over time, it will differentiate roles such that instrumental leadership and expressive leadership of the system are discriminated. 2) If the nuclear family consists in a defined 'normal' complement of the male adult, female adult and their immediate children, the male adult will play the role of instrumental leader and the female adult will play the role of expressive leader.
  I observe with irony that Zelditch's heterosexist hypotheses are regarded in sociology as objectively neutral and scientific, whereas nonheterosexist hypotheses are rarely even considered. —*Author*

and for this book in particular. Differential availability of data is also a problem for Zelditch, who notes that "certain societies were omitted merely because they were more difficult to gather material on than others," and "certain societies were included in the list of 75 simply because they were readily available."

My cross-cultural lesbian sample falls prey to the general methodological problem of availability of data. Inclusion or exclusion from the usable sample is determined by differential reporting of lesbian data by primary ethnographers.

My study of female sexuality indicates that there is a systematic bias in patriscientific methodology in both its conceptual model of the sexual world, and in the empirical methods of omitting lesbian data from the literature of record generally. However, there are notable exceptions to this rule: for example, Ford and Beach, and Kinsey. The sexuality studies of Kinsey, and Ford and Beach are so exceptional as to be considered classics in the field.

My lesbian sample of 30 societies is *disproportionately small in relation to the real world of lesbianism*—the result of differential reporting. The smallness of the sample reflects the low estimation patriscientists make of lesbianism, rather than an accurate estimate of the real world lesbian population.

The major methodological sources of this work derive from Murdock's bibliography and the *Human Relations Area Files (HRAF)*. I deal with three different subsamples drawn from Murdock's world samples. The sex ratio sample, the lesbian sample, and the sex segregation/integration sample are different; each is treated separately by chapter. In Appendix A, the three variables are brought together in cross-tabulated form.

SEX RATIO METHODOLOGY

My interest in sex ratios is based on the major hypothesis that high-female/low-male sex ratios are the sex ratios of women's liberation, while equal and high-male/low-female sex ratios characterize women's oppression. Since I theorize that women's oppression/-liberation is effected by societal sex ratios, I drew a world sample of 100 societal sex ratios from the *HRAF* first to disprove the patriscientific assumption that societal sex ratios are always approximately equal.

Further, since I hypothesized that original and early society is characterized by high-female/low-male sex ratios, I needed an empirical link to prehistoric society. The methodological approach to prehistoric social life through studying hunting and gathering society is an accepted social science methodology. To be sure, there are problems with this approach: For one, no hunters and gatherers studied in modern times have descended without change from our human ancestors of original society. Nevertheless, I decided to use the sex ratios of hunters and gatherers as a clue to prehistoric sex ratios in this book. Hunters and gatherers are still the best living human link to prehistory that social scientists have found to date.

PREHISTORIC SEX RATIOS

The methodological literature patriscientists use to study the prehistoric family consist of: 1) the social and physical lives of nonhuman primates, new and old world monkeys, the great apes; 2) family lives of hunters and gatherers of "wild provender" who have been studied in modern times; 3) the tools and home sites of prehistoric humans and "protohumans." None of these sources are perfect.

As stated before, it is my theoretical intuition that high-female/-low-male sex ratios characterize early human societies. Further, the higher social and economic status that marxists and feminists think women enjoyed in prehistory is a function of the females' numerical preponderance relative to a few males selected by the females to enter female society. The sex ratio that I propose characterizes original human society corresponds to the high-female/low-male sex ratios found among many nonhuman primates today in the wilds. While nonhuman primates supplied valuable clues for my sex ratio theory of origin, I concentrated on hunter/gatherers' sex ratios for disproof or proof of my contentions—mainly because this type of data was available to me in the *HRAF*.

As an indirect measure of prehistoric sex ratios, I use the societal sex ratios of hunting and gathering society. The test is simply this: If hunters and gatherers are found to have high-female/low-male sex ratios in either the adult or total population, then I regard this evidence as support for my theory that high-female/low-male sex ratios characterize early society. If, however, the societal sex ratios of hunters and gatherers are modally equal or high-male/low-female, then I will conclude that there is no empirical support for my sex ratio theory.

Since I have also posited that equal sex ratios and/or high-male/-low-female sex ratios characterize patriarchy, if I find that these ratios modally obtain in patrilocal or patrilineal societies, and that high-female/low-male sex ratios modally obtain in matrilocal or matrilineal societies, then I will regard this as empirical support for my theory that high-female/low-male sex ratios characterize gynosociety, and the other two sex ratios characterize patriarchy.

Since there is no coded summary of world sex ratio data contained in Murdock's 1957 or 1967 world samples, or in the *HRAF*, it was necessary to draw my own sex ratio subsample from the *HRAF*. Originally, I intended to draw my sex ratio sample from the exclusive universe of hunting and gathering societies—since my major theories regard prehistoric social organization. However, due to lack of information in the *HRAF* regarding hunting and gathering sex ratios, this plan proved impossible. I was only able to locate sufficient information on 18 hunting and gathering societal sex ratios out of a list of 91 such societies, listed in Murdock 1957. Since few generalizations could be inferred from such a small sample, I opted for another sample design.

I decided to keep the 18 hunting and gathering sex ratios, since they are prehistorically valuable; but to enlarge the sample, I decided to search for 15 to 20 societies with information available on sex ratios from each of Murdock's six world regions—in order to have a regionally representative world sample of societal sex ratios. This research design proved successful.

After examining some 162 societies in the *Human Relations Area Files* at City University in New York (CUNY-*HRAF*), I found 100 societies with enough information available to test my hypotheses. The empirical results of this research exercise are located in chapter 5.

SEX RATIO CALCULATIONS

A brief description of the procedure I used to calculate sex ratios, both total and adult, is in order. The 100 societies selected for hypothesis testing range in mean societal size from one Trumai village of 43 persons in the Mato Grosso of South America, to the entire 1926 Soviet Union society of 147,027,915 persons.

The calculation procedure I followed is this: I took the average sex ratio of all accounts I could find in the *HRAF*. I rarely used only one account of a society's sex ratio that could not be cross-checked or averaged out by other accounts. Most of the sex ratios used in this sample are derived from multiple calculations of the mean, then the grand mean, of all field censuses or official censuses found in the *HRAF*.

I felt that my calculations would be safer and closer to the true population sex ratio across time and society, if I based my sociology of numero-sexual society on the mathematical mean. Thus, I did not select the highest or lowest individual report of a societal sex ratio for use in my hypothesis test. Rather, I took the average sex ratio of all reports per society for use in my tables. The reader must keep in mind, then, that the numerical sexual proportions presented in this book are mean societal sex ratios.

Old Mother Goddess (ancient Turkey)
Çatalhöyük—neolithic, 6th millenium B.C.
Anadolu Medeniyetleri Museum, Ankara

Tables

TABLE 19. Reproductivity of Sex Ratios

MOSTLY FEMALE	NEAR EQUAL	MOSTLY MALE
1 female + 0 male = **0-1 offspring**	1 female + 1 male = **0-1 offspring**	0 female + 1 male = **0-1 offspring**
2 females + 1 male = **0-2 offspring**	2 females + 2 males = **0-2 offspring**	1 female + 2 males = **0-1 offspring**
3 females + 1 male = **0-3 offspring**	3 females + 3 males = **0-3 offspring**	1 female + 3 males = **0-1 offspring**
4 females + 1 male = **0-4 offspring**	4 females + 4 males = **0-4 offspring**	1 female + 4 males = **0-1 offspring**
5 females + 1 male = **0-5 offspring**	5 females + 5 males = **0-5 offspring**	1 female + 5 males = **0-1 offspring**
10 females + 1 male = **0-10 offspring**	10 females + 10 males = **0-10 offspring**	1 female + 10 males = **0-1 offspring**
50 females + 1 male = **0-50 offspring**	50 females + 50 males = **0-50 offspring**	1 female + 50 males = **0-1 offspring**
100 females + 1 male = **0-100 offspring**	100 females + 100 males = **0-100 offspring**	1 female + 100 males = **0-1 offspring**

TABLE 20. Adult Sex Ratios by Total Sex Ratios

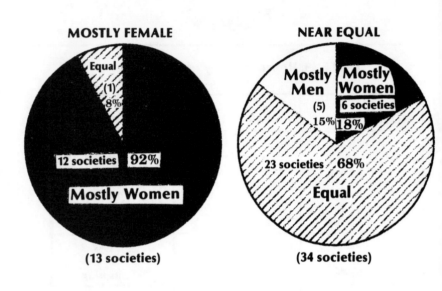

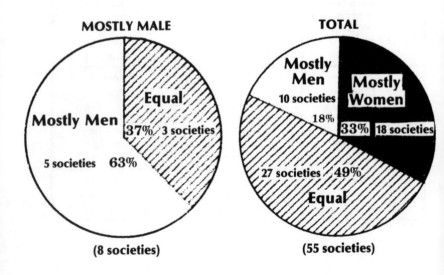

TABLE 21. Hunting and Gathering by Sex Ratios (Total Population)

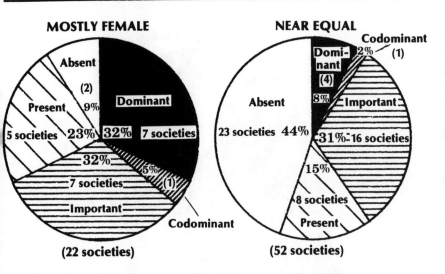

The categories within each pie graph express the **relative weight of hunting and gathering** among the societies sampled. The formal categories are as follows, moving from the greatest to the least relative weight of hunting and gathering: Dominant—Codominant—Important, but not major—Present, but unimportant—Absent.

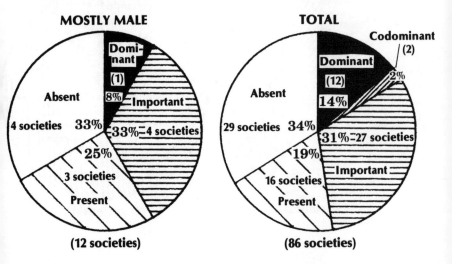

[See page 95 for an examination of the same data from a different angle]

TABLE 22. Sex Ratios (Total Pop.) by Marriage Form

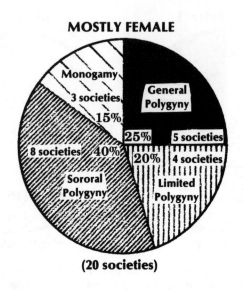

MOSTLY FEMALE

Monogamy
3 societies
15%

General
Polygyny

25%   5 societies

8 societies   40%

20%   4 societies

Sororal
Polygyny

Limited
Polygyny

(20 societies)

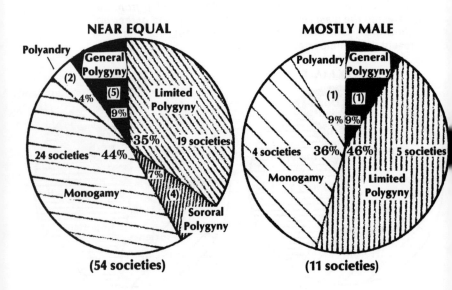

NEAR EQUAL

Polyandry
(2)
4%

General
Polygyny
(5)
9%

Limited
Polygyny
35%   19 societies

24 societies   44%

7%

(4)

Monogamy

Sororal
Polygyny

(54 societies)

MOSTLY MALE

Polyandry
(1)
9%

General
Polygyny
(1)
9%

4 societies   36%   46%   5 societies

Monogamy

Limited
Polygyny

(11 societies)

TABLE 23. Sex Ratios (Total Pop.) by Household Form

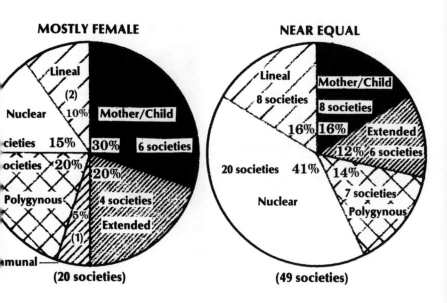

MOSTLY FEMALE

Lineal (2) 10%

Nuclear

cieties 15%

ocieties 20%

Polygynous 5%

(1)

munal

Mother/Child 30% 6 societies

20% 4 societies

Extended

(20 societies)

NEAR EQUAL

Lineal 8 societies 16%

Mother/Child 8 societies 16%

Extended 12% 6 societies

14%

7 societies Polygynous

20 societies 41% Nuclear

(49 societies)

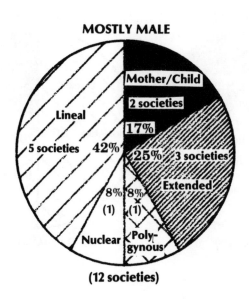

MOSTLY MALE

Lineal 5 societies 42%

Mother/Child 2 societies 17%

25% 3 societies Extended

8% (1) 8% (1)

Nuclear Polygynous

(12 societies)

TABLE 24. Sex Ratios by Family Structure

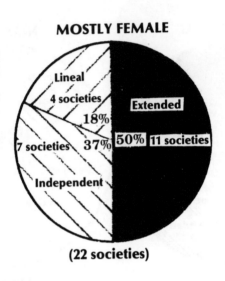

MOSTLY FEMALE

Lineal
4 societies
18%

Extended
50% 11 societies

7 societies 37%

Independent

(22 societies)

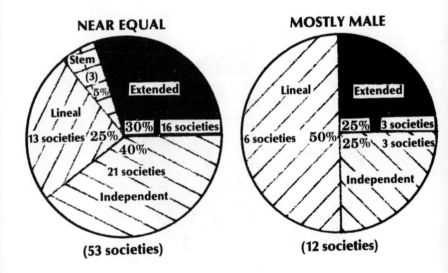

NEAR EQUAL

Stem
(3)
5%

Extended
30% 16 societies

Lineal
13 societies 25%
40%
21 societies
Independent

(53 societies)

MOSTLY MALE

Lineal
6 societies 50%

Extended
25% 3 societies
25% 3 societies

Independent

(12 societies)

TABLE 25. Sex Ratios by Mean Size of Local Communities

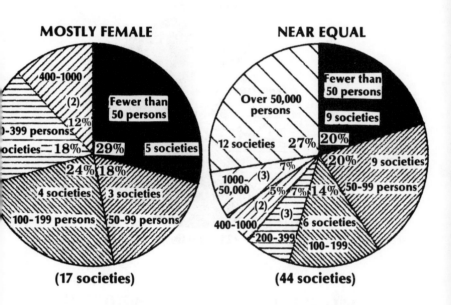

MOSTLY FEMALE

400-1000
(2)
12%
0-399 persons
ocieties — 18%
24% 18%
4 societies
100-199 persons
Fewer than 50 persons
29% 5 societies
3 societies
50-99 persons

(17 societies)

NEAR EQUAL

Over 50,000 persons
12 societies 27%
1000-50,000
(3) 7%
5% 7%
400-1000
(2)
200-399
14%
Fewer than 50 persons
9 societies
20%
20% 9 societies
50-99 persons
(3)
6 societies
100-199

(44 societies)

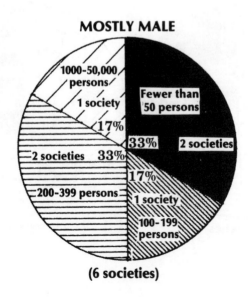

MOSTLY MALE

1000-50,000 persons
1 society
17%
2 societies 33%
200-399 persons
Fewer than 50 persons
33% 2 societies
17%
1 society
100-199 persons

(6 societies)

TABLE 26. Sex Ratios by Social Stratification

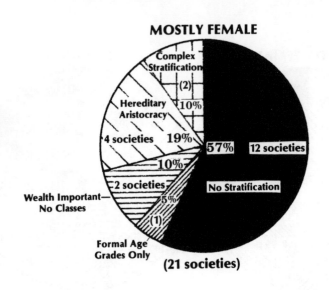

MOSTLY FEMALE

Complex Stratification (2) 10%

Hereditary Aristocracy 4 societies 19%

10%

2 societies

Wealth Important—No Classes

5% (1)

Formal Age Grades Only

57% 12 societies No Stratification

(21 societies)

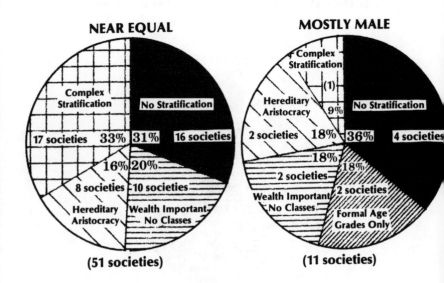

NEAR EQUAL

Complex Stratification 17 societies 33%

No Stratification 31% 16 societies

16% 20%

8 societies Hereditary Aristocracy

10 societies Wealth Important—No Classes

(51 societies)

MOSTLY MALE

Complex Stratification (1)

Hereditary Aristocracy 2 societies 18%

9%

No Stratification 36% 4 societies

18% 18%

2 societies Wealth Important—No Classes

2 societies Formal Age Grades Only

(11 societies)

TABLE 27. Sex Ratios (Total Pop.) by Descent

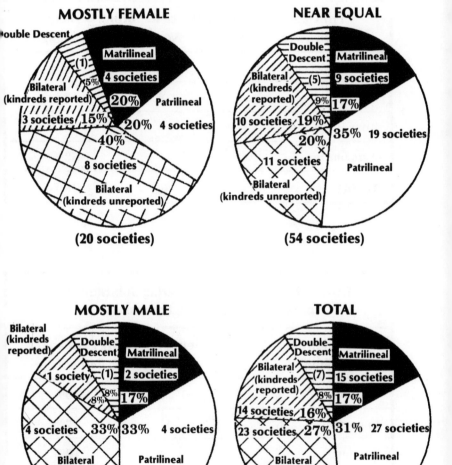

MOSTLY FEMALE

Double Descent
(1)
5%
Bilateral
(kindreds reported)
3 societies 15%
Matrilineal
4 societies
20%
Patrilineal
20% 4 societies
40%
8 societies
Bilateral
(kindreds unreported)

(20 societies)

NEAR EQUAL

Double Descent
(5)
Bilateral
(kindreds reported)
9%
10 societies 19%
20%
11 societies
Bilateral
(kindreds unreported)
Matrilineal
9 societies
17%
35% 19 societies
Patrilineal

(54 societies)

MOSTLY MALE

Bilateral
(kindreds reported)
Double Descent
(1)
1 society 8%
8%
4 societies 33%
Bilateral
(kindreds unreported)
Matrilineal
2 societies
17%
33% 4 societies
Patrilineal

(12 societies)

TOTAL

Double Descent
(7)
Bilateral
(kindreds reported)
8%
14 societies 16%
23 societies 27%
Bilateral
(kindreds unreported)
Matrilineal
15 societies
17%
31% 27 societies
Patrilineal

(86 societies)

TABLE 28. Principal Subsistence of Societies Reporting Lesbianism		
Principal Subsistence	**Societies Reporting Lesbianism**	
	Number	*Percentage*
Hunting & Gathering	6	**20%**
Fishing	4	**13%**
Animal Husbandry	4	**13%**
Agriculture	16	**53%**
TOTAL	**30**	**99%**

TABLE 29. Hunting and Gathering Subsistence of Societies Reporting Lesbianism		
Hunting & Gathering	**Societies Reporting Lesbianism**	
	Number	*Percentage*
Dominant	6	**20%**
Important, Not Major	11	**37%**
Present	3	**10%**
Absent	10	**33%**
TOTAL	**30**	**100%**

TABLE 30. Cultivated Plants of Societies Reporting Lesbianism

Cultivated Plants	Societies Reporting Lesbianism	
	Number	Percentage
Cereal Grains	12	40%
Roots or Tubers	4	13%
Tree Fruits	2	7%
Absent	12	40%
TOTAL	**30**	**100%**

TABLE 31. Settlement Patterns of Societies Reporting Lesbianism

Settlement Pattern	Societies Reporting Lesbianism	
	Number	Percentage
Nomadic Bands	8	28%
Compound Settlements	4	14%
Clusters of Hamlets	1	3%
Dispersed Homesteads	2	7%
Semi-Nomadic Communities	3	10%
Compact Villages	11	38%
TOTAL	**29**	**100%**

TABLE 32. Mean Size of Local Communities Which Report Lesbianism		
Number of People (mean)	**Societies Reporting Lesbianism**	
	Number	*Percentage*
Fewer than 50	4	13%
50—99	7	23%
100—199	3	10%
200—399	7	23%
400—1,000	2	7%
More than 1,000 not urban	0	0%
5,000—50,000	3	10%
More than 50,000	4	13%
TOTAL	**30**	**99%**

TABLE 33. Normal Marital Residence of Societies Reporting Lesbianism		
Marital Residence	**Societies Reporting Lesbianism**	
	Number	*Percentage*
Patrilocal	15	50%
Uxoripatrilocal	6	20%
Matrilocal	5	17%
Neolocal	2	7%
Bilocal	1	3%
Uxoribilocal	1	3%
TOTAL	**30**	**100%**

TABLE 34. Marriage in Societies Reporting Lesbianism		
Form of Marriage	**Societies Reporting Lesbianism**	
	Number	*Percentage*
Monogamy	8	**27%**
Limited Polygyny	8	**27%**
Sororal Polygyny	6	**20%**
General Polygyny	4	**13%**
Nonsororal Polygyny	3	**10%**
Limited Polygyny, preferably sororal	1	**3%**
TOTAL	30	**100%**

TABLE 35. Family in Societies Reporting Lesbianism		
Form of Family	**Societies Reporting Lesbianism**	
	Number	*Percentage*
Independent	16	**53%**
Extended	11	**37%**
Lineal	3	**10%**
Stem	0	**0%**
TOTAL	30	**100%**

TABLE 36. Household in Societies Reporting Lesbianism		
Form of Household	**Societies Reporting Lesbianism**	
	Number	*Percentage*
Mother/child	10	**34%**
Nuclear	10	**34%**
Polygamous	6	**21%**
Extended	1	**3%**
Stem	1	**3%**
Qualified Polygynous	1	**3%**
TOTAL	**29**	**98%**

TABLE 37. Marital Economic Exchange in Societies Reporting Lesbianism		
Marital Exchange	**Societies Reporting Lesbianism**	
	Number	*Percentage*
Bride-Price	10	**33%**
Bride Service	7	**23%**
Dowry	2	**7%**
Gift Exchange	1	**3%**
Sister of Groom exchanged for Bride	1	**3%**
No Material Considerations	9	**30%**
TOTAL	**30**	**99%**

TABLE 38. Segregation of Adolescent Boys in Societies Reporting Lesbianism		
Segregation of Adolescent Boys	**Societies Reporting Lesbianism**	
	Number	*Percentage*
Total	5	**17%**
Partial	6	**20%**
Absent	19	**63%**
SUM	**30**	**100%**

TABLE 39. Post-Partum Sex Taboos of Societies Reporting Lesbianism		
Post-Partum Sex Taboos	**Societies Reporting Lesbianism**	
	Number	*Percentage*
Longer than 2 years	3	**13%**
1—2 years	3	**13%**
6 months—1 year	3	**13%**
2—6 months	5	**22%**
Shorter than 1 month	7	**30%**
No Taboo	2	**9%**
TOTAL	**23**	**100%**

TABLE 40. Premarital Heterosex Norms of Societies Reporting Lesbianism

Premarital Heterosex	Societies Reporting Lesbianism	
	Number	Percentage
Insistence on virginity	8	29%
Prohibited	7	25%
Freely permitted	6	21%
Allowed	6	21%
Precluded by early marriage	1	4%
TOTAL	**28**	**100%**

TABLE 41. Social Stratification of Societies Reporting Lesbianism

Degree of Social Stratification	Societies Reporting Lesbianism	
	Number	Percentage
No stratification	9	30%
Wealth important, but no social classes	9	30%
Hereditary Aristocracy	5	17%
Complex Stratification	7	23%
TOTAL	**30**	**100%**

TABLE 42. World Distribution of Societies Segregating Adolescent Boys

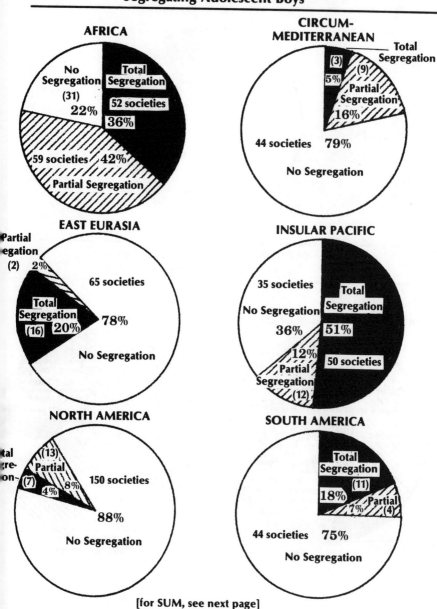

AFRICA

No Segregation (31) 22%

Total Segregation 52 societies 36%

59 societies 42% Partial Segregation

CIRCUM-MEDITERRANEAN

Total Segregation (3) 5%

(9) Partial Segregation 16%

44 societies 79%

No Segregation

EAST EURASIA

Partial Segregation (2) 2%

65 societies

Total Segregation (16) 20%

78%

No Segregation

INSULAR PACIFIC

35 societies No Segregation 36%

Total Segregation 51% 50 societies

12% Partial Segregation (12)

NORTH AMERICA

Total Segregation (7) 4%

(13) Partial 8%

150 societies

88%

No Segregation

SOUTH AMERICA

Total Segregation (11) 18%

Partial 7% (4)

44 societies 75%

No Segregation

[for SUM, see next page]

TABLE 42, World Distribution of Societies Segregating Adolescent Boys, *cont'd.*

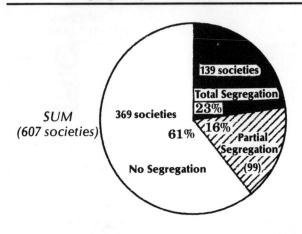

TABLE 43. Post-Partum Sex Taboos by Segregation of Adolescent Boys

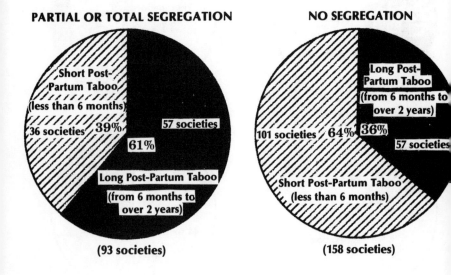

TABLE 44. Hunting and Gathering by Segregation of Adolescent Boys		
Segregation of Adolescent Boys	**Hunters and Gatherers**	
	Number	*Percentage*
Partially or Totally Segregated	10	**19%**
Absence of Segregation	44	**81%**
SUM	54	**100%**

TABLE 45. World Lesbian Sample

NORTH AMERICA (10)
   Blackfoot
   Crow
   Chiricahua
   Cocopa
   Kaska
   Klamath
   Kutenai
   Maricopa
   Navaho
   Ojibwa (Chippewa)

SOUTH AMERICA (3)
   Aymara
   Cagaba
   Maya

EAST EURASIA (2)
   Cantonese
   Chukchee (Reindeer)

AFRICA (6)
   Azande
   Dahomean (Fon)
   Herero
   Hottentot (Nama)
   Mbundu
   Tswana

INSULAR PACIFIC (5)
   Aranda
   Balinese
   Ifaluk (Woleians)
   Manus
   Samoans

CIRCUM-MEDITERRANEAN (4)
   Americans (New England)
   Athenian (450 B.C.)
   Bedouin (Rwala)
   Roman (A.D. 100)

Lesbian Hypothesis Test

My lesbian sample demonstrates that lesbianism is reported in all six of Murdock's world regions and supports the hypothesis that lesbianism is geographically widespread across human society. Lesbianism crosses all continents. Specific distribution of the sample is as follows: AFRICA, 6 (20%); CIRCUM-MEDITERRANEAN, 4 (13%); EAST EURASIA, 2 (7%); INSULAR PACIFIC, 5 (17%); NORTH AMERICA, 10 (33%); SOUTH AMERICA, 3 (10%). In this sample, lesbianism crosses all world regions, but unevenly.

TABLE 46. Female Control of Agriculture

23 societies where *agriculture is "dominant, i.e., the principal subsistence activity,"* and where *"females conduct the activity, male participation being negligible."*

AFRICA (1)
Kwere: Northeast Bantu

INSULAR PACIFIC (5)
Buka (Kurtatchi): Western Melanesia
Ifugac: Philippines and Taiwan
Loyalty Islanders (Lifu): Eastern Melanesia
Mangaians: Eastern Polynesia
Miriam: New Guinea

NORTH AMERICA (11)
Creek: eastern woodlands
Delaware (Munsee): eastern woodlands
Fox: prairie
Huron: eastern woodlands
Iroquois: eastern woodlands
Mandan: plains
Miami: prairie
Pawnee (Skidi): prairie
Shawnee: prairie
Wichita: prairie
Winnebago: prairie

SOUTH AMERICA (6)
Cayapa: Andes
Miskitu: Central America
Taino: Caribbean
Tucano (Cubeo): interior Amazonia
Tupinamba: eastern Brazil
Witoto: interior Amazonia

CIRCUM-MEDITERRANEAN (0)

EAST EURASIA (0)

TABLE 47. Agricultural Sexual Division of Labor Where the Female Share is Greater

47 societies where *agriculture is "dominant, i.e., the principal subsistence activity," and "both sexes participate, but the female share is appreciably greater."*

AFRICA (16)
Bassakomo: Nigerian plateau
Bete: Guinea coast
Dahomeans (Fon): Guinea coast
Hehe (Iringa): northeast Bantu
Ibo (Ezinihite): Guinea coast
Kabre: western Sudan
Kikuyu: northeast Bantu
Kpe (Kwiri): equatorial Bantu
Nika (Digo): northeast Bantu
Nsaw: equatorial Bantu
Safwa: northeast Bantu
Sukuma: northeast Bantu
Thonga: southern Bantu
Wute: Nigerian plateau
Yako (Umor): Guinea coast
Yao: central Bantu

NORTH AMERICA (3)
Cherokee: eastern woodlands
Choctaw: eastern woodlands
Natchez: eastern woodlands

EAST EURASIA (2)
Aryans (800 BC): north and
  central India
Nuri (Kafir): Middle East

CIRCUM-MEDITERRANEAN (1)
Wolof: Moslem Sudan

INSULAR PACIFIC (13)
Alfur (W Ceram): east Indonesia
Alorese (Atimelang): eastern
  Indonesia
Atayal: Philippines and Taiwan
Banaro: New Guinea
Manobo: Philippines and Taiwan
Mentaweians (N Pageh): western
  Indonesia
New Caledonians (Ajie): east
  Melanesia
Palauans: Micronesia
Rossell Islanders: west Melanesia
Samoans (Manua): west Polynesia
Tanimbarese: eastern Indonesia
Ulawans: west Melanesia
Yapese: Micronesia

SOUTH AMERICA (12)
Apalai: lower Amazon
Bacairi: Mato Grosso
Black Carib: Caribbean
Bush Negroes (Salamacca): Guiana
Camaracoto: Guiana
Carib (Barama River): Guiana
Cashinawa: interior Amazonia
Chama: interior Amazonia
Jivaro: interior Amazonia
Panare: Guiana
Trumai: Mato Grosso
Wapishana: Guiana

TABLE 48. Agricultural Sexual Division of Labor

130 societies where *agriculture is "dominant,*
"both sexes participate approximately

AFRICA (28)

Ashanti: Guinea coast
Bemba: central Bantu
Bongo: eastern Sudan
Chagga: northeast Bantu
Dera: Nigerian plateau
Dilling: eastern Sudan
Dogon: western Sudan
Gure: Nigerian plateau
Ibibio (Efik): Guinea coast
Jukun: Nigerian plateau
Kadara: Nigerian plateau
Karekare: Nigerian plateau
Kissi: Guinea coast
Koma: eastern Sudan
Konkomba: western Sudan
Lamba: central Bantu
Lovedu: southern Bantu
Luo: upper Nile
Margi (Kilba): Nigerian plateau
Matakam: Nigerian plateau
Mende: Guinea coast
Mesakin: eastern Sudan
Mumuye: Nigerian plateau
Shilluk: eastern Sudan
Shona (Hera): southern Bantu
Tenda (Coniagui): Guinea coast
Tiv: Nigerian plateau
Tullishi: eastern Sudan

NORTH AMERICA (2)

Cocopa: southwest
Yuchi: eastern woodlands

INSULAR PACIFIC (32)

Ambrym (Ranon): east Melanesia
Arapesh: New Guinea
Belu (Mountain): east Indonesia
Bougainville (Siuai): west Melanesia
Dobuans: west Melanesia
Dusun: west Indonesia
Chamorro (Saipan): Micronesia
Hanunoo: Philippines and Taiwan
Iban: west Indonesia
Ifaluk: Micronesia
Ili-Mandiri (E Flores): east Indonesia
Javanese: west Indonesia
Kapauku: New Guinea
Keraki: New Guinea
Kiwai: New Guinea
Kutubu: New Guinea
Mailu: New Guinea
Malaitans: west Melanesia
Malekulans (Seniang): east Melanesia
Minangkabau: west Indonesia
Nakanai (Western): west Melanesia
Nauruans: Micronesia
Rotinese: east Indonesia
Subanun (Sindangan): Philippines
  and Taiwan
Tagalog: Philippines and Taiwan
Tagbanua: Philippines and Taiwan
Tannese (Whitesands): east Melanesia
Tobelorese: east Indonesia
Toraja (Bare'e): east Indonesia
Trobrianders: west Melanesia
Wogeo: New Guinea
Yami: Philippines and Taiwan

Where Both Sexes Are Equal   TABLE 48

*i.e., the principal subsistence activity," and
equally in the activity."*

EAST EURASIA (40)
Abor: Himalayas
Akha: southeast Asia
Ao (Chongli): Assam and Burma
Baiga: south India
Bhil: north and central India
Bondo: south India
Burmese: Assam and Burma
Burusho: Himalayas
Cambodians: southeast Asia
Chakma: Assam and Burma
Dard (Shina): Himalayas
Garo: Assam and Burma
Gond (HillMaria): south India
Japanese: east Asia
Kachin (Jinghpaw): Assam, Burma
Karen: Assam and Burma
Khasi: Assam and Burma
Koreans: east Asia
Lakher: Assam and Burma
Lamet: southeast Asia
Lepcha: Himalayas
Lolo: east Asia
Malay (Trengganu): southeast Asia
Merina (Hova): Indian Ocean
Miao: east Asia
Mikir: Assam and Burma
Minchia: east Asia
Monguor: central Asia
Muong: southeast Asia
Nepalese (Kiranti): Himalayas
Okinawans: east Asia
Palaung (Katur): Assam and Burma
Rengma: Assam and Burma
Santal: north and central India
Sinhalese (Kandyan): Indian Ocean
Tanala (Menabe): Indian Ocean
Thado: Assam and Burma

CIRCUM-MEDITERRANEAN (16)
Bulgarians (Dragelevtsy): eastern
    Europe
Cheremis: eastern Europe
Czechs (Hana): east Europe
Danes (Lolland): northwest Europe
French (Provence): south Europe
Fur: Moslem Sudan
Georgians: Caucasia
Guanche: north Africa
Hungarians: east Europe
Italians (Sicily): south Europe
Kabyle: north Africa
Kanembu: Moslem Sudan
Konso: Ethiopia/Horn of Africa
Kunama: Ethiopia/Horn of Africa
Rumanians: east Europe
Serbs (Orasac): east Europe

SOUTH AMERICA (12)
Apinaye: east Brazil
Araucanians (Mapuche): Chile
    and Patagonia
Aymara (modern): Andes
Cagaba: Caribbean
Cayua: east Brazil
Chibcha: Andes
Inca: Andes
Mundurucu: lower Amazon
Paez: Andes
Palikur: lower Amazon
Sherente: east Brazil
Tenetehara: east Brazil

EAST EURASIA, *cont'd.*
Thai: southeast Asia
Tibetans (central): Himalayas
Vietnamese: southeast Asia

TABLE 49. Regional Distribution of the Sexual Division of Labor Where Agriculture is the Main Subsistence Type

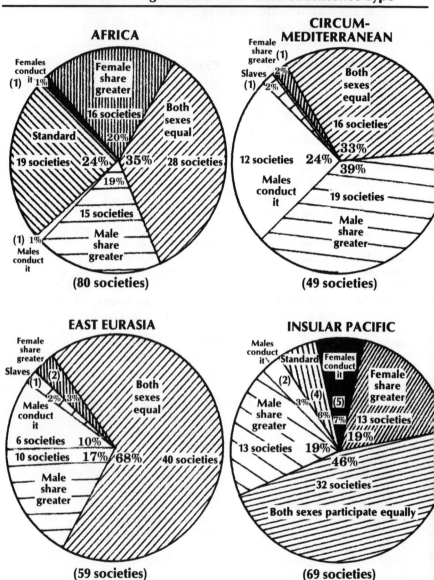

AFRICA

Females conduct it (1) 1%
Female share greater 16 societies 20%
Standard 19 societies 24%
Both sexes equal 28 societies 35%
15 societies 19%
Male share greater
(1) 1% Males conduct it
(80 societies)

CIRCUM-MEDITERRANEAN

Female share greater (1) 2%
Slaves (1) 2%
Both sexes equal 16 societies 33%
12 societies 24%
Males conduct it
19 societies 39%
Male share greater
(49 societies)

EAST EURASIA

Female share greater (2) 3%
Slaves (1) 2%
Males conduct it 6 societies 10%
10 societies 17%
Male share greater
Both sexes equal 40 societies 68%
(59 societies)

INSULAR PACIFIC

Males conduct it (2) 3%
Standard (4) 6%
Females conduct it (5) 7%
Female share greater 13 societies 19%
Male share greater 13 societies 19%
32 societies 46%
Both sexes participate equally
(69 societies)

TABLE 49. Regional Distribution of the Sexual Division of Labor in Agricultural Societies, *cont'd.*

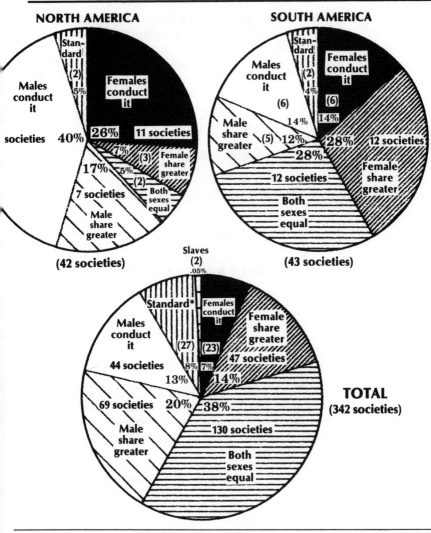

NORTH AMERICA

Standard (2) 5%
Males conduct it
societies 40%
Females conduct it
26% 11 societies
7%
17% (3) Female share greater
5% (2)
7 societies Both sexes equal
Male share greater
(42 societies)

SOUTH AMERICA

Standard (2) 4%
Males conduct it (6)
Females conduct it (6) 14%
14%
Male share greater (5) 12%
28% 12 societies
28% Female share greater
12 societies
Both sexes equal
(43 societies)

Slaves (2) .05%
Standard* (27)
Males conduct it
44 societies
Females conduct it (23)
Female share greater 47 societies
8% 7%
13% 14%
69 societies 20% 38%
130 societies
Male share greater
Both sexes equal
TOTAL (342 societies)

---

*The "standard division of labor by sex" involves a considerable amount of female labor. Murdock defines and codes this category as:

Standard division of labor by sex, i.e., men clear the land and women do the cultivation. (In column 3, men herd the women milk; in column 4, men do the major fishing and/or marine hunting and women do the minor shore or reef fishing and/or shellfishing; in column 5, men hunt and women gather.)

—G.P. Murdock, "World Ethnographic Sample," *American Anthropologist*, vol. 59, no. 4, August 1957, p. 668.

TABLE 50. Female Justice Organizations

In the following societies, if a woman is abused, the entire female population comes to harass the male offender.

AFRICA (5)

Bakalais: equatorial Africa
Beni Amer (Beja)*
Ibo (Ezinihite): Nigeria*
Kaffir*
Mpongwe

INSULAR PACIFIC (1)

Tasmanians (now extinct)

The source for the Ibo is Sylvia Leith-Ross. The rest of the sample derives from Ernest Crawley's *The Mystic Rose*, originally published in 1902 (London: Spring Books, 1965).

---

*This culture is indexed in George Peter Murdock's 1957 "World Ethnographic Sample," *American Anthropologist* 54,4: 664-87 (August 1957). Only those cultures which are indexed in Murdock, 1957 are usable in this study; those not indexed there are lost to the sample. —*Author*

TABLE 51. Societies with High-Female/Low-Male Adult Sex Ratios

Society	Location	Time	Percentage of Females
	AFRICA		
Kung	Pygmies & Khoisan	1926-28	57.6%
Lozi	Central Bantu	1958	65.4%
Chagga	Northeast Bantu	1891	'preponderance of women'
Fang	Equatorial Bantu	1936-50	59.1%
Mende	Guinea Coast	1921-31	57%
Nupe	Nigeria	1930	55%
Tiv	Nigerian plateau	1950	56.5%
	CIRCUM-MEDITERRANEAN		
Wolof	Moslem Sudan	1960	57.5%
Hausa	Moslem Sudan	1931	59.1%
Soviet Union	Eastern Europe, Northern Asia	1926	54.3%
	INSULAR PACIFIC		
Alorese	East Indonesia	1938-39	55.6%
Ifaluk	Micronesia	1905	58.9%
	NORTH AMERICA		
Yokuts	California	1805-33	54.8%
Blackfoot	Plains	1890	'preponderance of women'
Gros Ventre	Plains	1847	'preponderance of women'
Mandan	Plains	1870-72	'preponderance of women'
Crow	Plains	1862	'¼ more women than men'
	SOUTH AMERICA		
Callinago	Caribbean	1647	'multitude of women'
Jivaro	Interior Amazonia	1949	70.7%
Tehuelche	Chile & Patagonia	1833	75%
Caraja	East Brazil	1908	59.2%

Mean Year = 1895   **Mean Female/Male Sex Ratio = 59.7% to 40.3%**

TABLE 52. Regional Distribution of High-Female/ Low-Male Adult Sex Ratios

REGION	Number of Societies	Percentage
AFRICA	7	**33%**
CIRCUM-MEDITERRANEAN	3	**14%**
EAST EURASIA	0	**0%**
INSULAR PACIFIC	2	**10%**
NORTH AMERICA	5	**24%**
SOUTH AMERICA	4	**19%**
TOTAL	**21**	**100%**

TABLE 53. Societies with High-Male/Low-Female Total Population Sex Ratios

Society	Location	Time	Percentage of Females
	AFRICA		
Dorobo	Upper Nile	1929	40.8%
Rundi	Western Bantu	1948	26%
	CIRCUM-MEDITERRANEAN		
Siwans	Sahara	1897, 1927	42.5%
Georgians	Caucasia	1887-95	45.5%
	EAST EURASIA		
Toda	South India	1902	43.1%
Miao	East Asia	1850	39.2%
	INSULAR PACIFIC		
Lesu	West Melanesia		
Easter Islanders	East Polynesia	1882-92	45.2%
Maori	East Polynesia	1938	42.5%
	NORTH AMERICA		
Tlingit	Northwest coast	1890	45.6%
	SOUTH AMERICA		
Cagaba	Caribbean	1940-48	45.7%
Tapirape	Lower Amazon	1935-47	43.5%
Trumai	Mato Grosso	1938	41.9%

Mean Year = 1913   Mean Female/Male Sex Ratio = 41.8% to 58.2%

TABLE 54. Regional Distribution of High-Male/ Low-Female Total Population Sex Ratios		
REGION	*Number of Societies*	*Percentage*
AFRICA	2	15%
CIRCUM-MEDITERRANEAN	2	15%
EAST EURASIA	2	15%
INSULAR PACIFIC	3	23%
NORTH AMERICA	1	8%
SOUTH AMERICA	3	23%
TOTAL	**13**	**99%**

TABLE 55. Societies with High-Male/Low-Female Adult Sex Ratios			
Society	**Location**	**Time**	**Percentage of Females**
	AFRICA		
Dorobo	Upper Nile	1929	37%
Somali	Horn of Africa	1888	37.5%
	EAST EURASIA		
Toda	South India	1871	42%
	INSULAR PACIFIC		
Easter Islanders	East Polynesia	1882-92	42.5%
Maori	East Polynesia	1938	39.3%
	NORTH AMERICA		
Kaska	Arctic America	1944	42.1%
	SOUTH AMERICA		
Tapirape	Lower Amazon	1935-47	45.4%

Mean Year = 1912   Mean Female/Male Sex Ratio = 40.8% to 59.2%

Notes

Introduction

1. See *Dissertation Abstracts International*, Volume XXXIX, No. 11, 1979. My dissertation is available from University Microfilms International, Dissertation Copies, P.O. Box 1764, Ann Arbor, Michigan, 48106. Order No. 7910272.

    I want to thank Martin Oppenheimer, director of my dissertation committee, for safely steering my dissertation through the bureaucratic channels of Rutgers University, and for his lively and intelligent criticisms of my work. I also thank Mary S. Hartman for her support of my dissertation and for helping me to meet the high academic standards she requires of herself and her students; for introducing me to the academic discipline of women's studies; and for her generosity. I thank Adrienne Rich for her deep commitment to my dissertation, for the endless hours she spent with me trying to improve my language and sharpen my arguments. I thank Rhoda Blumberg for her gentle wit and sharp criticisms of my dissertation, which greatly improved my work. I think I had the best dissertation committee a student could ask for, and I will always remember them fondly. I also want to thank Eleanor Burke Leacock, outside reader of the dissertation from City University of New York, for her invaluable support of my data on sex ratios and lesbianism.

2. See Kate Millett's description of patriarchy in *Sexual Politics* (New York: Avon, 1971); and Mary Daly's work on patriarchy in *Gyn/Ecology* (Boston: Beacon Press, 1978).

3. George Weinberg, *Society and the Healthy Homosexual* (New York: St. Martin's Press, 1972). Weinberg coined the term, "homophobia." See Glossary, page *19i*, for more information on homophobia.

4. Mary Barnard, *Sappho, A New Translation* (Berkeley, CA: University of California, 1973), p. 54; see also Sarah Pomeroy, *Goddesses, Whores, Wives and Slaves: Women in Classical Antiquity* (New York: Shocken, 1976), pp. 53-56.

5. Pomeroy, *op. cit.*, p. 88.

6. Ernest Becker, ed. and translator, *The Politics of Aristotle* (New York: Oxford-Galaxy, 1962), pp. 75, 80-82.

7. Radicalesbians, *The Woman Identified Woman* (New York; pamphlet, 1970). See also Richard Lewinsohn, *A History of Sexual Customs* (Greenwich, Conn.: Premier-Fawcett, 1961), pp. 60-61.

8. Pomeroy, *op. cit.*, pp. 55-56. Due to the widespread suppression of information regarding lesbian hystory and gay history, John Lauritsen and David Thorstad, who wrote *The Early Homosexual Movement 1864-1935* (New York: Times Change Press, 1974), found it necessary to inform the North American public that the June 1969 Stonewall riots in Greenwich Village, New York City, do not mark the beginning of the gay liberation movement. On the contrary, Stonewall 1969 marked the 100th anniversary, and consequent rebirth, of lesbian and gay liberation. Thorstad and Lauritsen provide an excellent historical summary of the gay male movement in 19th century Germany. However, they only reserve two pages (17-19) for the lesbian feminists of the early European homosexual movement.

9. Lesbian separatism is the vanguard ideology of the international lesbian movement. Lesbian separatist ideology aims to create all-female culture and territory in what is now a male dominated planet. Lesbian separatism hopes to create all-female homelands where classism, racism, ageism, sexism and heterosexism do not exist, and where women's oppression will be a long forgotten nightmare.

Lesbian separatism began in the United States in 1971. A group of lesbian separatists in Washington, DC called the Furies (Rita Mae Brown, Charlotte Bunch, and others) is generally acknowledged to be the first separatist group—although, almost simultaneously, separatist groups appeared in New York City and in Seattle, Washington, with the Seattle separatists publishing *Amazon Analysis.* I am personally much more familiar with lesbian separatist hystory in New York City and will only present that here—although it must be noted that separatism spread rapidly throughout the U.S. in the 1970's, and each city had its own separatist hystory.

New York City: In 1971, a lesbian separatist group formed on the lower eastside of Manhattan (Morgan Murielchild, Frog, and other dykes composed it). In 1972, the Dyke Separatists, as they called themselves, *girl-cotted* a straight feminist conference at Barnard College, organized by Jill Johnston. Instead, they sent a statement read by Jane O'Wyatt, in which they denounced straight feminists as condescending oppressor/collaborators of lesbians. In May 1973, Morgan Murielchild published an article in *Coming Out Rage*, titled "Dyke Separatism." In the winter of 1973-74, C.L.I.T. (Collective Lesbian International Terrors) was formed by Maricla Moyano, Marsha Segerberg, and Susan Cavin; its first statement, "The Divorce Is Final," was published by *Off Our Backs* and by *Majority Report* (New York).

C.L.I.T. Statement #2, Collection 1 was written by Maricla Moyano, Marsha Segerberg, and Susan Cavin, and published by *Off Our Backs* in July 1974. The C.L.I.T. Papers, as this collection came to be called, was reprinted in *DYKE* magazine, winter 1975-76; in Montreal's *Long Time Coming*; and in New Zealand's *Lesbian Feminist Circle*; in London, Scotland, and Ireland; and was translated into German and published as a book titled, *Rufe Alle Lesben Bitte Kommen (Calling All Dykes, Please*

Come) in Berlin by Tomyris Press. *DYKE* magazine was founded by lesbian separatists Liza Cowan and Penny House in 1975, and published through 1978 in New York City. C.L.I.T. Statement #3, Collection 2, was published in *DYKE* magazine in the spring of 1976.

In May 1976, at a lesbian feminist conference held at public school 41 in New York, a workshop on lesbian separatism was held, and an ongoing group formed. In March 1977, this group opened Fort Dyke, the first lesbian separatist space in New York City—a storefront at 49-51 Prince Street in Manhattan. Fort Dyke was founded by Rhonda Gottlieb, Eileen Kane, Maricla Moyano, Susan Cavin, and Charoula Dontopoulos. In May 1977, the Fort Dyke Collective began publishing *Tribad*, a bimonthly lesbian separatist newsjournal. Both Fort Dyke and *Tribad* lasted until 1979.

C.L.I.T. Statement #4 was published in *Green Mountain Dyke News* (Bennington, Vermont) in 1980. Statements #4 and #5 were written by Maricla Moyano, Marsha Segerberg, Mecca Rylance and Susan Cavin. C.L.I.T. Statement #5 was published in *Big Apple Dyke News (B.A.D. News)*, vol. 1, Nos. 7 & 8, October and November 1981, in New York City.

Note: This brief summary only includes public lesbian separatist activities and writings in New York City—my apologies to those separatists I may have omitted due to lack of information.

10. See Glossary for definition of *patriscience*.

Chapter 1: Sex Devolution

1. Thanks to Adrienne Rich for coning the term, *hetero-feminist*, and for introducing it to me.

2. For example, the Lesbian Herstory Archives in New York City prefers to use the term, *herstory*, to refer to the life and times of women.

3. Besides Bachofen's *Mutterrecht* in 1861 and Engels' *Origin of the Family, Private Property and the State* (first published in 1884), the major 19th century contributions to the matriarchal school were made by: Lewis Henry Morgan, *Ancient Society* (Cambridge, Mass.: Belknap, 1964), whose discovery of matrilineage among the Iroquois was construed as a vestige of matriarchy persisting among indigenous peoples in transition from matriarchy to patriarchy; J. F. McLennan, *The Patriarchal Theory*, who in 1885 pinpointed the origin of the patriarchal family to the practice of "marriage by abduction" or female capture, and also drew attention to the practice of exogamy; J. Lubbock's *The Origin of Civilisation* (1870), in which "communal marriage" is regarded as a historical fact—Lubbock regarded the marriage ceremony as "expiation for marriage," and individual marriage as an infringement on communal rights; E. B. Tylor, who first applied statistics to the study of primitive marriage. Tylor's major works are: "A Method of Investigating the Development of Institutions," *Journal of American Anthropology*, 1899; *Researches into the Early History of Mankind*, 1878; and *Primitive Culture*, 1872. Tylor concludes that

the old communal maternal system was intervened upon by "marriage by capture" to produce individual marriage. See also Julius Lipper, *The Evolution of Culture* (New York: Macmillan, 1931), who linked the decline of female infanticide to the advent of bride price; Giraud-Teulon, *Les Origines de la Famille* (1874); Hewitt and Fison, "From Mother-right to Father-right," *JAI*, 1883; G.A. Wilen, *Das Matriarchat* (1884); and Robertson Smith, *Kinship and Marriage in Early Arabia* (1885), and others.

4. Elizabeth Fee, "The Sexual Politics of Victorian Social Anthropology" in *Clio's Consciousness Raised*, eds. Mary S. Hartman and Lois Banner (New York: Harper and Row, 1974), pp. 86-102.

5. Adrienne Rich, *Of Woman Born: Motherhood as Experience and Institution* (New York: Norton, 1976).

6. Lewis Henry Morgan, *League of the Ho-de-no-sau-nee or Iroquois* (New Haven: Human Relations Area Files, 1954).

7. Carol R. Ember and Melvin Ember, *Cultural Anthropology* (New York: Appleton-Century-Crofts, 1973), p. 40.

8. Frederick Engels, *The Origin of the Family, Private Property and the State*, with an introduction by Eleanor Burke Leacock (New York: International Publishers, 1972).

9. In *Origin...*, Engels characterizes the "consanguine" family as "extinct." Thus, he knew that no one would be able to locate a live tribe of such people. Kathleen Gough thinks there is insufficient evidence to either support or disprove Engels' family sequences. Precisely for this reason, Kate Millett finds the debate incapable of resolution.

It must be stated here that Tylor, Morgan, and Engels' uses of the terms, "savagery," "barbarism," and "civilization," are no longer acceptable in modern anthropology. In her "Introduction" to Engels' *Origin...*, Eleanor Burke Leacock explains that: "Contemporary terminologies generally refer instead to major productive techniques, such as 'food gathering' ('savagery') and 'food production' ('barbarism'). Food gatherers are usually referred to as 'hunters and gatherers' (although they also eat fish). Food producers are divided into an initial 'horticultural' phase, also called 'hoe agriculture,' 'slash and burn agriculture' or 'swidden agriculture,' and a more developed agricultural phase involving the use of the plow and/or systematic fertilization and/or irrigation. For a recent discussion of archaeological levels, see Robert J. Braidwood, 'Levels in Prehistory: A Model for the Consideration of the Evidence,' in Tax, 1960."

10. Both Morgan and Engels have been criticized by 20th century anthropologists for having drawn their conclusions regarding the "consanguine" and "punaluan" families not from evidence of actual group marriage among primitive peoples, but rather from the kinship terms Morgan found still in existence in Iroquois society. Modern anthropological evidence does not bear out Engels' and Morgan's conclusions regarding early society's communal sex arrangements. See Murdock 1957; Coult 1965; and Murdock 1967 regarding hunters and gatherers. All known

hunters and gatherers live in families, mostly nuclear, instead of communal households. Out of 175 hunting and gathering socieites in Murdock's 1967 survey, 47% live in nuclear families, 38% live in stem families, and only 14% in extended families, according to Kathleen Gough, *op. cit.*, p. 64.

11. Engels believed that the domestication of animals preceded cultivation of the soil. More recent anthropological research suggests that cultivation and pastoralism developed at the same time in the same environ as "progressively divergent and somewhat interdependent adaptions." (Latimore, 1957). See Karen Sacks, "Engels Revisited: Women, the Organization of Production, and Private Property," in *Toward an Anthropology of Women, op. cit.,* pp. 211-212. Cf. Marshall Sahlins, *Stone Age Economics* (1971), as cited in Sacks, *op. cit.*, regarding the complex differences between noncapitalist and capitalist production for exchange.

   In chapters 7 and 8, I will offer an alternative hypothesis on the patriarchal urge.

12. See Eleanor Burke Leacock's exceptional "Introduction" to Engels' *Origin..., op. cit.*

13. Cf. Embers, *op. cit.*, p. 39: "Edward Burnet Tylor (1832-1917), an Englishman, is generally considered to be the first professional anthropologist in that he was the first person to hold a university position in anthropology." See also Thorstein Veblen's *Leisure Class, op. cit..* See chapter 1, especially pp. 4-5, 14-15, 12, 14, 18.

   Veblen, having accepted Morgan's evolutionary sequence, traces the origin of the "leisure class" to the male occupations of "late savagery/early barbarism," during the transition from a peaceable to a consistently warlike habit of life.

   The "leisure class" becomes fully developed in the "higher stage of barbarism" of feudal Europe and Japan. The "leisure class" is, by custom, exempt from "industrial occupations" (manual labor, "drudgery," the "everyday work of getting a livelihood"). Their exemption is the economic expression of "superior rank." Honorable employments which are reserved for the "leisure class" are: warfare, government, religious observances and sports. According to Veblen, these "leisure class" employments derive from the male employments in the transition from "savagery to barbarism," whereas:

   > ...the women, are, by prescriptive custom, held to those employments out of which the industrial occupations properly develop at the next advance. The men are exempt from these vulgar employments and are reserved for war, hunting, sports, and devout observances... The man's occupation as it stands at the earlier barbarian stage is not the original out of which any appreciable portion of labor industry has developed... Virtually the whole range of industrial employments is an outgrowth of what is classed as women's work in the primitive barbarian community.

   Veblen posits that the institution of a "leisure class" is the outgrowth of an early discrimination by sex between "worthy employments (male) and "unworthy employments" (female). The "worthy employments are those which may be classed as exploit," according to Veblen, and involve the use of "force or fraud." Any activity that is of a "predatory nature" is considered at once noble, honorable and male.

Industry is the female realm, since industry is considered "unworthy" work by the male because "no appreciable element of exploit enters" into it. Veblen defines industry as: "the effort that goes to create a new thing, with a new purpose given it by the fashioning hand of its maker out of passive (brute) material." In Veblen's theoretical universe, man's work is not the productive labor Marx and Engels posit, but rather "an acquisition of substance by seizure." Veblen observes:

> Under this common-sense barbarian appreciation of worth or honor, the taking of life—the killing of formidable competitors whether brute or human—is honorable in the highest degree. And this high office of slaughter...casts a glamor of worth over every act of slaughter and over all the tools and accessores of the act. Arms are honorable, and the use of them...becomes a honorific employment. At the same time, employment in industry (female) becomes correspondingly odious, and,...the handling of the tools and implements of industry falls beneath the dignity of able-bodied men.

According to Veblen, the ancient male occupation of "predatory exploit" historically becomes synonymous with the patriarchal "leisure class's" code of "predatory exploit." I would argue that rape is one of the major forms of male predatory exploit.

Veblen's study of the early sexual division of labor reveals a striking difference in the productive relations of the sexes. According to Veblen, woman's productive relation to nature is industry and tool technology; man's is predatory exploit and weapons technology. Marx, in his theoretical universe, did not recognize the hystorical sexual differential, and gave woman no stated productive role of her own. Instead Marx designates "man's relationship to nature" as industry and technology—and omits the critical woman's relationship to nature in his theory.

Both Marx and Engels misjudged the amount and importance of women's work in social production. Sacks, *op. cit.*, writes that: "Engels believed that men were always the collectors or producers of subsistence. It has since become clear that for gathering/hunting societies the reverse is closer to the norm (Lee and Devore, 1968); and for horticultural societies, it is often the women's horticultural activities which are the basis of subsistence." Kathleen Gough, *op. cit.*, thinks women probably invented horticulture. See also Judith Brown, "Iroquois Women: An Ethnohistoric Note," in *Toward an Anthropology of Women, op. cit.*, p. 250. Brown concludes that Iroquois women "controlled the factors of agricultural production." See also Ann Oakley, *Woman's Work: The Housewife, Past and Present* (New York: Vintage-Random, 1974). Oakley contends that: "In their role as agriculturalists, women produced the bulk of the country's food supply." My own evidence on the sexual division of labor in agricultural societies, which is presented in chapter 7, corroborates these contentions that women, in the majority of agricultural societies (59%) in Murdock 1957, perform half to most to all of the agricultural labor in those societies. Even Engels' own statistics in *The Condition of the Working-Class in England* (1845) reveal that more than half of the factory workers in the British empire in 1839 were women.

14. Franz Boas, "The Limitation of the Comparative Method in Anthropology," *Race, Language, and Culture* (New York: Macmillan, 1940). Boas' "historical particularism" begins the 20th century emphasis on data collection and the end of 19th century grand theory.

15. A similar movement away from 19th century evolutionary theory and into heavy data collection and structural functionalist analysis has occurred in the field of sociology in the 20th century, as well. The originators of both fields, anthropology and sociology, were grand theorists and evolutionists. I find it ironic that patriscientists in sociology or anthropology consider evolutionary theory below the academic standards of their field.

16. The British school of "diffusionists" includes: G. Elliot Smith, Wiliam J. Perry, and W. H. R. Rivers. The German-Austrian diffusionist school was led by Fritz Graebner and father Wilhelm Schmidt. The diffusionists in the late 19th and early 20 centuries held that "people borrow from other cultures because they are basically uninventive," according to the Embers, *op. cit.*, p. 42. This school is now dead.

17. Bronislaw Malinowski, "The Group and the Individual in Functional Analysis," *American Journal of Sociology*, vol. 44, 1939, pp. 938-964.

18. A. R. Radcliffe-Brown, *Structure and Function in Primitive Society* (London: Cohen and West, 1952).

19. Claude Lévi-Strauss, *The Elementary Structures of Kinship* (Boston: Beacon, 1969). Cf. Eleanor Leacock's critique of Lévi-Strauss, "The Changing Family and Lévi-Strauss, or Whatever Happened to Fathers?", *Social Research*, vol. 44, No. 2, summer 1977.

20. Julian Steward, "The Concept and Method of Cultural Ecology," in *Theory of Culture Change*, pp. 30-42.

21. Leslie A. White, *The Science of Culture, op. cit.* White's other major work is *The Evolution of Culture* (1959).

    V. F. Calverton, "Modern Anthropology and the Theory of Cultural Compulsives," in *The Making of Man*, ed., V. F. Calverton (Westport, Connecticut: Modern Library/Greenwood, 1931), pp. 3-8.

    Today, patri-anthropologists generally consider evolutionist theory outdated. However, not all 20th century anthropologists did. In the 1930's Leslie A. White and the "neo-evolutionists" attacked Boas and argued that Morgan and Tylor's evolutionary approach was correct from the start. Also in the 1930's, V. F. Calverton analyzed and defended the 19th century evolutionists. Calverton presents an interesting and unique interpretation of the attraction toward and reaction against 19th century social evolutionary theory in the field of anthropology:

    > If, before 1859, western civilization found its intellectual continuity in Biblical doctrine, after 1859 it found its new continuity in the doctrine of evolution... The Darwinian theory of natural selection made survival synonymous with advance... In other words, the Darwinian

doctrine of evolution and the consequences of its logic proffered the best justification of the *status quo* of 19th century Europe that had appeared in generations. It harmonized perfectly with the philosophy of the ruling class of that day... It was in this cultural milieu that anthropology had its origins... Beginning with E. B. Tylor's *Primitive Culture* in 1872, the main history of anthropological thought in the 19th century is concerned with the application of the doctrine of evolution to the interpretatrion of man's past... Influenced particularly by Morgan, these anthropologists of the evolutionary school soon concluded that society had passed through certain definite stages, a constant progression from the lower to the higher, in which modern civilization stood as an apex toward which all the past had converged. Not content, for instance, with tracing the development of marriage through its various forms, these men were equally concerned with proving that monogamy was the ultimate stage in marital evolution... As long as Morgan's doctrine was concerned only with the past, and in its evolutionary emphases pointed to the present as something of an ultimate in the moral process — as in the case of monogamy — there was no terror in its proposition. The moment, however, that the radicals insisted upon interpreting evolution as a relative instead of an absolutistic concept, the danger began. No longer could the institutions of 19th century civilization be looked upon as a culmination of evolutionary advance... Private property and the family, therefore, were but part of a process and not a fulfillment of it. In fact, in accordance with the evolutionary progression postulated by the radicals, these institutions were destined to disappear with the next advance in the social process. Once the doctrine of evolution was seen to carry in its wake the possibilities of destruction as well as construction, a new set of justifications was needed to defend the permanency of the prevailing values... Private property was declared an instinct, fundamental to all social life... Monogamy, the specific form of the family dominant at the time, was declared the basic form of marriage of the human species... In these ways, 19th century institutions were saved from the danger of change and decay. No matter in what direction evolution occurred, private property and the family were inviolable... The class-logic at work here is obvious. Anthropology was thus made to serve as an excellent prop for the support of middle-class ethics.

22. Some other 20th century "neo-evolutionists" are: V. Gordon Childe, "Archaeological Ages as Technological Stages," *The Journal of the Royal Anthropological Institute of Great Britain and Ireland*, vol. 74, 1944; Childe, *Man Makes Himself* (New York: Oxford University Press, 1939); Marshall Sahlins and Elman Service, *Evolution and Culture* (Ann Arbor: University of Michigan Press, 1960). See also Julian Steward, *Theory of Culture Change* (Urbana: University of Illinois Press, 1955); Elman Service, *Primitive Social Organization: An Evolutionary Perspective* (New York: Random, 1968), pp. 5-6, 195-203.

23. Carol R. Ember and Melvin Ember, *Cultural Anthropology* (New York: Appleton-Century-Crofts, 1973), p. 41.

Twentieth century patriscientific interpretation of anthopological data does not support the contentions of marxists, evolutionists, "neo-evolutionists," and matriarchists that matrilineage represents a universal historical stage in human society which precedes patrilineage. The Embers summarize the general patri-anthropological objections to such theories of predetermined evolution:

> The predetermined evolutionism of Tylor, Morgan, and others of the 19th century is rejected today (at least outside the Soviet Union). First, predetermined evolutionist theories cannot satisfactorily account for why there is unequal development—why, for instance, some societies today are in Upper Savagery and others are in Civilization. The 'psychic unity of mankind' that was postulated to account for parallel development cannot also account for differential development in time. Second and more important, we have some evidence that societies do not necessarily progress through such stages. Some societies have 'regressed' or have even become extinct. Other societies may have 'progressed' to civilization, but some of them have not passed through all of the postulated stages. If the sequence is not inevitable, evolution cannot be said to be predetermined, and we must look elsewhere to explain the evolution of culture.

24. There is a matriarchal tradition among classicists such as Joseph Campbell, Robert Graves, Erich Neumann, James Frazer, and Jane Ellen Harrison. Cf. Merlin Stone, *When God Was a Woman* (New York: Dial, 1976).

25. Even with such evidence as that presented by James Mellaart of *Catal Huyak*, critics such as Ake Hultkranz, "Bachofen and the Mother Goddess: An Appraisal After One Hundred Years," *Ethnos*, vol. 26, 1961, pp. 75-85, do not accept it.

26. Ruby Rohrlick-Leavitt, Barbara Sykes and Elizabeth Weatherford, "Aboriginal Woman: Male and Female Anthropological Perspectives," in *Toward an Anthropology of Women,* (New York: Monthly Review Press, 1975), p. 111.

27. David F. Aberle, "Matrilineal Descent in Cross-Cultural Perspective," in *Matrilineal Kinship*, eds. David M. Schneider and Kathleen Gough (Berkeley: University of California Press, 1962), pp. 655-727.

28. *Ibid.*, pp. 655-727. Aberle writes:

> Even if we could assert confidently that matriliny first arose in conjunction with horticulture, or that it is an invariant feature of first adaptive horticulture everywhere, it would still not be a stage in general evolution. For some hunters and gatherers, some fishers, and some pure pastoralists would belong to the same stage as some horticulturists... I abjure efforts to decide whether matriliny preceded patriliny, or *vice versa*, since these efforts assume that the question is one of general evolution.

29. *Ibid.*, p. 677. See Table 17-4, "Descent and Types of Subsistence." Aberle found that 56%, of 47 out of the 84 matrilineal societies, were dominantly characterized by horticultural subsistence. See also pp. 664-5. See Table 17-3 in Aberle.

30. Kathleen Gough, "The Origin of the Family," Reiter (ed.), *Toward an Anthropology of Women* (New York: Monthly Review Press, 1975), p. 73. She writes:

     Among apes and monkeys, it is almost always males who leave the troop or are driven out. Females stay closer to their mothers and their original site; males move about, attaching themselves to females where availability and competition permit.

     Removal of the wife to the husband's home or band may have been a relatively late development in societies where male cooperation in hunting assumed overwhelming importance. Conversely, after the development of horticulture (which was probably invented and is mainly carried out by women), those tribes in which horticulture predominated over stock raising were mostly likely to be or to remain matrilocal and to develop matrilineal descent groups with a relatively high status of women. But where extensive hunting of large animals, or later, the herding of large domesticates, predominated, patrilocal residence flourished and women were used to form alliances between male-centered groups. Upper Paleolithic hunters produced female figurines that were obvious emblems of fertility. The cult continued through the Mesolithic and into the Neolithic period. Goddesses and spirits of fertility are found in some patrilineal as well as matrilineal societies, but they tend to be more prominent in the latter. It is thus possible that in many areas even late Stone Age hunters had matrilocal residence and perhaps matrilineal descent, and that in some regions this pattern continued through the age of horticulture and even — as in the case of the Nayars of Kerala and the Minangkabau of Sumatra — into the age of plow agriculture, of writing, and of the small-scale state.

31. Kate Millett, *Sexual Politics* (New York: Avon, 1971), p. 152.

32. The oppressors at the top of the male dominance hierarchies usually tend to see themselves as highly evolved — while they view those oppressed at the bottom of male dominance hierarchies as "unfit," and unevolved.

     Earlier in the chapter, Rich and Fee criticized male matriarchist theory of evolutionary progress; I have already criticized that patriarchal position. Now the marxist theory of evolutionary sequences relevant to women are based primarily on Engels' synthesis of Bachofen, Morgan, Marx, and Darwin's theories of evolution. Other subsequent marxists have economically applied their own interpretations of Engels' theory on women — for example, Bebel, Lenin, Stalin, Mao, Castro and others. See August Bebel, *Women Under Socialism*, translated by Daniel De Leon, with an introduction by Lewis Coser (New York: Schocken Books, 1975); V.I. Lenin, *Women and Society* (New York: 1938); Lenin's *Collected Works*, vols. 19 and 26 (Moscow: Progress Publishers); Clara Zetkin, *Lenin on the Woman Question* (New York: 1934); Joseph Stalin, *Anarchism or Socialism?* (New York: 1951); and *Quotations from Chairman Mao Tse-Tung* (Peking: Foreign Languages Press, 1967).

     See also Sheila Rowbotham's discussion of the 19th century exchanges between the feminist and socialist movements in *Hidden from History: Rediscovering Women in History from the 17th Century to the Present*

(New York: Vintage, 1976). chapters 6-23, pp. 31-166. See also Hilda Scott, *Does Socialism Liberate Women? Experiences from Eastern Europe* (Boston: Beacon, 1975), chapter 3, "The Enemy is Challenged"; and Evelyn Reed, *Woman's Evolution: From Matriarchal Clan to Patriarchal Family* (New York: Pathfinder, 1975).

In his *Problems of Leninism*, Stalin argues: "The dialectical method therefore holds that the process of development should be understood not as a movement in a circle, not as a simple repetition of what has already occurred, but as an onward and upward movement, as a transition from an old qualitative state to a new qualitative state, as a development from the simple to the complex, from the lower to the higher."

There are many historical "moments" of marxist macrocosmic evolutionary theory to know, too many to discuss here; but I do want to briefly criticize the full circle movement from stateless, propertyless, communal, egalitarian, original society to the establishment of patriarchy, patrilineage, the heterosexual monogamian family, women's oppression, slavery, private property, class, state; the evolution of labor from slavery through feudal serfdom to capitalist wage labor, and the evolution of society from capitalist to socialist to communist, where the abolition of the state, private property, and the recreation of communal, egalitarian society occurs. Here I am mainly interested in the beginning and the endpoint of marxist evolutionary theory from a female point of view.

The communist vision of classless, propertyless, stateless, communalistic, egalitarian society is self-consciously based on Marx, Morgan, and Engels' conception of ancient matriarchy, which is original and prehistoric society. The marxist vision of future society, where the first becomes last and the last becomes first, has of course been called "religious" by capitalist scholars — but that is not the point for women.

Although I am aware that marxists do not consider evolution as "a movement in a circle," I think these evolutionary sequences *are* circular for women, but not for men. That is, men do end up in a different and probably better place historically than they started. However, the patriarchal sequences which destroy the sexual equality posited in the matriarchal sequences cannot be considered progressive for women. While patriarchy may be an up trip for men, it is a down trip for women. It appears to lesbian feminists and separatists that women lost everything from the advent of patriarchy and were enslaved for thousands of years, so that men could evolve to the point where women were from the beginning. Patriarchal oppression of women is neither progressive, nor necessary for women. Patriarchy is a pointless, violent digression for women. Generally all male ideologies seek to justify patriarchy.

The evolution of patriarchy is the devolution of gynosociety. While men feel as if they are going historically up, women feel as if they are going down. Sexual evolution in patriarchy seems more like a series of male-manic/female-depressive episodes than a steady progressive climb for both sexes. High male status in patriarchy is obviously based on low female status.

Determining the sex of the social twins, evolution and devolution, is about as trickly as determining paternity: For what child is legitimate in gynosociety is "illegitimate" in patriarchy, and *vice versa.*

Now there is one other moment in marxist evolution that bothers me, aside from the communist logic that derives from the aforementioned sequence that women need communism in order to create classless, egalitarian, communalistic societies; when the fact of the matter is communism needs women in order to create classless, egalitarian, communalistic societies. Hystorically, women created the first classless, egalitarian, communalistic societies millenia before Marx and Engels dreamed of reading about Iroquois matriarchy. It is not only communist societies which need women; all societies, as well as society itself, need women to embody, to materialize social relations. This critical maintenance need of all patriarchal states to exploit women's reproductive and productive resources, energy, and labor—to exploit female sexuality—has led to what I call *vulgar feminism.*

Vulgar feminism is male capitalization and further exploitation of female attempts at liberation, using feminist slogans such as "equal pay for equal work" for male purposes, when female reserve labor is needed for a patriarchal project or political movement. I think all male polities and political movements, including marxists, display frequent opportunistic behavior to women, which is unacceptable to feminists. Vulgar feminism will be discussed presently, but here I want to finish my critique of marxist evolution in relation to women.

The other sequence of marxist evolution that is disturbing is this: Although Marx and Engels recognize that the enslavement of women, the wife by the husband, is the first form of human slavery, the evolution of women's slavery in patriarchy is dropped in Marx's discussion of the evolution of labor form slavery to serfdom to wage labor.

The evolution of women's slavery becomes romanticized in heterosexist terms in Marx and Engels' work, although initially they recognize heterosexual monogamian marriage as slavery. Woman's slavery runs parallel to Marx's general stage of labor, historically. "Marriage by abduction," or the capture of women, is the first form of human slavery. First, women are taken by rape, sheer brute force. At the next stage, women are sold by their parents under father-right into the patrilocal household (marriage by purchase) through the time of feudal serfdom. It is in the modern period of patriarchal labor history, as wage labor develops under capitalism, where the worker contractually sells his labor, that women are allowed to sell themselves, or to contractually arrange their own marriages. While the male capture of the female body is the first form of slavery, the male purchase of female heterosex is the first commodity exchange, according to Martin Oppenheimer.

Furthermore, in *Capital*, vol. 1, Marx wrote of the close material relationship between unpaid labor and "surplus-value." Yet he never connected women's work in the home, housework, with the original and continuing source of unpaid labor, the command over which Marx defined as capital:

> Capital, therefore, is not only, as Adam Smith says, the command over labor. It is essentially the command over unpaid labor. All surplus-value, whatever particular form (profit, interest, or rent) it may subsequently crystallize into, is in substance the materialization of unpaid labor. The secret of the self-expansion of capital resolves intself into having the disposal of a definite quantity of other people's unpaid labor.

Marx also writes that "the ownership of past unpaid labor is thenceforth the sole condition for the appropriation of living unpaid labor on a constantly increasing scale." In view of these definitions, it is not merely rhetorical to say that capital and its expansion is originally and currently based on the past and present mountains of "wages due" women.

Generally, vulgar feminism is the distortion and misuse of feminist principles or concepts to exploit women for male advantage. For example, capitalist Madison Avenue advertising techniques use the stylistic image of "the liberated woman" to sell capitalist products to a new market of women who want to be real liberated women.

Vulgar feminism takes many forms, and is not only confined to the world of capitalist enterprise. Male political movements have capitalized on the vulgar feminist approach to add more women to their ranks by rhetorically claiming to work for the eradication of women's oppression—when in actuality, no concrete political actions are being taken to overturn male supremacy inside or outside male political organization. Furthermore, their real interest in women is not to throw the full weight of the male political machinery behind women's issues, women's rights, women's liberation, or the women's movement—but rather to get more women working for their particular political cause, which essentially has nothing to do with the liberation of women. Thus, vulgar feminists are opportunists, political or economic.

Unfortunately, the "motherhood cult" of socialism (praise mother with medals for all the fine sons she gives the revolution) falls into the wastebasket of vulgar feminism. Mao, I think, was particularly brilliant in his blending of vulgar feminism with China's agricultural need for more laborers. In *The Little Red Book* or *Quotations from Chairman Mao Tse-tung*, the following passages in consecutive order explain what I mean by Mao's vulgar feminism:

> In agricultural production our fundamental task is to adjust the use of labor power in an organized way and to encourage women to do farm work.
>
> In order to build a great socialist society, it is of the utmost importance to arouse the broad masses of women to join in productive activity. Men and women must receive equal pay for equal work in production. Genuine equality between the sexes can only be realized in the process of the socialist transformation of society as a whole.
>
> With the completion of agricultural cooperation, many cooperatives are finding themselves short of labor. It has become necessary to arouse the great mass of women who did not work in the fields before to take their place on the labor front... China's women are a vast reserve of labor power. This reserve should be tapped in the struggle to build a great socialist country.
>
> Enable every woman who can work to take her place on the labor front, under the principle of equal pay for equal work. This should be done as quickly as possible.

It is not that farmwork will liberate women; rather, China needed farmwork done, and women represented a "vast reserve of labor power." Sometimes this vulgar feminist streak in marxist history leads marxists to insist that women need socialism, when it is truer to say that socialism needs women.

See Oedipussy Tudde's discussion of U.S. patriarchal "ec(cop)tation" (economic co-optation) of lesbian fashion and how the "liberated woman" gets coopted, in her C.L.I.T. article, "Fashion Politics and the Fashion in Politics," *Off Our Backs*, July 1974.

See the following works by Mao Tse-Tung (as cited in *Quotations...*, *op. cit.*): "Our Economic Policy," 23 January 1934, in his *Selected Works*, vol. 1, p. 142; introduction to "Women Have Gone to the Labor Front," vol. 1, 1955; introduction to "Solving the Labor Shortage by Arousing the Women to Join in Production," *The Socialist Upsurge in China's Countryside*, vol. 2, 1955; and his introduction to "On Widening the Scope of Women's Work in the Agricultural Co-operative Movement," *The Socialist Upsurge in China's Countryside*, vol. 1, 1955.

33. The *New York Times* misplaces the majority of articles on women, even feminist articles—and this is the ultimate insult—under its section titled, "Family/Style."

34. Cf. Mariarosa Dalla Costa, "Women and the Subversion of the Community," in *The Power of Women and the Subversion of the Community* (Briston, England: Falling Wall Press).

35. Juliet Mitchell, *Women's Estate* (New York: Pantheon, 1971), pp. 80-81, 102-3, 120.

36. Kathleen Gough, "The Origin of the Family," in *Toward an Anthropology of Women*, ed. Rayna R. Reiter (New York: Monthly Review Press, 1975).

37. Simone de Beauvoir, *The Second Sex* (New York: Bantam, 1970), p. 52.

38. Kate Millett, *Sexual Politics* (New York: Avon, 1971). See also Gayle Rubin, "The Traffic in Women: Notes on the 'Political Economy' of Sex," *Toward an Anthropology of Women, op. cit.*, pp. 160-3. Rubin criticizes the position that women's oppression is located only inside capitalism, with this argument: "...to explain women's usefulness to capitalism is one thing. To argue that this usefulness explains the genesis of the oppression of women is quite another."

39. Susan Brownmiller, *Against Our Will* (New York: Bantam, 1976), p. 2.

40. *Ibid.*, p. 6.

41. Nancy Myron and Charlotte Bunch, "Introduction," *Lesbianism and the Women's Movement* (Baltimore: Diana, 1975), p. 10.

42. Barbara Solomon, "Taking the Bullshit by the Horns," in *Lesbianism and the Women's Movement, op. cit.*, p. 42.

43. Charlotte Bunch, "Lesbians in Revolt," in *Lesbianism and the Women's Movement, op. cit.*, p. 31.

44. *Ibid.*, p.32. See also Eli Zaretsky, "Capitalism, the Family and Personal Life," *Socialist Revolution*, January-June 1973.

Eli Zaretsky has learned a lesbian feminist analysis of heterosexuality. As he writes:

In addition, Engels does not challenge the natural or biological basis of the family insofar as it has persisted into the present. That basis is the sexual division of labor—for example, the responsibility of women for child care—and heterosexuality. Heterosexuality is the precondition for the sexual division of labor; the division of labor, by insuring the reciprocal dependence of the sexes, gives rise to the 'bias towards heterosexuality.' Engels portrays the sexual division of labor as a natural or spontaneous phenomenon that derives its oppressive meaning only through the growth of commodity production. He assumes that under socialism the family will embody the traditional division of labor (to the extent that its productive forces have been fully socialized) and that it will be based upon heterosexuality.

45. Purple September, "The Normative Status of Heterosexuality," in *Lesbianism and the Women's Movement, op. cit.*, pp. 81-83.

46. Rita Mae Brown, "The Shape of Things to Come," in *Lesbianism and the Women's Movement, op. cit.*, p. 71.

47. Peter L. Berger and Thomas Luckmann, *The Social Construction of Reality* (Garden City, NY: Anchor-Doubleday, 1967); see Berger and Luckmann's discussion of "The Foundations of Knowledge in Everyday Life," pp. 10, 19-46.

   The phenomenon of marginals challenging taken-for-granted conformist reality can be metaphorically understood by another sociological analogy: If the heterosexual feminist's version of life in the group is the Simmelian insider's version, then the lesbian feminist's view resembles the classic outsider, Simmel's "stranger," who knows there is life outside the group.

   The eyes of the "marginal" have always been highly respected in the field of sociology. Lewis Coser contends that many of the masters of sociological thought were marginals, especially Marx and Veblen. Lesbian feminists, from their position of marginality, hold that there is life for women after death, after the patriarchal family.

   For more on marginality, see Simmel's essay on "The Stranger," *The Sociology of Georg Simmel, op. cit.*, pp. 402-8. Also, see Lewis Coser, *Masters of Sociological Thought: Ideas in Historical and Social Context* (New York: Harcourt Brace Jovanovich, 1971); see Coser's essays on "Karl Marx: Isolation and Double Marginality," pp. 83-6, and "Thorstein Veblen: A Marginal Man," pp. 296-9.

48. Linda Gordon, *Woman's Body, Woman's Right: A Social History of Birth Control in America* (New York: Grossman-Viking, 1976), pp. 231, 238.

49. Ellen Agger, Lorna Boschman, Betty Burcher, Judy Quinlan, Patrice Simister, Watson, Ellen Woodsworth, and Francie Wyland, "Lesbian and Straight," *All Work and No Pay: Women, Housework and the Wages Due*, eds. Wendy Edmond and Suzie Fleming (Bristol, England: Power of Women Collective and Falling Wall Press, 1975), pp. 21-5. See also Selma James, *Sex, Race, and Class* (Bristol, England: Falling Wall Press, 1975); *Wages for Housework Women Speak Out, May Day Rally Toronto* (Toronto: Amazon Press, 1975).

   The "Wages Due Collective, Toronto, Canada" analyzes the economics of "Lesbian and Straight":

   The perspective that results in the demand for Wages for Housework recognizes that housework is not women's biological destiny. We have all been raised to think that we will 'naturally' do the cooking, cleaning, raising children, looking after men, because we are all women. Wages for Housework says that we do this work because we are trained to do this work, because the State needs us to do this work. Heterosexuality is part of the definition of our housework. It is a role that has bveen imposed on us by and for the benefit of capital. Heterosexuality is the morality that says that all women 'naturally' serve men sexually and in other ways—emotionally, physically, etc. We know that many women are lesbians, many women are 'frigid,' many women are celibate, so we know that heterosexuality is not in our genes, but in our training for the work that we must do. We create and service the workers of the world (including ourselves). The existence of lesbianism points out to us that this work is not the result of our biological nature. Lesbianism exposes sexual servicing as WORK. Wagelessness guarantees our servitude.

The "Wages Due Collective, Toronto," points not only to the existence of lesbianism, but to the existence of prostitution as evidence that "sex is work." They also see lesbianism as "worker's control":

The existence of lesbianism helps define the sexual needs of women. It is the expression of all women's need to control our own sexuality, just as demanding community controlled daycare is an expression of our need to be free from the responsibility of training new workers... Lesbianism is workers' control. Because lesbianism is a refusal to sexually service men it is a fight against that work. One of the crucial working conditions of heterosexuality is isolation of women from each other.

A strategic difference between Margaret Small and "Wages Due Toronto" is that Small sees the lesbian as outside of production, reproduction and heterosexuality. "Wages Due" demands wages for all women, including lesbians.

50. Margaret Small, "Lesbians and the Class Position of Women," in *Lesbianism and the Women's Movement, op. cit.*, p. 58.

Chapter 2: Lesbian Origins

---

1. Lesbian and gay scholar/activists in the movement interpret Ruth and Naomi's relationship as lesbian. Although straight scholars may cling to the contention that Naomi and Ruth had only a mother-in-law/daughter-in-law relationship, in the old testament "Book of Ruth" in the bible, it is written: "And Ruth said, Entreat me not to leave thee, or to return from following after thee; for whither thou goest, I will go; and where thou lodgest, I will lodge: thy people shall be my people, and thy God my God: Where thou diest, will I die, and there will I be buried: the Lord do so to me, and more also, if aught but death part thee and me." (Ruth, 1.16-17).

2. I am aware of the fact that many scholars of patri-classics heatedly attempt to refute even Sappho's lesbianism, even as Sappho writes: "Afraid of losing you/I ran fluttering/like a little girl/after her mother." See *Sappho, A New Translation*, by Mary Barnard (Berkeley: University of California,

1973, p. 54). However, Mary Barnard and Sarah Pomeroy accept Sappho's lesbianism. See Sarah Pomeroy, *Goddesses, Whores, Wives and Slaves: Women in Classical Antiquity* (New York: Shocken, 1976), pp. 53-56. Pomeroy writes: "Many modern scholars have vehemently denied that Sappho's sentiments occasioned overt erotic activity. The Greeks certainly realized that Sappho wrote about the sexual activities of women... In Greek literature generally, references to the women of Lesbos connoted unusually intense eroticism, both homosexual and heterosexual. Anacreon, writing in the generation after Sappho, complained that the girl from Lesbos whom he desired 'gapes after some other woman.' The homosexual reputation of Lesbian women was the theme of Lucian's fifth 'Dialogue of the Courtesans,' written in the second century A.D. On the other hand, in Athenian comedy the verbs *lesbiazein* and *lesbizein* ('to play the Lesbian') and other references to the women of Lesbos connote enthusiasm for all sorts of sexual experiences and 'whorish behavior.'"

3. *The Politics of Aristotle*, translated and eidted by Ernest Barker (New York: Oxford-Galaxy, 1962). pp. 75, 82. See also Dacier's translation of Plutarch; Edward Carpenter, *Intermediate Types Among Primitive Folk: A Study in Social Evolution* (New York: Mitchell Kennerly, 1914), pp. 112-13. Carpenter writes: "...In the very early times—bordering on the prehistoric and matriarchal—love of a homosexual or Uranian kind had a far wider scope and acknowledged place in social life than in later days... And, with regard to the special peoples we are dealing with in this chapter, it may be desirable here to point out that this impulse among the early Greek peoples was by no means confined to the men, but was active and salient among the women also. Plutarch in his *Lycurgus* (c. 18) wrote of *paiderastia* among the Spartans: "This sort of love was so much in fashion among them that the most staid and virtuous matrons would own publicly their passion to a modest and beautiful virgin." Aristotle wrote of the Spartan women: "Another criticism of the Spartan constitution turns on the indulgence permitted to women... In all constitutions, therefore, where the position of women is poorly regulated, one-half of the citizen body must be considered as left untouched by the laws. This is what actually happened at Sparta. The legislator who made the Spartan code intended to make the whole citizen body hardy; but if he fulfilled that intention, as he obviously did, in regard to the men, he has wholly neglected to achieve it in regard to the women, who indulge in all sorts of license and live a luxurious life... There was wisdom in the earliest author of myths when he paired Ares and Aphrodite: the facts show that all martial races are prone to passionate attachments either to men or to women. It was attachments of the latter sort which were common in Sparta; and the result was that, in the days of her hegemony, affairs largely fell into the hands of women. But what is the difference between governors being governed by women and women being actually governors? The results are the same...during the Theban invasions; unlike the women of other states, they were of no use whatever, and caused more confusion than the enemy. We may admit that the license enjoyed by women seems to have come about originally at

Sparta in a way which is easy to understand. The men were absent on expeditions for long periods..."

4. Aristotle, *op. cit.*, pp. 80-82. Aristotle compares the Spartan, Cretan and Carthaginian constitutions in "Actual States which Approach the Ideal," and concludes that constitutionally "Crete [was] possibly the model of Sparta." Aristotle writes further that: "The Cretan type of constitution is allied to the Spartan... It may well have been the model on which the constitution of Sparta was generally based, indeed, this is said to be the case... Tradition records that Lycurgus, when he relinquished the office of guardian to king Charillus and went abroad, spent most of his time in Crete, to which he was drawn by ties of connection—the people of Lyctus (one of the cities of Crete) being a colony from Sparta... These Spartan settlers adopted the form of law which they found existing among the inhabitants at the time of their settlement. The adoption of these ancient laws by the Spartan colonists in Crete may help us to undetstand why they are still in vogue among the serfs of the island, as a body of law supposed to go back as far as the times of Minos... The legislation of Crete contains a number of ingenious devices intended to encourage an abstemious form of diet in the interest of the state; it also includes a provision for the segregation of women, to prevent them from having too many children, and it sanctions homosexual connections."

5. *Ibid.*, p. 75. Aristotle writes that: "...The citizens are dominated by their wives. (But the Celts are an exception to this general rule: so, too, are such peoples as openly approve of homosexual attachments)."

6. Sarah Pomeroy, *Goddesses, Whores, Wives and Slaves: Women in Classical Antiquity* (New York: Schocken, 1976), p. 88. Pomeroy thinks that some of the prostitutes of classical Athens were lesbians—which is especially interesting, in view of Bachofen's theory of hetaerist origins. She writes: "Though Plato invented a fable—attributing the story to Aristophanes—in which he purported to explain the natural origin of female homosexuality, we have no solid evidence of lesbian relationships actually occurring among citizen women... We do know, on the other hand, that prostitutes in Athens enjoyed not only a full range of heterosexual diversions, but homosexual relations as well—again, on the basis of vase paintings showing phallic devices designed for simultaneous use by two women. But the gap between respectable women and prostitutes was so wide that we cannot begin to infer from one group to the other, rather, we must consider the latter a case unto themselves." Pomeroy has been accused by feminists of classism in her studies of the women of antiquity. Her last sentence explains why. Although Pomeroy is academically correct to separate the life of the citizen woman from that of the prostitute in terms of social stratification, it must be remembered that both are women of Athens. The lesbian prostitutes (hetaera) of classical Athens will be used in this study as a societal case of reported lesbianism for "Athenians (450 B.C.)," as indexed in Murdock's 1957 "World Ethnographic Sample."

7. Dr. Richard Lewinsohn, *A History of Sexual Customs* (Greenwich, Conn.: Premier-Fawcett, 1961), pp. 60-1. He writes: "In Lesbos, as in

Athens, admiration of beauty could not be divorced from sex, and many women took delight in one another... The Greeks bestowed on women who indulged in this practice the contemptuous name of *tribades*, from *tribein*—to rub one's body against that of another. Sappho and Lesbos remained, however, the symbols of female homosexuality. Lucian says that the *tribades* are Lesbians, who are indifferent to men and behave together as though they were man and wife. Both Lucian and the Roman poets Juvenal and Martial have more to say on Lesbian love, which seems to have been more widely practiced in imperial Rome than in ancient Greece." See also Helen Diner, *Mothers and Amazons: The First Feminine History of Culture* (Garden City, NY: Anchor-Doubleday, 1973), p. 201. Diner writes of the "lesbian practices" at the rites of Bona Dea, the Roman goddess, who was celebrated exclusively by women: "Lesbian practices and holy obscenities, in honor of Bona Dea especially, exceeded the cultic rites of African rain priesteses, for primitive peoples have always considered rain the consequence of erotic stimulation of a divinity."

8. See Plato's "Symposium" in Jowett's *The Republic and Other Works of Plato* (Garden City, NY: International Collectors Library).

9. Pomeroy, *op. cit.*, pp. 55-6.

10. Bethe, as cited in Edward Carpenter, *Intermediate Types Among Primitive Folk: A Study in Social Evolution* (London: Allen and Unwin, 1919).

11. Carolyn Niethammer, *Daughters of the Earth: The Lives and Legends of American Indian Women* (New York and London: Collier-Macmillan, 1977), p. 229.

12. M. Kay Martin and Barbara Voorhies, *Female of the Species* (New York and London: Columbia University Press, 1975), pp. 84-107.

13. Niethammer, *op. cit.*, pp. 229-30. See also George Devereaux, "Institutionalized Homosexuality of the Mohave Indians," *Human Biology*, vol. 9, 1937, pp. 498-527; and Douglas Crawford McMurtrie, "A Legend of Lesbian Love Among the North American Indians," *Urologic and Cutaneous Review*, April 1914, pp. 192-3.

14. Jonathan Katz, *Gay American History: Lesbians and Gay Men in the U.S.A.* (New York: Crowell, 1976).

15. Edward Winslow Gifford, "The Kamia of the Imperial Valley," *U.S. Bureau of American Ethnology Bulletin*, no. 97 (Washington, DC: Government Printing Office, 1931), p. 12.

16. *HRAF*, New York Public Library, microfiche, OF 7 Bali, 4:Belo E-5 (1931-1939).

17. Robert Graves, *The Greek Myths*, vol. 1 (Baltimore: Penguin, 1964), p. 30. See Diner, *op. cit.*, pp. 2-4.

18. Sherry B. Ortner, "Is Female to Male as Nature is to Culture?", *Women, Culture and Society*, eds. Michelle Zimbalist Rosaldo and Louise Lamphers (Stanford, CA: Stanford University Press, 1974), pp. 67-87.

Chapter 3: Amazon Origin Theories

1. I have no information on Australian Amazon reportings. I am indebted to Maricla Moyano for her discussions of Amazons with me throughout my research for this chapter, for sharing her own research on the Amazons with me, and for translating difficult Spanish passages on the Amazons.

2. Emmanuel Kanter, *The Amazons: A Marxian Study* (Chicago: Charles H. Kerr, 1926); Donald J. Sobol, *The Amazons of Greek Mythology* (South Brunswick and New York: A.S. Barnes and Co., 1973); J.J. Bachofen, *Myth, Religion, and Mother-Right: Selected Writings of J.J. Bachofen* (Princeton, NJ: Princeton University/Bollingen Series LXXIV, 1973); Robert Graves, *The Greek Myths*, vol. 1 (Baltimore: Penguin, 1964); and many other reporters of Amazons.

3. J. Desmond Clark, *The Prehistory of Africa* (Southampton, England: Thames and Hudson, 1970), p. 15.

4. Sobol, *op. cit.*, pp. 13-28.

5. Plutarch, *Lives of the Noble Greeks*, ed. Edmund Fuller (New York: Dell-Laurel, 1959), pp. 30-1. Plutarch writes of the Amazon invasion of Athens: "Concerning his voyage into the Euxine Sea, Philochorus and some others write that he made it with Hercules, offering him his service in the war against the Amazons... The Amazon invasion of Attica...would seem to have been no slight or womanish enterprise. For it is impossible that they should have placed their camp in the very city, and joined battle close by the Pnyx and the hill called Museum, unless, having first conquered the country around about, they had thus with impunity advanced to the city. That they made so long a journey by land, and passed the Cimmerian Bosphorus, when frozen, as Hellanicus writes, is difficult to be believed. That they encamped all but in the city is certain, and may be sufficiently confirmed by the names that the places hereabout yet retain, and the graves and monuments of those that fell in the battle. Both armies being in sight, there was a long pause and doubt on each side which should give the first onset; at last Theseus, having sacrificed to Fear, in obedience to the command of an oracle he had received, gave them battle; and this happened in the month of Boedromion, in which to this very day the Athenians celebrate the Feast Boedromia. Clidemus, desirous to be very circumstantial, writes that the left wing of the Amazons moved toward the place which is yet called Amazonium and the right towards the Pnyx, near Chrysa, that with this wing the Athenians, issuing from behind the Museum, engaged, and that the graves of those that were slain are to be seen in the street that leads to the gate called the Piraic, by the chapel of the hero Chalcodon; and that here the Athenians were routed, and gave way before the women, as far as to the temple of the Furies, but, fresh supplies coming in from the Palladium, Ardettus, and the Lyceum, they charged their right wing, and beat them back into their tents, in which action a great number of the Amazons were slain. At length, after four months, a peace was concluded between them by the mediation of Hippolyta... We are also told that those of the Amazons that were wounded were privately sent away by Antiope to

Chalcis, where many by her care recovered, but some that died were buried there in the place that is to this time called Amazonium. That this war, however, was ended by a treaty is evident, both from the name of the place adjoining to the temple of Theseus, called, from the solemn oath there taken, Horcomosium; and also from the ancient sacrifice which used to be celebrated to the Amazons the day before the Feast of Theseus."

6. Columbus, Cortés, Magellan, Orellana, Raleigh, and other Italian, Spanish, Portuguese, and English explorers of the New World reported the presence of Amazon societies at the time of discovery. These sightings will be discussed later in the chapter.

7. Sir Richard Burton, *A Mission to Gelele, King of Dahome* (London: Routledge and Kegan Paul, 1966); Melville J. Herskovits, *The Myth of the Negro Past* (Boston: Beacon, 1958), p. 67. Herskovits writes: "The institution of polygamy reached fantastic proportions, for any woman who took the fancy of the ruler was liable to be claimed for his harem. In Dahomey, also, where centralization of authority and the despotic exercise of power were most developed, battalions of women warriors were kept as nominal wives of the ruler, and hence unapproachable by another man. Many women were thus not permitted normal life, which from the point of view of population policy prevented the kingdom from reproducing the numbers needed to support the expense, in human life and wealth, of its expansionist policy, and eventually contributed to its downfall."

In *Our Primitive Contemporaries* (New York: Macmillan, 1967), pp. 575-6, George Peter Murdock describes the Amazon armies of Dahomey: "The real military strength of Dahomey resides in its standing army, which is organized into a right wing, a center, and a left wing. The two wings commanded respectively by the *Gau* and the *Posu*, are composed largely of the palace guards, the court attendants, the sons of chiefs, and certain classes of criminal. These men are organized into regiments, each with its officers and distinctive uniform. But the shock troops of the army, the best disciplined and most redoubtable warriors, are those of the center, a body composed of about 2,500 female soldiers—the far-famed Dahomean 'Amazons.' From among the marriageable girls of his dominion, the king selects a certain proportion to grace his harem, and from the rest two special officers choose the most promising as soldiers. The Amazons are officially called 'wives' of the king, and they live in a special quarter of the palace, but they do not actually form a part of the harem. Like the other palace women, however, they are strictly segregated from all contact with men, even at public ceremonies. They go armed at all times and accompany the king's wives or their slaves whenever these women leave the palace grounds. All men who encounter a contingent of the king's women on the road, scamper into the bushes or out of sight as though for their lives. Not all Amazons are virgins; married women convicted of crime are often inducted into the corps in lieu of other punishment. Amazon officials, corresponding, as we have seen, to all the male administrative offices of state, govern the female population of the palace. From the point of view of their arms, the Amazons are divided into five branches: the musketeers or main body; the blunderbuss women or veterans, called upon only in emergencies; the elephant huntresses, the most daring warriors of all and equally renowned for their exploits in the chase; the razor women, a small group armed with huge razor-shaped knives especially designed for decapitating enemy chiefs; and the archeresses, a body of young girls prominent only in parades. These various elements are distributed among the three battalions into which the Amazon corps is divided. Each unit has its own uniform, headdress, and officers. The Amazons keep their persons neat and their weapons in good order. They execute rigorous practice maneuvers such as charging through hedges of thorns which cruelly lacerate their bodies. In battle they display a fearlessness, determination, and ferocity, the likes of which their French conquerors admit having encountered nowhere else in Africa." The degeneration of Amazons in late patriarchy in the service of male kings, which also occurs in Siam and Persia, is a topic in need of research.

8. Annie M.D. Lebeuf, "The Role of Women in the Political Organization of African Societies," in *Women of Tropical Africa*, ed. Denise Paulme (Berkeley: University of California Press, 1971), p. 36.

9. Irving A. Leonard, "Conquerors and Amazons in Mexico," *The Hispanic American Historical Review*, vol. 24, no. 4, November 1944, p. 562. See also Celeste Turner Wright, "The Amazons in Elizabethan Literature," *Studies in Philology*, vol. XXXVII, 1940, pp. 433-56.

10. Lebeuf, *op. cit.*, p. 36.

11. Sobol, *op. cit.*

12. *New York Herald-Tribune*, 2 December 1964, as cited in Sobol, *op. cit.*

13. *Encyclopaedia Britannica, Macropaedia*, vol. 1 (Chicago: Benton, 1974), p. 649; *Collier's Enclopedia*, vol. 1, 1971, p. 627; Bertram T. Lee and M.C. Heaton, *The Discovery of the Amazon according to the Account of Friar Gaspar de Carvajal* (New York: American Geographic Society, 1934).

14. Alexander F. Chamberlain, "Recent Literature on the South American 'Amazons,'" *Journal of American Folk-Lore*, vol. 14, 1911, pp. 16-20; Paul Ehrenreich, *The Myths and Legends of the Primitive Peoples of South America* (Berlin 1905); Georg Friederici, *The Amazons of America* (Leipzig 1910). I want to thank Martin Oppenheimer for his invaluable translation from the German, of Friederici's critical passage establishing the lesbianism of some South American Amazons, to be discussed later.

15. Leonard, *op. cit.*

16. Filippo Pigafetta, *Relatione del reame di Congo e della circonvicine per Filippo Pigafetta* (Rome: 1591); English translation by Margarite Hutchinson and John Murray, 1881.

17. J.L. Myres, *Herodotus and Anthropology*, p. 138. As cited in Kanter, *op. cit.*, p. 58.

18. Philip Slater, *The Glory of Hera: Greek Mythology and the Greek Family* (Boston: Beacon, 1968), p. 393, footnote 24.

19. *Ibid.*, pp. 392-4.

20. Although Helen Diner, *Mothers and Amazons: The First Feminine History of Culture*, ed. and trans. by John Philip Lundin (New York: Anchor-Doubleday, 1973), makes an interesting case for the hystoricity of the Amazons.

21. Emmanuel Kanter, *The Amazons: A Marxian Study, op. cit.*, pp. 12-14.

22. I could find no Amazons in Engels' work either.

23. Irving Leonard, "Conquerors and Amazons in Mexico," *The Hispanic American Historical Review*, vol. 24, no. 4, November 1944, pp. 561-79.

24. *Ibid.*, pp. 561-2.

25. Chapters 157-178 describe the Amazons' defeat of the christians at Constantinople. The Amazons fought on the side of "Armato, king of Persia," who had invited all "pagan princes" to unite to recapture the city, according to Leonard.

26. Garcirodríguez de Montalvo, *Sergas de Esplandian* (1510), chapter 157. He writes: "...Know ye that on the right hand of the Indies there is an island called California, very close to the Earthly Paradise, inhabited by Black women without a single man among them..."

27. Diner, *op. cit.*, p. 95.

28. This theory Kanter attributes to Max Duncker, Leonhardt, A. Reinach, and Meyer.

29. J.J. Bachofen, *Myth, Religion, and Mother-Right: Selected Writings of J.J. Bachofen* (Princeton University, 1973).

30. *Ibid.*, p. 104.

31. *Ibid.*, p. 105.

32. George Boas, "Preface" to Bachofen, *op. cit.*, p. xviii.

33. Kanter, *op. cit.*, p. 16.

34. *Ibid.*, p. 18.

35. *Ibid.*, pp. 31-2.

36. According to Martin Oppenheimer's translation, Friederici refers here to lesbianism. This establishes an hystorical connection between lesbians and Amazons.

37. Friederici, *op. cit.*, pp. 17-18.

38. Chamberlain, *op. cit.*, cites Richard Lasch, "On the South American Amazon-Legend" (1910).

39. Chamberlain, *op. cit.*, pp. 16-17.

40. *Ibid.*, p. 19.

41. See chapters 4 and 5 for further sex ratio analysis.

42. This is Jerry Brown's term.

43. Oscar Lewis, "Manly-hearted women among the North Piegan," *American Anthropologist*, vol. 43, 1941, pp. 173-87.

44. Pero de Magalhaes, *The Histories of Brazil* (1576), translated by John B. Stetson, Jr. (New York: Cortes Society, 1922), p. 89. Magalhaes writes that the "true significance" of the name Orellana gave the Amazon River is this: "...He had fought with women in the upper part of the river when

he made his voyage of discovery in 1541." Sobol, *op. cit.*, p. 118, reports: "Orellana was attacked along the river Marnaon in South America by bands of Tapuyas savages in whose ranks, he claimed, were armed females."

45. The reader will note that any discussion of South and Central American Amazons or Antillean Amazons involves not only the Spanish, Portuguese, and Italian accounts, but also the accounts of the native Americans as well. Thus, patriscientists not only have to discredit the European accounts of Amazons, but the native American accounts also. This process is best illustrated by Leonard, *op. cit.*, p. 573, as he tries to explain away the reports of Amazons in the state official documents of captain Hernando Cortés to his emperor Charles 5, as well as Diego de Velázquez, the governor of Cuba in 1518, who made contractual agreements with Cortés regarding the Amazons. See "Instrucción que dió el capitán Diego Velázquez en la isla Fernandina en 23 de octubre de 1518 al capitán Hernando Cortés," *Colección de documentos inditos para la historia de España* (112 vols., Madrid, 1842-1895). See especially vol. 1, p. 403. In Velázquez's *Instrucciones* (item 26 of the document), he instructs Cortés to reconnoiter: "Also where and in what direction are the Amazons, who are nearby according to the Indians whom you are taking with you." Leonard falls back on his racism to discount Cortés' and Velázquez's expectation in this way: "That the Indians accompanying the expedition are cited as authority for this expectation need not be taken too seriously, for it is quite possible that the idea was merely a projection from the minds of Velázquez and Cortés resulting from a recent reading or hearing which they unconsciously imposed upon the half-comprehending and over-awed Indians, who then returned it to the true authors." Leonard's theory is little more than a halfbaked racist, bourgeois psychological theory of history based on literature.

46. Dietrich von Bothmer, *Amazons in Greek Art* (Danford Oxford, 1957); Mary Benett, *Religious Cults Associated with the Amazons* (New York: AMS Press, 1967). Sobol, *op. cit.*, p. 12, reports that: "Since the 15th century, paintings ranging from a group of two and three figures to entire battle scenes, or Amazon-machies, have come from the leading European studios, including those of Rubens and Delacroix." They depict "Theseus's victorious defense of Athens and the meeting of Alexander the great and Thalestris, queen of the Amazons. Tasso's female crusader ranks a close third, being a particular favorite of the Italians." Artists generally represent Virtue as an Amazon, as in the Virginia state seal in the United States of America. Sobol continues: "Virtue rests her right hand on a spear. Her left foot holds down Tyranny, a male figure dressed as a Greek warrior." German literature and art history also offer a wealth of information on the Amazons.

47. Paul Hofmann, "Women Active Among Radicals in West Europe," *New York Times*, 16 August 1977. Hofmann writes that: "An 'Amazon complex' is said to be running out of control in West Germany these days, as psychologists and experts in social sciences debate why so many young

women have become terrorists. A good half of the unflattering pictures on the latest wanted posters in office buildings are of women... In Italy, young women have been implicated in most of the terrorist conspiracies that are plaguing the country. Scores of women are in jail on suspicion of having committed political violence... In Sweden, the Netherlands and other countries of Western Europe, young women are active in anarchism... Yet the ratio of women activists in the present day underground networks and urban guerrilla groups of Western Europe and Latin America is strikingly high. West German police officials speak of a 'women's club' that, they say, is the hard core of the clandestine revolutionary movement. Several Italian and West German sociologists and news commentators, all of them men, have suggested over the last few weeks that the significant female membership in radical and terrorist groups was an unwelcome consequence of the women's liberation movement. 'Women, unfortunately, can be particularly fanatical,' said Hildegard Hamm-Brucher, a minister of state in the West German foreign ministry, who was interviewed by the daily *Die Welt* of Hamburg... A patron of the arts in Dusseldorf, Gabriele Hankel, suggested that young women were suffering from an 'Amazon complex' that was running wild, and been deeply disturbed in their relationship with their parents."

I think it is interesting that when the sex ratios shift in revolutionary movements to a very high incidence of women relative to men, it is at this point that sociologists, psychologists, and news commentators in patriarchy begin to speak of an "Amazon complex." In an indirect fashion, this phenomenon alerts us to the importance of sex ratios in social organization and how this effects the form social organization will take. Specifically, the phenomenon indirectly supports my rather obvious contention that Amazons are associated with extremely high-female/low-male sex ratios, in the sociology of knowledge of a great many societies—even in late patriarchy.

48. My research has found Amazon/lesbian hystorical connections in Dahomey, on Lesbos, among the Tapuyes of Amazonia, among South American Indians decribed by Friederici, *op. cit.*, and among the Celts. Jean Markale, *Women of the Celts (La Femme Celt)*, translated by A. Mygind, C. Hauch, and P. Henry (London: Gordon Cremonesi, 1975), p. 39. Markale writes: "Like all other peoples, the Celts knew homosexuality... There are also signs of clandestine homosexuality in the institution of women warriors, corresponding to the ones found in association with Lesbians which flourish all over the world."

49. Kanter, *op. cit.*, p. 18. Kanter writes that: "...The Amazons were important historical characters, which even to this day marxian historians do not realize." Engels never mentions Amazons, even though he used Bachofen's work, which is saturated with Amazons.

Chapter 4: Sex Ratio Theory

1. *The Sociology of Georg Simmel*, translated and edited by Kurt H. Wolff (New York: Free Press, 1950), pp. 87-104. See especially Simmel's essay, "The Quantitative Determination of Group Divisions and of Certain Groups," pp. 105-117; "The Isolated Individual and the Dyad," pp. 118-44; "The Triad," pp. 145-69; and "The Importance of Specific Numbers for Relations Among Groups," pp. 170-7 (that is, chapters 1-5, part II). See also pp. 109-10.

2. Simmel is best remembered in contemporary North American sociological literature for his microscopic analysis of small group interaction, his classic essays on "faithfulness," the "stranger," the "secret," "The Metropolis and Mental Life"; his work on "piety," "Superordination and Subordination," his concept of "formal sociology," his contrast of the individual's personal relations in small groups with the alien objectivity of large organizations characteristic of the external world, especially in urban industrial society; his pioneering work on the functions of social conflict (revived by Lewis Coser in the 1950's)—and, of course, for his original formulation and analysis of the "dyad" and "triad."

3. Susan Cavin, "A Social Connection Between Simmel and Cooley: Simmel's Antecedent Social Relationship by the Dyad and Cooley's Imaginary Social Relations," Rutgers University, unpublished paper, 1971-2, 76 pages; Susan Cavin, "A Re-examination of Simmel: 'On the Significance of Numbers for Social Life,'" Rutgers University, unpublished paper, 1975, 52 pages. Both of these papers were written in Peter Berger's theory courses at Rutgers. The first became my master's thesis at Rutgers University, 1973.

4. Marvin Harris, *Cannibals and Kings, op. cit.*

5. Simmel, *op. cit.*, p. 87.

6. Cf. C. R. Carpenter, "Societies of Monkeys and Apes," in *Primate Social Behavior*, ed. C. H. Southwick (Princeton, NJ: Van Nostrand, 1963), pp. 29, 31, 32, 40; Solly Zuckerman, *The Social Life of Monkeys and Apes* (London: Routledge and Kegan Paul, 1932); Marshall Sahlins, "The Origins of Society," *Scientific American*, vol. 203, no. 3, September 1960, pp. 76-87. Sahlins' work supports the thesis that the majority of males lead either a "solitary life outside of or on the fringes of the horde," and that: "there are typically more adult females than adult males within the horde, sometimes, as in the case of the howler monkeys, three times as many." See also Evelyn Reed, *Women's Evolution: From Matriarchal Clan to Patriarchal Family* (New York and Toronto: Pathfinder Press, 1975), p. 65; Lila Leibowitz, "Perspectives on the Evolution of Sex Differences," in *Toward an Anthropology of Women,* (New York: Monthly Review Press, 1975), pp. 25-33. In "The Origin of the Family," *op. cit.*, Kathleen Gough reports: "Chimpanzees, and also South American howler monkeys, live in loosely structured groups (as in most monkey and ape societies), with a preponderance of females."

7. Reed, *Women's Evolution..., op. cit.*, pp. 63-4.

8. *Ibid.*, p. 65.
9. Kathleen Gough, "The Origin of the Family," Reiter, ed., *Toward an Anthropology of Women, op. cit.*, p. 55.
10. Lila Leibowitz, "Perspectives on the Evolution of Sex Differences," *Toward an Anthropology of Women, op. cit.*, p. 35.
11. Gough, *op. cit.*, p. 57.
12. *Ibid.*
13. Leibowitz, *op. cit.*, pp. 25-6.
14. Gough, *op. cit.*, p. 57.
15. Sahlins, "The Origins of Societies," *op. cit.*, p. 81; and Carpenter, *op. cit.*, pp. 29-32.
16. Frederick Engels, *The Origin of the Family, Private Property and the State* (New York: International Publishers, 1972).
17. August Bebel, *Women Under Socialism*, translated by Daniel De Leon, (New York: Schocken, 1971), pp. 127-66.
18. *Ibid.*, p. 127.
19. *Ibid.*, pp. 128-31. Bebel reports sex ratio data on five world areas: Europe, 51.2% female to 48.8% male; "North America and Islands (1880-1890), 49.5% female to 50.5% male; "Central American and the West Indies" (1877-1889), 48.5% female to 51.5% male; "South America total" (1872-1891), 48.7% female to 51.3% male; "Russian Possessions, total" (1885), 47.3% female to 52.7% male; "total population in Asia" (1877-1891), 48.9% female to 51.1% male.

    Hong Kong in 1889 had the lowest female population relative to male, reported by Bebel: 29% female relative to 71% male. Hawaii in 1890 rates second lowest female sex ratio: 34.8% female relative to 65.2% male. The finding that bothers Bebel most is that even under these mostly near-equal sex ratios in the 19th century, not all women are married to men.
20. Marvin Harris, "Why Men Dominate Women," *New York Times*, 13 November 1977, pp. 46, 115-23. See especially p. 116.
21. *Ibid.*, pp. 118-19.
22. *Ibid.*
23. Claude Levi-Strauss, *The Elementary Forms of Kinship* (Boston: Beacon, 1969), p. 38.
24. Elman Service, *Profiles in Ethnology* (New York: Harper & Row, 1971), chapter 9, "The Jivaro of South America," see p. 196. Service writes: "Constant warfare has caused a considerable numerical predominance of women in Jivaro society, and a consequent prevalence of polygyny."
25. Cf. George Peter Murdock, "World Ethnographic Sample," *American Anthropologist*, 59:664-687 (August 1957), p. 686. There are only 4 out of 554 societies in Murdock's 1957 sample where polyandry obtains. Three of these polyandrous societies are located in East Eurasia, while one is present in the Insular Pacific. Polyandry may be the result of a disturbed balance of the sexes, or it may under under near equal sex ratios. There are two forms of polyandry: 1) where the husbands of a woman are brothers; or 2) where the husbands of a woman may not be

related kin. The number of children in polyandrous families is reportedly low; in India, sometimes four to five brothers will only have three to four children or less. Polyandry is not generally considered a "primitive institution." It is theoretically a patriarchal institution that is actually less widespread than "woman-marriage."

See also D.N. Majumdar, *Races and Cultures of India* (London: Asin Publishing House, 1961), pp. 199-222, chapter X, "Family and Marriage in Polyandrous Society."

26. Georg Simmel, "On the Significance of Numbers for Social Life," *The Sociology of Georg Simmel*, trans. and ed. Kurt H. Wolff (New York: Free Press, 1950); see also Simmel, "The Numbers of Members as Determining the Sociological Form of the Group," *The American Journal of Sociology*, VIII, no. 1, 1-16, July 1902; no. 2, 158-196, September 1902.

Chapter 5: High Female Societies

1. I thank Rhoda Goldstein and Martin Oppenheimer, both of Rutgers University, for their criticism and suggestions in developing this chapter. Dr. Oppenheimer first suggested that I test my hypotheses on sex variables in the *Human Relations Area Files*, which proved to be a great asset to this work. I must credit Mary S. Hartman, Adrienne Rich, and Janet Siskind for their criticisms which necessitated my drawing an original sex ratio sample upon which to test my sex ratio hypotheses. These criticisms led to the discovery of critical empirical support for my sex ratio theories. I am deeply grateful for their help and encouragement.

See Appendix B: Methodology, for general research design and for sex ratio methodology. My sex ratio sample of 100 societies is drawn from the *Human Relations Area Files (HRAF)* at City University of New York. All information directly on sex ratios in this book derive from the HRAF/-CUNY. See also *HRAF Source Bibliography* (New Haven: Human Relations Area Files, Inc., 1976). The *Human Relations Area Files* originated at Yale University, and is published in New Haven, Connecticut. The *HRAF* is housed at several universities; the *HRAF* that I used throughout this study is located at CUNY on 42nd Street in New York City.

George Peter Murdock's compilation of cross-cultural data and his outlines of cultures have been invaluable to this study. See G.P. Murdock, *Outline of World Cultures* (New Haven: Human Relations Area Files, Inc., 1963); G.P. Murdock, Clellan S. Ford, Alfred E. Hudson, Raymond Kennedy, Leo W. Simmons, John W.M. Whiting, *Outline of Cultural Materials*, vol. 1 (New Haven: Human Relations Area Files, Inc., 1967); Murdock, *Ethnographic Atlas* (Pittsburgh: University of Pittsburgh Press, 1967); Murdock, "World Ethnographic Sample," *American Anthropologist*, vol. 59, no. 4, August 1957.

2. For more sex ratio data, see Appendix C: Tables. The data on "mean size of local communities" derives from Murdock's 1967 *Ethnographic Atlas, op. cit.*, pp. 51-2, column 31. The other tables derive information from

Murdock's 1957 "World Ethnographic Sample, *op. cit.* All information directly on sex ratios derives from the *HRAF.*

3. It is my theory that high-male/low-female total and adult populations characterize the societal sex ratios of patriarchal transition. In *Goddesses, Whores, Wives and Slaves...,* *op. cit.,* pp. 68-70, Sarah Pomeroy presents evidence on sex ratios from skeletal remains from classical Greece, which — according to gynologists — represents a society in transition to western patriarchy. Pomeroy writes: "J. Lawrence Angel's studies of skeletal remains indicate that the average adult longevity in Classical Greece was 45.0 years for males and 36.2 for females. Other sorts of studies give lower figures for both sexes, but all agree that females predeceased males by an average of five to ten years. Without the intervention of war — which would seletively affect the mortality of males — the sex differences in longevity alone would be responsible for a large ratio of men to women in the population... What proportion of the citizenry was male, what proportion female?... Homosexuality, anal intercourse, recourse to prostitutes and slaves or dislike of women, and the preference for a sexually inactive wife continued to be adaptations for population control... The Athenians understood that the simplest means of controlling the growth of the population was by increasing or decreasing the number of females who could produce citizen children... In normal times, when citizen men outnumbered citizen women, there was not enough brides for each man to be able to marry... It must be recognized that ancient literary sources may merely take note of the children who mattered most: that is, the boys. But a casual survey definitely gives the impression of a preponderance of male children among well-known Athenians... Johannes Kirchner's classical work, *Prosopographica Attica,* shows that, of 346 families, 271 had more sons than daughters and that the ratio of boys to girls is roughly five to one."

Pomeroy gives further information on the sex ratio of Greece's dark age (c. 1,000-600 B.C.): "The male-female population ratio at this period is startling: The Agora burial plot by the Tholos shows almost twice as many male burials as female, and the study of *prothesis* and *ekphora* vases also show more male burials than female. This imbalance could be explained away by speculating that more men were honored with prestigious burials than women. But Homer, who is probably relating a Bronze Age tradition, although he may be reflecting the Dark Age, states that Priam had fifty sons but only twelve daughters; Nausicaa is an only daughter with a number of brothers; Andromache mentions her seven brothers. We have also seen that some Greek colonies were founded by men alone... An ecologically sound method of limiting population is the destruction of the reproducing members of the group, the females, and the most likely reason for sexual imbalance in a population is female infanticide. While it cannot be proven beyond doubt that newborn females were selectively eliminated, the evidence seems to point that way." See also Pomeroy, *op. cit.,* p. 140 regarding high-male/low-female sex ratios, and pp. 227-8 for her summary of the sex ratios of classical antiquity: "In

18 B.C. according to the historian Cassius Dio there were more upper-class men than women. Such is my perception of the ratio of males to females, not only in the Roman upper class in the days of Augustus, but, with few exceptions, in all social strata throughout classical antiquity. A selection from the crude and haphazard data of various periods and places in antiquity shows that males outnumbered females by at least two to one. These are the sex ratios to be deduced from the funerary artifacts of the Dark Age and Archaic period, the prosopographical [biographical] studies of propertied families in classical Athens, sepulchral inscriptions of slaves and freedmen in the early empire, and the list of children receiving the alimentary fund at Veleia. Were there actually fewer females than males in antiquity, or is the apparent disproportion between the sexes illusory? Demographers point out that when a census is taken in an underdeveloped country, women are not adequately counted... Either women were undernumerated when living and undercommemorated after death to an extent that can only be described as startling, or there actually were fewer women than men, or both of these factors operated simultaneously." For further information on upper-class and slave sex ratios in Roman antiquity, see Pomeroy, *op. cit.*, pp. 164 and 194. Thanks to Mary Hartman for her informative discussions of Pomeroy and historical sex ratios at patriarchal transition with me.

4. Hortense Powdermaker, "Vital Statistics of New Ireland (Bismarck Archipelago) as revealed in genealogies," *Human Biology*, vol. 3, 1931, pp. 351-75; see especially page 366. Cf. G. H. L. F. Pitt-Rivers, *The Clash of Culture* (London: 1927), as cited in Powdermaker.

5. Henry Ling Roth, *The Aborigines of Tasmania*, assisted by Marion E. Butler, preface by Edward B. Tylor (London: Kegan Paul, Trench, Trubner, 1890). Card 29, *HRAF* microfiche.

6. Paul Schebesta, *Die Negrito Asiens*, II Band, Ethnographie der Negrito (Halbband, Wirtschaft and Soziologie Wien-Modling, St.-Gabriel-Verlag, 1954 and 1957).

7. W. Lloyd Warner, "Mahkarolla and Murngin Society," in *A Black Civilization: A Social Study of an Australian Tribe* (New York: Harper & Bros., 1958).

8. Ronald M. Berndt, "Murngin (Wulamba) Social Organization," *American Anthropologist*, vol. 57, 1955, pp. 84-106.

9. Evans-Pritchard, "Some Aspects of Marriage and Family Among the Nuer," *HRAF* microfiche, New York Public Library, 42nd St., New York.

10. See Rafael Karsten, "The Head Hunters of western Amazonas: the life and culture of the Jibaro Indians of eastern Ecuador and Peru (Helsingfors, Central-tryckeriet, 1935); and Bengt Danielsson, "Some attraction and repulsion patterns among Jibaro Indians: a study in sociometric anthropology," *Sociometry*, 12 (1949): 83-105.

Chapter 6: Cross-Cultural Lesbianism

1. Although this chapter is primarily concerned with human lesbianism, a brief section on cross-species lesbianism is fascinating, and the best place to begin this empirical investigation of the expanse of female sexuality.

   Lesbianism has been observed among numerous subprimate mammals: domestic cats, horses, lions, dogs, rabbits, pigs, sheep, guinea pigs, cattle, rats, mice and hamsters, according to Clellan Ford's and Frank Beach's study of *Patterns of Sexual Behavior* (Scranton, Penn.: Harper & Bros — Hoeber, 1952), pp. 138-43.

   In *The Great Apes: A Study of Anthropoid Life* (New Haven: Yale University Press, 1929), Ada and Robert Yerkes report homosexual "copulatory play" among chimpanzees, and obliquely suggest a female gibbon's lesbian attraction to a human female:

   > It has been remarked by various authorities that some at least of the gibbons tend to be more reserved toward man than toward women, and in some instances to exhibit very marked preferences. This obviously may be due on the one hand to the treatment received by the animal from persons, or, on the other, to sex interest. We have observed the latter in a mature female wau-wau. (p. 259).

   Wainwright Churchill, in *Homosexual Behavior Among Males: A Cross-Cultural and Cross-Species Investigation* (Englewood Cliffs, NJ: Prentice-Hall-Prism, 1971), adds more animals and information to the queer list:

   > Objective observation of the sexual behavior of lower animals has revealed that sexual contacts between individuals of the same sex occur in almost every species of mammal that has been extensively studied. Homosexual behavior, for example, has been observed by scientists among monkeys, dogs, bulls, rats, porcupines, guinea pigs, goats, horses, donkeys, elephants, hyenas, bats, mice, lions, rabbits, cats, raccoons, baboons, apes and porpoises. (pp. 60-1).

   See also A.C. Kinsey, W.B. Pomeroy, C.E. Martin, and P.H. Gebbhard, *Sexual Behavior in the Human Female* (Philadelphia: W.B. Saunders, 1953), pp. 448-50. Kinsey, *et. al.* write: "The impression that infrahuman mammals more or less confine themselves to heterosexual activities is a distortion of the fact which appears to have originated in man-made philosophy, rather than in specific observations of mammalian behavior. Biologists and psychologists who have accepted the doctrine that the only natural function of sex is reproduction, have simply ignored the existence of sexual activity which is not reproductive. They have assumed that heterosexual responses are a part of an animal's innate, 'instinctive' equipment, and that all other types of sexual activity represent 'perversions' of the 'normal instincts.' Such interpretations are, however, mystical. They do not originate in our knowledge of the physiology of sexual response, and can be maintained only if one assumes that sexual function is in some fashion divorced from the physiologic processes which control other functions of the animal body. It may be true that heterosexual contacts outnumber homosexual contacts in most species of mammals, but it would be hard to demonstrate that this depends upon the 'normality' of heterosexual responses, and the 'abnormality' of homosexual responses."

Solly Zuckerman reports in *The Social Life of Monkeys and Apes* that the mounting of one female by another is common among baboons. Ford and Beach inform that:

> Mounting of one female by another is not confined to the primates. It is, in fact, common among many subprimate mammals... There are several indications that the appearance of malelike behavior in females is closely related to a condition of sexual arousal. For example, female rabbits normally do not ovulate unless they have copulated with a buck [male rabbit]. But when one estrous doe [female rabbit] mounts another and executes vigorous copulatory thrusts, the *mounting animal* may ovulate afterward. Furthermore, this type of behavior is, for many species, closely associated with estrus, the time at which the female is sexually receptive. Stockbreeders have long been aware of this fact and have taken the occurrence of masculine behavior as a reliable sign of receptivity on the part of the female showing the temporary sexual inversion. Sows that are ready to breed are often said to 'go boaring,' mares in heat are said to 'horse,' and cows to 'bull.' Laboratory investigations of female guinea pigs demonstrate that mounting behavior shown toward other females is a regular precursor or accompaniment of the estrous condition. This form of behavior is induced in spayed females by injections of the same ovarian hormones that produce feminine receptivity. A female hormone is not essential to mounting behavior in all species, however, for spayed rats and dogs are known to display such behavior without any endocrine treatment. (pp. 141-2).

It seems queer to me that stockbreeders and sexuality researchers routinely consider lesbian mounting (known in heterosexist literature as "masculine" behavior or "sexual inversion") as a "reliable sign" of heterosexuality among females. This reasoning is inverted.

Aside: The concept and term, "inversion," which is central to Marx's brilliant theoretical construct of "ideology," is also the 19th century term for "true homosexuality." "Inverts" are true homosexuals. This is an interesting subliminal terminology spillover. In the late 1970's, "inversion" was the term used by the Weather Underground to denote resurfacing from underground to aboveground political work. This word has been through many political changes in the last two centuries.

If it is the practice of many female mammals to display lesbian sexuality initially at estrus, this is a powerful piece of information. It disproves the heterosexist contention that all animals are "instinctually" heterosexual, but it also reveals that commonly lesbianism hystorically precedes heterosexuality or the heterosexual act among female primates and mammals.

On 23 November 1977, the *New York Times* indexed a new discovery in the "News Summary" under the subsection, "Health/Science," titled: "Widespread Lesbianism is found among Seagulls." Molly and George Hunt of the University of California at Irvine spent three years studying 1,200 pairs of western seagulls on Santa Barbara Island, described as "an uninhabited rock about 40 miles southwest of Los Angeles." The *New York Times* reported these findings:

A university research team says that about 14% of the female seagulls on an island off the California coast are lesbians, calling it the first solid evidence of widespread homosexuality among wild birds. One of the female gulls assumes a male role and the birds form stable unions like those of heterosexual seagulls: they go through the motions of mating, lay sterile eggs and defend their nests like other couples, the report said. No evidence of homosexuality among male birds was found. 'We were absolutely astounded' at the discovery, said Dr. George Hunt of the University of California at Irvine. 'This sort of thing has not been found before and was clearly not what we anticipated.' (p. A-12).

This is an important finding, due to the fact that generally patriscientists report only male homosexuality, when they report homosexuality at all— implying that lesbianism is rare or absent. The patriscientific practice of either omitting or underreporting lesbian sexuality holds across the study of both human and nonhuman animal societies, with only a few classic exceptions. The Hunt evidence is indeed rare.

This brief section on cross-species lesbianism does not exhaust the subject. Nevertheless, it does empirically support the hypothesis that lesbianism occurs across nonhuman mammalian society. Lesbianism has been observed among: baboons, gibbons, chimpanzees, domestic cats, horses, lions, rabbits, dogs, pigs, sheep, guinea pigs, cattle, rats, hamsters, mice, goats, porcupines, elephants, bats, hyenas, raccoons, donkeys, and porpoises. Among wild birds, lesbianism has been observed among seagulls in significant statistical numbers.

The remaining sexuality hypotheses in chapter 6 will be tested on George Peter Murdock's 1957 "World Ethnographic Sample" of 565 societies. These 30 societies, which report lesbianism and are at the same time indexed in Murdock 1957, form the data base of my hypothesis tests on female sexuality.

2. The regional distribution of the 565 societies coded in Murdock 1957, *op. cit.*, is as follows: Africa—116 societies (21%); Circum-Mediterranean— 76 societies (14%); East Eurasia—85 societies (15%); Insular Pacific—99 societies (17%); North America—110 societies (19%); South America—77 societies (14%).

3. *Ibid.*, p. 686. Murdock's Table 2, "Regional Variations in the Incidence of Plural Marriages," reveals that 75% of world society prefers to practice some form of polygyny.

4. Thanks to Janet Siskind of Rutgers University for differentiating between these two phenomena, and suggesting a separate section on "woman-marriage."

5. Gough, cited in Marvin Harris, *Culture, People, Nature: An Introduction to General Anthropology* (New York: Crowell, 1975), p. 318.

6. *Ibid.*

7. Melville J. Herskovits, "A Note on 'Woman Marriage' in Dahomey, *Africa*, vol. 10, no. 3, 1937.

8. Herskovits, *The Myth of the Negro Past* (Boston: Beacon, 1958), p. 172.

9. Carolyn Niethammer, *Daughters of the Earth: The Lives and Legends of*

American Indian Women (London and New York: Collier, 1977).

10. Lewis, *op. cit.*

11. Jonathan Katz, *Gay American History: Lesbians and Gay Men in the U.S.A.* (New York: Crowell, 1976), pp. 293-8.

12. Magalhaes, *op. cit.*

13. D. Taraore, "Yaro Ha ou mariages entre femmes chez les Bobo Nienege," *Journal de la Société des Africanistes*, vol. XI, 1941, pp. 197-200; cited in M. Perlman and M.P. Moal, "Analytical Bibliography," in Paulme (ed.), *Women of Tropical Africa* (Berkeley and Los Angeles: University of California Press, 1971), p. 240.

14. McMurtrie, in Katz, *op. cit.*, p. 322.

15. Churchill, *op. cit.*, p. 61.

16. Ford and Beach, *op. cit.*, p. 133.

17. A.C. Kinsey, W.B. Pomeroy, C.E. Martin, and P.H. Gebbhard, *Sexual Behavior in the Human Female* (Philadelphia: W.B. Saunders, 1953).

18. K.B. Davis, *Factors in the Sex Life of Twenty-Two Hundred Women* (New York: Harper & Bros., 1929).

19. *Ibid.*; see also Frank S. Caprio, *Female Homosexuality* (New York: Citadel Press, 1954), p. 56.

20. Shere Hite, *The Hite Report: A Nationwide Study of Female Sexuality* (New York: Dell, 1976).

21. G.V. Hamilton, *A Research in Marriage* (New York: A.C. Boni, 1929).

22. C. Landis and M.M. Bolles, *Personality and Sexuality of Physically Handicapped Women* (New York: Paul Hoeber, 1942).

23. Sidney Abbott and Barbara Love, "Is Women's Liberation a Lesbian Plot?", in *Woman in Sexist Society: Studies in Power and Powerlessness*, eds. Vivian Gornick and Barbara K. Moran (New York: Mentor-New American Library, 1972), p. 603.

24. Havelock Ellis, "Sexual Inversion," *Studies in the Psychology of Sex* (New York: Random House, 1936), vol. 2, p. 124.

25. Edward Westermarck, *The Origin and Development of Moral Ideas* (London:O Macmillan, 1926), vol. II, chapter XLIII, "Homosexual Love," pp. 456-89.

26. *Ibid.*, pp. 464-5.

27. Margaret Mead, *Coming of Age in Samoa* (New York: William Morrow, 1930).

28. *Ibid.*, p. 285.

29. Tobias Schneebaum, *Keep the River On Your Right*, as cited in Bob McCubbin, *The Gay Question: A Marxist Appraisal* (New York: World View Publishers, 1976), p. 6.

30. G.W. Henry, *Sex Variants* (New York: Paul S. Hoeber, 1941). See also Alan P. Bell and Martin S. Weisberg, *Homosexualities* (New York: Simon and Schuster, 1978).

31. Hite, *op. cit.*, p. 229. See Tables on pp. 230, 231, 612-18.

32. Bridget Overton, and editor at *Lesbian Tide* (vol. 8, no. 2, September/-

October 1978, p. 20) wrote: "Books Confiscated — *The Joy of Lesbian Sex* and *The Joy of Gay Sex* were two of a dozen confiscated from three bookstores in Lexington, Kentucky. This was the city's initial enforcement of a new anti-porno law that prohibits the display of sexually explicit material in premises frequented by minors. And in a separate action, B. Dalton Book Company, headquartered in New York, has banned the display of both books in its 300 stores. Store managers have been advised to keep the books off the selling floor and to make them available to adult customers only on request."

Chapter 7: Sex Separation

1. See Evelyn Reed, *Women's Evolution: From Matriarchal Clan to Patriarchal Family* (New York and Toronto: Pathfinder Press, 1975), on sex segregation among primates as a natural safeguard for the female.
2. The oldest historical data I have on sexual segregation is reported by Aristotle on Crete. See *The Politics of Aristotle, op. cit.,* p. 82.
3. Most of the data presented here on "female languages" is derived from the work of Ernest Crawley, *The Mystic Rose: A Study of Primitive Marriage and of Primitive Thought in its Bearing on Marriage* (London: Spring Books, 1965), pp. 77-83.
4. *South American Cultures, op. cit.,* p. 122.
5. Crawley, *The Mystic Rose..., op. cit.,* p. 77.
6. Edward Westermarck, *The History of Human Marriages,* as cited in Crawley, *The Mystic Rose..., op. cit.,* p. 83.
7. *Ibid.*
8. *Ibid.,* p. 79.
9. *Ibid.*
10. *Ibid.,* pp. 79-80.
11. Robert Briffault, *The Mothers: A Study of the Origin of Sentiments and Institutions* (New York: Macmillan, 1952).
12. *Ibid.,* p. 65.
13. George Peter Murdock, *Ethnographic Atlas,* Pittsburg: University of Pittsburg Press, 1967, pp. 63, 67, 71, 75, 79, 83, 87, 91, 95, 99, 103, 107, 111, 115, 119, 123.
14. *Ibid.,* p. 53.

Chapter 8: Women's Liberations

1. Marjorie Topley, "Marriage Resistance in Rural Kwangtung," in *Women in Chinese Society,* eds. Margery Wolf and Roxane Witke (Stanford, CA: Stanford University Press, 1975), pp. 67-88. Topley writes: "For approximately one hundred years, from the early 19th to the early 20th century, numbers of women in a rural area of the Canton delta either refused to marry or, having married, refused to live with their husbands. Their resist-

ance to marriage took regular forms. Typically they organized themselves into sisterhoods. The women remaining spinsters took vows before
a deity, in front of witnesses, never to wed. Their vows were preceded by
a hairdressing ritual resembling the one traditionally performed before
marriage to signal a girl's arrival at social maturity. This earned them the
title 'women who dress their own hair,' *tzu-shunii.* The others, who were
formally married but did not live with their husbands, were known as *pu
lo-chia,* 'women who do not go down to the family,' i.e., women who
refuse to join their husband's family." See J. Dyer Ball, *Things Chinese*
(Shanghai: 1925), p. 6, regarding evidence of female language among
these marriage resistant sisterhoods in China.

2. *Hysteconomy* is the hystory of women's labor; it is, as well, the basal
   structure of all economies.

3. *Webster's...*, *op. cit.*, pp. 1165-6.

4. I learned this term from Irene Mascolo.

5. This is Mary Daly's concept.

6. Kathleen Gough, "Variation in Preferential Marriage Forms," in *Matrilineal Kinship, op. cit.*, pp. 614-30.

7. Yolanda Murphy, *Women of the Forest* (New York: Columbia University
   Press, 1974); Robert F. Murphy, *The Trumai Indians of Central Brazil*
   (Seattle: University of Washington Press, 1955).

8. Ruby Rohrlich-Leavitt, Barbara Sykes, and Elizabeth Weatherford,
   "Aboriginal Woman: Male and Female Anthropological Perspectives,"
   in *Toward an Anthropology of Women, op. cit.*, pp. 111-12.

9. Paula Webster, "Matriarchy: A Vision of Power," in *Toward an Anthropology of Women, op. cit.*, p. 154.

10. Judith Van Allen, "'Aba Riots' or Igbo 'Women's War'? Ideology, Strati-
    fication, and the Invisibility of Women," in *Women in Africa: Studies in
    Social and Economic Change*, eds. Nancy J. Hafkin and Edna G. Bay
    (Stanford: Stanford University Press, 1976), pp. 59-85. Van Allen writes:
    "The term, 'Women's War,' in contrast to 'Aba Riots,' retains both the
    presence and the significance of the women, for the word 'war' in this
    context derived from the pidgin English expression, 'making war,' an
    institutionalized form of punishment employed by Igbo women and also
    known as 'sitting on a man.' To 'sit on' or 'make war on' a man involved
    gathering at his compound at a previously agreed upon time, dancing,
    singing scurrilous songs detailing the women's grievances against him
    (and often insulting him along the way by calling his manhood into
    question), banging on his hut with pestles used for pounding yams, and,
    in extreme cases, tearing up his hut (which usually meant pulling the roof
    off). This might be done to a man who particularly mistreated his wife,
    who violated the women's market rules, or who persistently let his cows
    eat the women's crops. The women would stay at his hut all night and
    day, if necessary, until he repented and promised to mend his ways."

11. Topley, *op. cit.*

12. Exceptions to this rule are the works of Thorstein Veblen, W.I. Thomas,
    and the empirical works produced by the Kinsey Institute.

Bibliography

Abbott, Sidney, and Love, Barbara. "Is Women's Liberation a Lesbian Plot?", in Gornick and Moran (eds.), *Woman in Sexist Society*. New York: New American Library, 1971.

Aberle, David F. "Matrilineal Descent in Cross-Cultural Perspective," in Schneider and Gough (eds.), *Matrilineal Kinship*. Berkeley: University of California Press, 1962.

Adams, Kathleen Joy. "The Barama River Caribs of Guyana Restudied: 40 Years of Cultural Adaptation and Population Change." Ph.D. dissertation, Case Western University, 1972.

Arensberg, Conrad Maynadier, and Kimball, Solon Toothaker. *Family and Community in Ireland*. Cambridge: Harvard University Press, 1940.

Bachofen, Johann Jacob. *Myth, Religion, and Mother Right: Selected Writings*. Translated by Ralph Manheim, with a preface by George Boas, and introduction by Joseph Campbell. Princeton, NJ: Princeton University Press, 1967.

Batchelor, John. *Ainu Life and Lore: Echoes of a Departing Race*. Tokyo: Kyobunkwan, 1927.

Beaglehole, Pearl, and Beaglehole, Ernest. *Ethnology of Pukapuka*. Honolulu: Bernice P. Bishop Museum, 1938.

Bebel, August. *Women Under Socialism*. Translated by Daniel DeLeon, with a new introduction by Lewis Coser. New York: Schocken, 1971.

Berndt, Ronald. "Murngin (Wulamba) Social Organization." *American Anthropologist*, 57:834-106 (1955).

Boas, Franz. *Race, Language and Culture*. New York: Free Press, 1966.

Bogoras, Waldemar. *The Chukchee*. New York: G. E. Stechert, 1904.

Bohannan, Paul. *Tiv Farm and Settlement*. London: Her Majesty's Stationary Office, 1957.

Boker, H., and von Bulow, F.W. *The Rural Exodus in Czechoslovakia*. Geneva: P.S. King and Son, 1935.

Bouroncle Carreón, Alfonso. "Contribución al estudio de los Aymaras," *América Indígena*, 24: 129-169, 233-269 (1964).

Bowers, Alfred William. *Mandan Social and Ceremonial Organization.* Chicago: University of Chicago Press, 1950.

Briffault, Robert. *The Mothers: A Study of the Origin of Sentiments and Institutions.* New York: Macmillan, 1952.

Brown, Judith. "Iroquois Women: An Ethnohistoric Note," in Reiter (ed.), *Toward an Anthropology of Women.* New York: Monthly Review Press, 1975.

Brownmiller, Susan. *Against Our Will: Men, Women and Rape.* New York: Bantam, 1975.

Calverton, V. F., ed. *The Making of Man.* Westport, Conn.: Modern Library, 1931.

Carpenter, C. R. "Societies of Monkeys and Apes," in Southwick (ed.), *Primate Social Behavior.* Princeton, NJ: Van Nostrand, 1963.

Carpenter, Edward. *Intermediate Types Among Primitive Folk: A Study in Social Evolution.* London: Allen and Unwin, 1919.

Carter, William E. *Aymara Communities and the Bolivian Agrarian Reform.* Gainesville, Florida: University of Florida Press, 1965.

Chamberlain, Alexander. "Recent Literature on the South American 'Amazons'," *Journal of American Folklore,* 24: 16-20 (1911).

Childe, V. Gordon. *Man Makes Himself.* New York: New American Library, 1951.

Chinnery, E. W. *Studies of the Native Population of the East Coast of New Ireland.* Canberra: H. J. Green Government Printer, 1931.

Churchill, Charles Wesley. *The City of Beirut: A Socio-economic Survey.* Beirut: American University of Beirut, 1954.

Churchill, Wainwright. *Homosexual Behavior Among Males: A Cross-Cultural and Cross-Species Investigation.* Englewood Cliffs, NJ: 1967.

Clark, J. Desmond. *The Prehistory of Africa.* Southampton, England: Thames and Hudson, 1970.

Cline, Walter Buchanan. *Notes on the People of Siwah and El Garah in the Libyan Desert.* Menasha, Wisconsin: Banta, 1936.

Cook, Sherburne F. *The Aboriginal Population of the San Joaquín Valley, California.* Berkeley: University of California Press, 1955.

Cooper, John Montgomery. "Patagonian and Pampean Hunters," in Steward (editor), *Handbook of South American Indians.* Washington DĊ: Government Printing Office, 1946.

Coser, Lewis. *Masters of Sociological Thought: Ideas in Historical and Social Context.* New York: Harcourt Brace Jovanovich, 1971.

Coult, Allan D. *Cross Tabulations of Murdock's World Ethnographic Sample.* St. Louis: University of Missouri, 1965.

Covarrubias, Miguel. *Island of Bali.* New York: Knopf, 1938.

Crawley, Ernest. *The Mystic Rose: A Study of Primitive Marriage and of Primitive Thought in its Bearing on Marriage.* London: Spring Books, 1965.

Crocker, Walter Russell. *Nigeria: A Critique of British Colonial Administration.* London: George Allen and Unwin, 1936.

Crosby, K. H. "Polygamy in Mende Country," *Africa,* 10: 249-264 (1937).

Culwick, Geraldine Mary. *A Dietary Survey among the Zande of the South-Western Sudan.* Khartoum: Agricultural Publications Committee for the Ministry of Agriculture, Sudan Government, 1950.

Damn, Hans. *The Central Carolines.* Hamburg: Friederichsen DeGruyter, 1938.

Danielsson, Bengt. "Some Attraction and Repulsion Patterns among Jibaro Indians: A Study in Sociometric Anthropology," *Sociometry,* 12: 83-105 (1949).

Davis, Katherine Bement. *Factors in the Sex Life of Twenty-Two Hundred Women.* New York: Harper and Bros., 1929.

DeBeauvoir, Simone. *The Second Sex.* New York: Knopf, 1953.

DeLaguna, Frederica. *The Story of a Tlingit Community: A Problem in the Relationship Between Archaeological, Ethnological, and Historical Methods.* Washington, DC: Smithsonian Institute, 1960.

Devereaux, George. "Institutionalized Homosexuality of the Mohave Indians," *Human Biology,* 9: 498-527 (1937).

Diner, Helen. *Mothers and Amazons: The First Feminine History of Culture.* Edited and translated by John Philip Lundin, introduced by Brigitte Berger. Garden City, NY: Anchor-Doubleday, 1973.

Djamour, Judith. *Malay Kinship and Marriage in Singapore.* London: Athlone Press, 1958.

Dobritzhofer, Martin. *An Account of the Abipones, an Equestrian People of Paraguay.* Translated from Latin by Sara Coleridge. London: J. Murray, 1822.

Downes, Roger Meaden. *The Tiv Tribe.* Kaduna: Government Printer, 1933.

Drapkin, I. *Contribution to the Demographic Study of Easter Island.* Honolulu: Bernice P. Bishop Museum, 1935.

Dubois, Cora. *The People of Alor: A Social-Psychological Study of an East Indian Island.* Minneapolis: University of Minnesota Press, 1944.

Elwin, Verrier. *The Muria and their Ghotul.* Bombay: Oxford University Press, 1947.

Engelhardt, Alexandr Platonovich. *A Russian Province of the North.* Translated from Russian by Henry Cooke. Westminister: Archibald Constable, 1899.

Engels, Frederick. *The Origin of the Family, Private Property and the State.* Introduced by Eleanor Burke Leacock. New York: International Publishers, 1972.

Erlich, Vera St. *Family in Transition: A Study of 300 Yugoslav Villages.* Princeton, NJ: Princeton University Press, 1966.

Fee, Elizabeth. "The Sexual Politics of Victorian Social Anthropology," in Hartman and Banner (eds.), *Clio's Consciousness Raised.* New York: Harper and Row, 1974.

Ferrars, Max, *Burma.* London: Low Marston, 1901.

Field, Henry. *Contributions to the Anthropology of Iran.* Chicago: Field Museum of Natural History, 1939.

Firth, Raymond Williams. *Malay Fishermen: Their Peasant Economy.* London: Kegan Paul, Trench, Trubner, 1946.

Flannery, Regina. *The Gros Ventres of Montana: Part I, Social Life.* Washington, DC: Catholic University of America, 1953.

Ford, Clellan S., and Beach, Frank A. *Patterns of Sexual Behavior.* Scranton, Penn.: Harper and Bros.-Hoeber, 1952.

Gifford, Edward Winslow. "The Cocopa," *University of California Publications in American Archaeology and Ethnology*, 31: 294 (1933).

Gluckman, Max. *Economy of the Central Barotse Plain.* Livingstone, Northern Rhodesia (Zambia): Rhodes-Livingstone Institute, 1941.

Goldenweiser, Alexander A. *On Iroquois Work.* Canada: Geological Survey Summary Reports, 1912: 464-475.

Gordon, Linda: *Woman's Body, Woman's Right: A Social History of Birth Control in America.* New York: Grossman-Viking, 1976.

Gorer, Geoffrey. *Himalayan Village: An Account of the Lepchas of Sikkim.* London: M. Joseph, 1938.

Gough, Kathleen. "The Origin of the Family," in Reiter (ed.), *Toward an Anthropology of Women.* New York: Monthly Review Press, 1975.

Gould Davis, Elizabeth. *The First Sex.* Baltimore: Penguin, 1971.

Grattan, F.J.H. *An Introduction to Samoan Custom.* Apia, Western Samoa: Samoa Printing and Publishing Co., 1948.

Graves, Robert. *The Greek Myths.* Baltimore: Penguin, 1955.

Grigolia, Alexander. *Custom and Justice in the Caucasus: The Georgian Highlanders.* Philadelphia: 1939.

Gullick, J.M. *Indigenous Political Systems of Western Malaya.* London: Athlone Press, 1958.

Gurdon, Philip Richard Thornhagh. *The Khasis.* London: D. Nutt, 1907.

Hall, Edward T., and Pelzer, Karl J. *The Economy of the Truk Islands: An Anthropological and Economic Survey.* Honolulu: U.S. Commercial Company Economic Survey, 1946.

Halpern, Joel Martin. *A Serbian Village.* New York: Columbia University Press, 1958.

Hamilton, G.V. "A Study of Sexual Tendencies in Monkeys and Baboons," *Journal of Animal Behavior*, 4 (1914).

Harris, Marvin. *Culture, People, Nature: An Introduction to General Anthropology.* New York: Crowell, 1975.

————. "Why Men Dominate Women," *New York Times*, 13 November 1977, pp. 46, 115-23.

Hart, Charles William, and Pilling, Arnold R. *The Tiwi of North Australia.* New York: Holt, 1960.

Herskovits, Melville J. "A Note on 'Woman Marriage' in Dahomey," *Africa*, 10, 3:335-341 (1937).

————. *The Myth of the Negro Past.* Boston: Beacon, 1941.

————. *Life in a Haitian Village.* New York: Octagon Books, 1964.

Hilger, Inez M. *A Social Study of One Hundred Fifty Chippewa Indian Families of the White Earth Reservation of Minnesota.* Washington, DC: Catholic University of America Press, 1939.

Hill, Polly. *Rural Hausa: A Village and a Setting.* Cambridge: At the University Press, 1972.

Hite, Shere, *The Hite Report: A Nationwide Study of Female Sexuality.* New York: Dell, 1976.

Hobley, C.W. "Anthropological Institute of Great Britain and Ireland, 33: 323-359 (1903).

Hofmann, Paul. "Women Active Among Radicals in West Europe," *New York Times*, 16 August 1977.

Hogbin, Herbert Ian. *The Island of Menstruating Men: Religion in Wogeo, New Guinea.* Scranton, Penn.: Chandler Publishing, 1970.

Holmberg, Allan R. *Nomads of the Long Bow: The Siriono of Eastern Bolivia.* Washington, DC: Government Printing Office: 1950.

Honigmann, John Joseph. *Culture and Ethos of Kaska Society.* New Haven: Yale University Press, 1949.

Howitt, A. W., and Fison, L. "From Mother-right to Father-right," *Journal of Anthropological Institute,* 12: 30-46 (1883).

Hrdlicka, Ales. *Physiological and Medical Observations among the Indians of Southwestern United States and Northern Mexico.* Washington, DC: Smithsonian Institution, Bureau of American Ethnology, 1908.

Hunter, William Wilson. "Statistical Account of the Khasi and Jaintia Hills," in *A Statistical Account of Assam.* London: Trubner, 1879.

Huntingford, G. W. B. *The Southern Nilo-Hamites.* London: International African Institute, 1953.

India. *National Council of Applied Economic Research: Techno-economic Survey of Kerala.* New Delhi: National Council of Applied Economic Research, 1962.

Islavin, Vladimir. "The Samoyed in their Domestic and Social Life." St. Petersburg, Russia: Ministerstva Gosudarstvennykh Imushchest, 1847.

James, Selma. *Sex, Race, and Class.* Bristol, England: Falling Wall Press, 1975.

Jenness, Diamond. *The Life of the Copper Eskimos.* Ottawa: F. A. Acland, King's Printer, 1922.

Kanter, Emmanuel. *The Amazons: A Marxian Study.* Chicago: Charles H. Kerr, 1926.

Karsten, Rafael. *The Head Hunters of Western Amazonas: The Life and Culture of the Jibaro Indians of Eastern Ecuador and Peru.* Helsingfors: Central-Tryckeriet, 1935.

Katz, Jonathan. *Gay American History: Lesbians and Gay Men in the U.S.A.* New York: Crowell, 1976.

Kelly, William Henderson. *The Papago Indians of Arizona: A Population and Economic Study.* Tucson: Bureau of Ethnic Research, University of Arizona, 1963.

Kramer, Augustin, and Nevermann, Hans. *Ralik-Ratak.* Hamburg: Friederichsen, DeGruyter, 1938.

Kroeber, A.L. "The Tubatulabal," in *Handbook of the Indians of California*. Washington, DC: Smithsonian Institute, 1925.

LaBarre, Weston. *The Aymara Indians of the Lake Titicaca Plateau, Bolivia*. Menasha, Wisconsin: American Anthropological Association, 1943.

Landor, Arnold Henry Savage. *Alone with the Hairy Ainu*. London: Murray, 1893.

Lauritsen, John, and Thorstad, David. *The Early Homosexual Rights Movement (1864-1935)*. New York: Times Change Press, 1974.

Leach, Edmund Ronald. *Pul Eliya, a Village in Ceylon: A Study of Land Tenure and Kinship*. Cambridge: University Press, 1961.

League of Nations. *European Conference on Rural Life, 1939, Lithuania*. Geneva: League of Nations, 1939.

Lebeuf, Annie M.D. "The Role of Women in the Political Organization of African Societies," in Paulme (ed.), *Women of Tropical Africa*. Berkeley and Los Angeles: University of California Press, 1971.

Leibowitz, Lila. "Perspectives on the Evolution of Sex Differences," in Reiter (ed.), *Toward an Anthropology of Women*. New York: Monthly Review Press, 1975.

Levi-Strauss, Claude. *The Elementary Structure of Kinship*. Boston: Beacon, 1969.

Lippert, Julius. *The Evolution of Culture*. New York: Macmillan, 1931.

Lowie, Robert Harry. *Social Life of the Crow Indians*. New York: American Museum of Natural History, 1912.

McClintock, Walter: *The Old North Trail, or Life Legends and Religion of the Blackfoot Indians*. Lincoln, Nebraska: University of Nebraska, 1968.

McCubbin, Bob: *The Gay Question: A Marxist Appraisal*. New York: World View Publishers, 1976.

McCulloch, Merran. *The Ovimbundu of Angola*. London: International African Institute, 1952.

McMurtrie, Douglas C. "Marriages Between Women." *Alienist and Neurologist*, 23: 497-499 (1902).

Maine, Henry. *The Early History of Institutions*. London: 1875.

Mair, Lucy Philip. *An African People in the Twentieth Century*. London: G. Routledge and Sons, 1934.

Majumdar, D.N. *Races and Cultures of India*. London: Asin Publishing House, 1961.

Mao Tse-Tung, *Quotations from Mao Tse-Tung*, Peking: Foreign Languages Press, 1967.

Marshall, Lorna. "Marriage among the !Kung Bushmen," *Africa*, 29: 335-364 (1959).

Marshall, William E. *A Phrenologist among the Todas*. London and New York: Macmillan, 1906.

Martin, M. Kay and Voorhies, Barbara. *Female of the Species*. New York and London: Columbia University Press, 1975.

Marx, Karl. *Capital*, vol. 1. New York: International Publishers, 1972.

Mason, Leonard. "Relocation of the Bikini Marshallese: A Study in Group Migration." Ph.D. dissertation, Yale University, 1954.

Masters, William Murray. "Rowanduz: A Kurdish Administrative and Mercantile Center." Ph.D. dissertation, University of Michigan, 1953.

Mead, Margaret. *Coming of Age in Samoa*. New York: William Morrow, 1930.

Metraux, Alfred. "Ethnography of the Chaco," in Steward (ed.), *Handbook of South American Indians*. Washington, DC: Government Printing Office, 1946, 197-370.

————. *Ethnology of Easter Island*. Honolulu: Bernice P. Bishop Museum, 1935.

Mickey, Margaret Portia. *The Cowrie Shell Miao of Kweichow*. Cambridge: Peabody Museum-Harvard University, 1947.

Millett, Kate. *Sexual Politics*. New York: Avon, 1971.

Mitchell, Juliet, *Woman's Estate*. New York: Pantheon, 1971.

Morgan, Lewis Henry. *The League of the Ho-De'No-Sau-Nee, Iroquois*. New Haven: Human Relations Area Files, 1954.

————. *Ancient Society*. Edited by Eleanor Burke Leacock. Cleveland: World Publishing Co., 1963.

Mukherjea, Charulal. *The Santals*. Calcutta: A. Mukherjee, 1962.

Murdock, George Peter. *Our Primitive Contemporaries*. New York: Macmillan, 1934.

————. "World Ethnographic Sample," *American Anthropologist*, 59: 664-687 (August 1957).

————. *Outline of World Cultures*. New Haven: Human Relations Area Files, Inc., 1963.

————. *Ethnographic Atlas*. Pittsburgh: University of Pittsburg Press, 1967.

Murphy, Robert Francis, and Quain, Buell. *The Trumai Indians of Central Brazil*. Locus Valley: J.J. Augustin, 1955.

Myron, Nancy, and Bunch, Charlotte, eds. *Lesbianism and the Women's Movement*. Baltimore: Diana Press, 1975.

Nadel, Siegfried Frederick. "The Kede: A Riverain State in Northern Nigeria," in Fortes and Evans-Pritchard (eds.), *African Political Systems*. London: Oxford University Press for the International African Institute, 1940: 164-195.

Niethammer, Carolyn. *Daughters of the Earth: The Lives and Legends of American Indian Women*. London and New York: Collier, 1977.

Oakley, Ann. *Woman's Work: The Housewife, Past and Present*. New York: Vintage-Random, 1974.

Ortner, Sherry. "Is Female to Male as Nature is to Culture?", in Rosaldo and Lamphere (eds.), *Woman, Culture, and Society*. Stanford: Stanford University Press, 1974.

Paine, Robert. *Coast Lapp Society II: A Study of Economic Development and Social Values*. Tromso: Universitets forlaget, 1965.

Parsons, Talcott, and Bales, Robert F. *Family, Socialization and Interaction Process*. New York: Free Press, 1955.

Petrov, Ivan. "The Limit of the Innuit Tribes on the Alaska Coast," *American Naturalist*, 16: 567-575 (1882).

Plutarch. *Lives of the Noble Greeks*. New York: Dell-Laurel, 1959.

Pomeroy, Sarah. *Goddesses, Whores, Wives, and Slaves: Women in Classical Antiquity*. New York: Schocken, 1975.

Powdermaker, Hortense. "Vital Statistics of New Ireland (Bismarck Archipelago) as revealed in genealogies," *Human Biology, 3: 351-375 (1931)*.

——————. *Life in Lesu: The Study of a Melanesian Society in New Ireland*. Foreword by Clark Wissler. New York: Norton, 1933.

Powell, H.A. "Competitive Leadership in Trobriand Political Organization," *Royal Anthropological Institute of Great Britain and Ireland*, 90: 118-145 (1960).

Prescott, James. "Body Pleasure and the Origins of Violence," *Bulletin of Atomic Scientists*, November 1975, p. 10f.

Radcliffe-Brown, A.R. *Structure and Function in Primitive Society*. London: Cohen and West, 1952.

Redfield, Robert, and Villa Rojas, Alfonso. *Chan Kom: A Maya Village*. Chicago: University of Chicago Press, 1934.

Reed, Evelyn. *Woman's Evolution: From Matriarchal Clan to Patriarchal Family*. New York and Toronto: Pathfinder Press, 1975.

Reichard, Gladys A. *Social Life of the Navajo Indians: with some attention to minor ceremonies.* New York: Columbia University Press, 1928.

Reichel-Dolmatoff, Gerardo. "Los Kogi: una triba de la Sierra Nevada de Santa Marta, Colombia," *Instituto Ethnológico Nacional*, 4: 1-319 (1949/1950).

Reynolds, Barrie. *Magic, Divination and Witchcraft among the Barotse of Northern Rhodesia.* London: Chatto and Windus, 1963.

Rich, Adrienne. *Of Woman Born.* New York: Norton, 1976.

Richards, Audrey I. "The Assimilation of the Immigrants and the Problem for Buganda," in Richards (ed.), *Economic Development and Tribal Change: A Study of Immigrant Labour in Buganda.* Cambridge: W. Heffer and Sons for the East African Institute of Social Research, 1954: 161-223.

Rivers, William Halse. *The Todas.* London and New York: Macmillan, 1906.

Rohrlich-Leavitt, Ruby; Sykes, Barbara; and Weatherford, Elizabeth. "Aboriginal Woman: Male and Female Anthropological Perspectives," in Reiter (ed.), *Toward an Anthropology of Women.* New York: Monthly Review Press, 1975.

Roscoe, John. *The Baganda: An Account of their Native Customs and Beliefs.* London: Macmillan, 1911.

Rubin, Gayle. "The Traffic in Women: Notes on the 'Political Economy' of Sex," in Reiter (ed.), *Toward an Anthropology of Women*, New York: Monthly Review Press, 1975.

Rush, Florence. "Freud and the Sexual Abuse of Children: The Freudian Cover-Up," *Chrysalis: A Magazine of Women's Culture*, 1: 31-45 (1977).

Sahlins, Marshall. "The Origin of Society," *Scientific American*, 203: 76-87 (September 1960).

————. *Stone Age Economics.* Chicago: Aldine, 1972.

Sanders, Irwin Taylor. *Balkan Village.* Lexington, Kentucky: University of Kentucky Press, 1949.

Sappho. New translation by Mary Barnard. Berkeley and Los Angeles: University of California Press, 1953.

Schlippe, Pierre de. *Shifting Cultivation in Africa: The Zande System of Agriculture.* London: Routledge and Kegan Paul, 1956.

Schram, Louis M.J. *The Monguors of the Kansu-Tibetan Border. Part II: Religious Life.* Philadelphia: American Philosophical Society, 1957.

Scott, Hilda. *Does Socialism Liberate Women? Experiences from Eastern Europe*. Boston: Beacon, 1975.

Senftt, Arno. "Journey of the Royal District Official Senftt in Yap to the Western Carolines," *Deutsches Kolonialblatt*, 15: 12-14 (1904).

Service, Elman. *Primitive Social Organization*. New York: Random House, 1968.

Simmel, Georg. *The Sociology of Georg Simmel*. Translated, edited and with an introduction by Kurt H. Wolff. New York: Free Press, 1950.

Slater, Philip. *The Glory of Hera: Greek Mythology and the Greek Family*. Boston: Beacon, 1968.

Slocum, Sally. "Woman the Gatherer: Male Bias in Anthropology," in Reiter (ed.), *Toward an Anthropology of Women*. New York: Monthly Review Press, 1975.

Smith, Robertson. *Kinship and Marriage in Early Arabia*. Boston: Beacon, 1903.

Smith, Watson, and Roberts, John Milton. *Zuni Law: A Field of Values*. Cambridge: Harvard University, 1954.

Sobol, Donald. *The Amazons of Greek Mythology*. London: Thomas Yoseloff Ltd., 1973.

Spier, Leslie. *Klamath Ethnology*. Berkeley: University of California Press, 1930.

Steggerda, Morris. *Maya Indians of Yucatán*. Washington, DC: Carnegie Institute of Washington, 1941.

Taylor, Douglas Macrae. "The Interpretation of some Documentary Evidence on Carib Culture," *Southwestern Journal of Anthropology*, 5: 379-392.

———. *Source Book for Social Origins*. Chicago and London: University of Chicago Press, 1909.

Thompson, Laura. *Fijian Frontier*. Introduction by Bronislaw Malinowski. San Francisco: American Council, Institution of Pacific Relations, 1940.

Tiger, Lionel. *Men In Groups*. New York: Vintage-Random, 1970.

Titiev, Mischa. *Old Oraibi: A Study of the Hopi Indians of Third Mesa*. New York: Kraus Reprint, 1971.

Topley, Marjorie. "Marriage Resistance in Rural Kwangtung," in Wolf and Witke (eds.), *Women in Chinese Society*. Stanford, CA: Stanford University Press, 1975: 67-88.

Turnbull, Colin M. *The Mbuti Pygmies: An Ethnographic Survey*. New York: American Museum of Natural History, 1965.

Tudde, Oedipussy. "Fashion Politics and the Fashion in Politics," in the C.L.I.T. Papers in *Off Our Backs*, 88: 17-19, July 1974.

Tylor, E.B. "On a Method of Investigating the Development of Institutions," in Kroeber and Waterman (eds.), *Source Book in Anthropology*. New York: Harcourt, Brace, 1931.

———. *Primitive Culture*. New York: Harper and Row, 1958.

———. *Researches into the Early History of Mankind*. Chicago and London: University of Chicago Press, 1964.

Veblen, Thorstein. *The Theory of the Leisure Class: An Economic Study of Institutions*. New York: Modern Library, 1934.

Von Bothner, Dietrich. *Amazons in Greek Art*. London: Oxford, 1957.

Waller, Wynne, Jr. *The Population of Czechoslovakia*. Washington, DC: Government Printing Office, 1953.

Warner, W. Lloyd. "Mahkarolla and Murngin Society," in *A Black Civilization: A Social Study of an Australian Tribe*. New York: Harper and Row, 1958.

Westermarck, Edward. *The History of Human Marriage*. London: Macmillan, 1903.

———. *The Origin and Development of Moral Ideas*. London: Macmillan, 1926.

Weltfish, Gene. *The Lost Universe; with a closing chapter on 'The Universe Regained.'* New York and London: Basic Books, 1965.

Wheeler-Voegelin, Erminie. *Tubatulabal Ethnography*. Berkeley: University of California Press, 1938.

White, Leslie. *The Science of Culture*. New York: Farrar, Straus and Cudahy, 1949.

Yalman, Nur. *Under the Botree: Studies in Caste, Kinship, and Marriage in the Interior of Ceylon*. Berkeley and Los Angeles: University of California Press, 1971.

Yasa, Ibrahim. *Hasanoglan: Socio-Economic Structure of a Turkish Village*. Ankara: Yeni Matbaa, 1957.

Yerkes, Ada, and Yerkes, Robert. *The Great Apes: A Study of Anthropoid Life*. New Haven: Yale University Press, 1929.

Zaretsky, Eli. *Capitalism, the Family and Personal Life*. Santa Cruz, CA: Loaded Press, 1973.

Zuckerman, Solly. *The Social Life of Monkeys and Apes*. London: Routledge and Kegan Paul, 1932.

Name Index

Hofmann, Paul: 77, 251-2.
Homer: 256.
Hunt, George: 259-60.
Hunt, Molly: 259-60.

Jacobs, Julius: 135.
Joan of Arc: 7.
Johnston, Jill: 229.

Kanter, Emmanuel: 67, 72-3, 78, 252.
Katz, Jonathan: 46, 122, 132.
King, Martin Luther: 36n.
Kinsey, Alfred: 133, 195, 258-9.
Kollontai, Alexandra: 127n.

Landis, C.: 135.
Lasch, Richard: 74.
Leacock, Eleanor Burke: 115, 228, 231.
Leibowitz, Lila: 41, 88, 90.
Lenin, Vladimir Ilyich: 18, 127n.
Leonard, Irving: 68-70, 250, 251.
Lévi-Strauss, Claude: 13, 93-4.
Lewinsohn, Richard: 245-6.
Lewis, Oscar: 75.
Lipper, Julius: 231.
Love, Barbara: 135.
Lubbock, J.: 230.

Magellan, Ferdinand: 65, 248.
Maine, Henry: 23i, 23, 28.
Mao Tse-tung: 240-1.
Markale, Jean: 252.
Martin, M. Kay: 45.
Marx, Karl: 22i, 18, 27, 34, 67, 169, 233, 238, 239-40, 242, 259.
McLennan, John Ferguson: 230.
McMurtrie, Douglas: 133.
Mead, Margaret: 135-6.
Millett, Kate: 30, 33, 231.
Mitchell, Juliet: 18, 33, 34.
Moal, M.P.: 132.
Montalvo, Garcirodríguez de: 69, 250.
Morgan, Elaine: 88n.
Morgan, Lewis Henry: 22i, 18, 26, 27, 231, 234, 235, 236, 237, 238.
Moyano, Maricla: 2, 229, 230, 247.
Murdock, George Peter: 29, 95, 119, 122-3, 124, 126, 147, 179, 184, 186, 193, 194, 195, 196, 197, 245, 254, 260.
Murielchild, Morgan: 229.
Murphy, Ed: 25i.

Naomi (of the old testament): 43, 243.
Nestle, Joan: 16i.
Niethammer, Carolyn: 45, 131.

Oppenheimer, Martin: 228, 239, 249, 255.
Orellana, Francisco de: 76, 248, 250-1.
Ortner, Sherry: 49.
O'Wyatt, Jane: 229.

Parsons, Talcott: 23i, 18, 28, 194.
Perlman, M.: 132.
Pigafetta, Filippo: 65.
Pitt-Rivers, G.H.L.F.: 113, 115.
Plato: 43-4, 245.
Plutarch: 43, 247-8.
Pomeroy, Sarah: 44, 244, 245, 256-7.
Powdermaker, Hortense: 113-15.
Priam (Trojan king): 256.

Raleigh, Walter: 248.
Reed, Evelyn: 86-7, 90.
Rich, Adrienne: 19i, 25, 228, 230, 255.
Rodríguez, Barboza: 74.
Rohrlich-Leavitt, Ruby: 28, 174.
Roth, Henry Ling: 115.
Rothery, G.C.: 74.
Rubin, Gayle: 34, 241.
Ruth (of the old testament): 43, 243.
Rylance, Mecca: 230.

Sacks, Karen: 34.
Sahlins, Marshall: 41, 90, 253.
Sappho: 2, 43, 44, 119, 243-4, 246.
Schebesta, Paul: 116.
Schneebaum, Tobias: 136.
Segerberg, Marsha: 229, 230.
Service, Elman: 94, 254.
Simmel, Georg: 13, 81-2, 242, 253.
Siskind, Janet: 255, 260.
Slater, Philip: 66, 67.
Small, Margaret: 243.
Smith, Adam: 239.
Sobol, Donald: 251.
Solomon, Barbara: 35.
Solomon, king: 84n.
Stalin, Joseph: 18, 127n, 238.
Stone, Merlin: 22i, 27.
Sykes, Barbara: 28, 174.
'Sylvia': 25i.

Subject Index

abduction of women: 26, 91, 165. *see also* 'marriage by capture.'

Abipon (of South America): 100, 107, 108.

abortion: 163n, 176.

academia, male: *see* patriscience.

adolescence: 41, 50, 54, 90, 94, 135, 138n, 141, 144, 148-52, 179-80, 182, 184, 186-7, 213, 215-17.

adultery: 44.

adult females: 41, 42-3, 62, 90, 141, 151.

adult males: 50-1, 55, 90, 141-2, 162.

Africa: 95, 103, 107, 108, 109, 110, 123, 126, 246; matrilineal societies in, 63, 65, 66, 67, 69, 248-9; woman-marriage in, 131; female languages in, 143, 144; segregation of adolescent boys in, 149-50.

age: 21, 206.

agriculture: 91, 237; and sex ratios, 104, 105, 110, 111, 112; and lesbianism, 124, 126, 208; and the sexual division of labor, 153, 154-7, 218-22.

Algeria: 63, 65.

all-female societies: 4, 44, 63, 84, 161, 169, 172.

all-male societies: 86, 87.

Alorese (of east Indonesia): 225.

Alout (of arctic America): 108.

Amarakaeri (of Peru): 122, 136.

Amazonas, Brazil: 65, 75-6, 143.

Amazons: 4, 12, 25, 48, 49, 50, 63-80, 84, 144, 164, 170, 247-52.

Americans, North (New England): 122, 123.

anarchy: 164, 173.

Anatolia (ancient Turkey): 63.

androgyny: in Plato's origin myth, 44; in Mohave tradition, 45-6.

Angola: 65.

animal husbandry: and sex ratios, 104, 105, 110, 111; and lesbianism, 124, 127, 208; and the sexual division of labor, 153.

animals, male exploitation of: 26-7, 30, 86-7, 173.

anthropology: 21, 23, 26, 27, 33, 34, 75, 92, 93-5, 113, 115-18, 120, 122, 129-33, 175, 234, 235.

anti-gay culture: 10; *see also* heterosexism.

anti-patriarchy: 22-3.

Aranda (Pacific islanders): 122, 123.

archaeology: 28, 196.

Argentina: 122.

aristocracy: 126, 206, 214.

Armenia: 65.

art: 43, 63, 68, 77, 161.

asexuality: *16i*, 8, 30, 40, 41, 42, 45, 53, 164. *see also* celibacy.

Asia: 63; *see* East Eurasia.

Asia Minor: 63, 69.

Asian Americans: 10.

Athens: 43, 64, 70, 122, 123, 244, 245-6, 256, 257. *see also* Greece.

aunt: 139.

aunt/niece relationship: 58, 141.

avunculocality: 29; defined, *16i*.

Aymara (of South America): 122, 123.

Azande (of Africa): 122, 123.

baboons: 86-7, 88.

Babylonians: 101.

bachelors: 150.

Bali (Pacific islanders): 46, 122, 123, 135.

Bantu, central (Africa): 29, 107.

Bavenda (of South Africa): 131.

Berbers (of north Africa): 143, 144.

betrayal of women (by heterosexist women): 37.

bible: 2n, 43, 48n, 55n, 84n, 165-6n, 234, 243.

bilateral descent: *16i*.

bilocality: *16i*, 106, 210.

biological constant: 22.

biological variables: 21-2, 30.

biology, female: 22, 23, 35, 173.

bisexuality: 8, 40, 41, 42, 45, 48, 78,